Refactoring

Visit **informit.com/ruby** for a complete list of available products.

The **Addison-Wesley Professional Ruby Series** provides readers with practical, people-oriented, and in-depth information about applying the Ruby platform to create dynamic technology solutions. The series is based on the premise that the need for expert reference books, written by experienced practitioners, will never be satisfied solely by blogs and the Internet.

Addison-Wesley Cisco Press EXAM/CRAM IBM Press. QUE PRENTICE HALL SAMS | Safari

Refactoring

Ruby Edition

Jay Fields
Shane Harvie
Martin Fowler

with Kent Black

Addison-Wesley

Upper Saddle River, NJ • Boston • Indianapolis • San Francisco
New York • Toronto • Montreal • London • Munich • Paris • Madrid
Cape Town • Sydney • Tokyo • Singapore • Mexico City

The publisher offers excellent discounts on this book when ordered in quantity for bulk purchases or special sales, which may include electronic versions and/or custom covers and content particular to your business, training goals, marketing focus, and branding interests. For more information, please contact:

U.S. Corporate and Government Sales
(800) 382-3419
corpsales@pearsontechgroup.com

For sales outside the United States please contact:

International Sales
international@pearson.com

Visit us on the Web: informit.com/aw

Library of Congress Cataloging-in-Publication Data is on file.

ISBN-13: 978-0-321-98413-5

ISBN-10: 0-321-98413-7

This product is printed digitally on demand. This book is the paperback version of an original hardcover book.

First printing October 2009

Associate Publisher
Mark Taub

Acquisitions Editor
Greg Doench

Managing Editor
Kristy Hart

Project Editor
Andy Beaster

Copy Editor
Geneil Breeze

Indexer
Erika Millen

Proofreader
Jennifer Gallant

Technical Reviewers
Chad Fowler
Clinton Begin
Justin Gehtland

Publishing Coordinator
Michelle Housley

Cover Designer
Chuti Prasertsith

Compositor
Jake McFarland

"To Dana, the love of my life, thank you for your endless patience and support"

—Jay Fields

"To Jan, my sounding board for many a bad idea and questionable opinion, thank you for never judging"

—Shane Harvie

"For Cindy"

—Martin Fowler

Contents

Foreword

I remember what it was like to learn object-oriented (OO) programming; As I learned OO, I was left with a low-grade tension—a feeling that I was missing something. Some new concepts felt simple and familiar in a way that told you there was a depth underlying them waiting to be discovered. That can be an unsettling feeling.

I read the literature on design patterns with great interest but, disappointingly, derived little enlightenment. I talked to other developers, browsed the Web, read books, and perused source code but remained convinced that there was something important that wasn't coming through. I understood how the tools of object orientation worked, but I was unable to apply them in a way that *felt* right to me.

Then I picked up the first edition of this book.

Software is not created in one inspired moment. The usual focus on the *artifacts* of the development process obscures the fact that software development is in fact a process. More specifically, as *Refactoring* taught me, it is a series of small decisions and actions all made through the filter of a set of values and the desire to create something excellent.

Understanding that software development is a constant activity and not a static event helps us to remember that code can and should be organic. Good code is easy to change. Bad code can incrementally be made easier to change. Code that's easy to change is fun to work with. Code that's hard to change is stressful to work with. And the more changes you make, without refactoring it, the more stressful working with it becomes.

So becoming a software developer is less about what good code is than about how to *make* good code. Software doesn't just spring into being. It's created by humans, one keystroke at a time. Refactoring is the book from which I learned how to do that process well. It taught me how to sit down and write great code, one tiny piece at a time.

When I initially read *Refactoring*, I was on a small team whose responsibility was to help larger groups write better software. At meetings and code reviews,

I would carry the hard-covered book around with me, wielding it as both a weapon and a shield. I was passionate about my job and (more strongly) the craft of software development, and I'm sure that the developers we worked with often dreaded the sight of me and this book heading toward their cubicles. I didn't so much refer to the book's contents in these meetings as just have it with me as a reminder of what it represented for me: Our work can be great if we always remember that it should be great and we take the simple steps to *make* it great.

Looking back on that time with the advantage of hindsight, I realize that the languages and tools we were using were working against us. The techniques in this book were born out of Smalltalk development. In a dynamic environment, refactoring flourishes. So it's only fitting that they should be reborn here in Ruby. As a longtime Rubyist it is thrilling to see the book that made such a profound difference for me become available to developers who speak Ruby as their primary programming language.

Refactoring: Ruby Edition will serve as a guiding light for a new generation of Rubyists who will learn to create better, more flexible software and (I hope) to love the craft of software development as much as I have.

—Chad Fowler
Co-Director, Ruby Central, Inc.
CTO, InfoEther, Inc.

Preface

Just over a decade ago I (Martin) worked on a project with Kent Beck. This project, called C3, became rather known as the project that marked the birth of extreme programming and helped fuel the visibility of what we now know as the agile software movement.

We learned a lot of things on that project, but one thing that particularly struck me was Kent's methodical way of continually reworking and improving the design of the system. I had always been a fan of writing clear code, and felt it was worthwhile to spend time cleaning up problematic code to allow a team to develop features swiftly. Kent introduced me to a technique, used by a number of leading Smalltalkers, that did this far more effectively than I had done it before. It's a technique they called *refactoring*, and soon I wanted to talk about it wherever I went. However, there was no book or similar resource I could point people to so that they could learn about this technique themselves. Kent and the other Smalltalkers weren't inclined to write one, so I took on the project.

My *Refactoring* book was popular and appears to have played a significant role in making refactoring a mainstream technique. With the growth of Ruby in the past few years, it made sense to put together a Ruby version of the book, this is where Jay and Shane stepped in.

What Is Refactoring?

Refactoring is the process of changing a software system in such a way that it does not alter the external behavior of the code yet improves its internal structure. It is a disciplined way to clean up code that minimizes the chances of introducing bugs. In essence when you refactor you are improving the design of the code after it has been written.

Many people find the phrase *improving the design after it has been written* rather odd. For many years most people believed that design comes first, and the coding comes second. Over time the code gets modified, and the integrity of the system, its structure according to that design, gradually fades. The code slowly sinks from engineering to hacking.

Refactoring is the opposite of this practice. With refactoring you can take a bad design, chaos even, and rework it into well-designed code. Each step is simple, even simplistic. You move an instance variable from one class to another, pull some code out of a method to make into its own method, and push some code up or down a hierarchy. Yet the cumulative effect of these small changes can radically improve the design. It is the exact reverse of the normal notion of software decay.

With refactoring you find the balance of work changes. You find that design, rather than occurring all up front, occurs continuously during development. You learn from building the system how to improve the design. The resulting interaction leads to a program with a design that stays good as development continues.

What's in This Book?

This book is a guide to refactoring; it is written for a professional Ruby programmer. Our aim is to show you how to do refactoring in a controlled and efficient manner. You learn to refactor in such a way that you don't introduce bugs into the code but instead methodically improve the structure.

It's traditional to start books with an introduction. Although I agree with that principle, I don't find it easy to introduce refactoring with a generalized discussion or definitions. So we start with an example. Chapter 1 takes a small program with some common design flaws and refactors it into a more acceptable object-oriented program. Along the way we see both the process of refactoring and the application of several useful refactorings. This is the key chapter to read if you want to understand what refactoring really is about.

In Chapter 2 we cover more of the general principles of refactoring, some definitions, and the reasons for doing refactoring. We outline some of the problems with refactoring. In Chapter 3 Kent Beck helps us describe how to find bad smells in code and how to clean them up with refactorings. Testing plays an important role in refactoring, so Chapter 4 describes how to build tests into code with a simple testing framework.

The heart of the book, the catalog of refactorings, stretches from Chapter 5 through Chapter 12. This is by no means a comprehensive catalog. It is the beginning of such a catalog. It includes the refactorings that we have written down so far in our work in this field. When we want to do something, such as Replace Conditional with Polymorphism, the catalog reminds us how to do it in a safe, step-by-step manner. We hope this is the section of the book you come back to often.

Refactoring in Ruby

When I wrote the original *Refactoring* book, I used Java to illustrate the techniques, mainly because Java was a widely read language. Most of the refactoring techniques apply whatever the language, so many people have used the original book to help them in their refactoring outside Java.

But obviously it helps you to learn refactoring in the language that you mostly program in. With many people learning the Ruby language, and with refactoring being a core part of the Ruby culture, we felt it was particularly important to provide a way for Rubyists to learn about refactoring—particularly if they don't have a background in curly-brace languages.

So Jay and Shane took on the task of going through my original book, and reworking it for Ruby. They started with the original text and meticulously went through it to remove all the Javaisms and rework the text to make sense in a Ruby context. They are experienced Ruby programmers who also have a good background in Java and C#, so they have the right background to do this well.

They also added some new refactorings that are particular to Ruby. Truth be told most of the refactorings are the same as those you need in any other object-oriented language, but there are a few new ones that come into play.

Who Should Read This Book?

This book is aimed at a professional programmer, someone who writes software for a living. The examples and discussion include a lot of code to read and understand.

Although it is focused on the code, refactoring has a large impact on the design of a system. It is vital for senior designers and architects to understand the principles of refactoring and to use them in their projects. Refactoring is best introduced by a respected and experienced developer. Such a developer can best understand the principles behind refactoring and adapt those principles to the specific workplace.

Here's how to get the most from this book without reading all of it.

- **If you want to understand what refactoring is**, read Chapter 1; the example should make the process clear.
- **If you want to understand why you should refactor**, read the first two chapters. They will tell you what refactoring is and why you should do it.
- **If you want to find where you should refactor**, read Chapter 3. It tells you the signs that suggest the need for refactoring.
- **If you want to actually do refactoring**, read the first four chapters completely. Then skip-read the catalog. Read enough of the catalog to know roughly what is in there. You don't have to understand all the details. When you actually need to carry out a refactoring, read the refactoring in detail and use it to help you. The catalog is a reference section, so you probably won't want to read it in one go.

We wrote this book assuming you haven't come across refactoring before and haven't read the original book, so you can treat this as a fully blown introduction to the subject. You start with either this book or the original, depending on which language you prefer as your focus.

I Have the Original Book—Should I Get This?

Probably not. If you're familiar with the original book you won't find a lot of new material here. You'll need to adjust the original refactorings to the Ruby language, but if you're like us you shouldn't find that an inordinate challenge.

There are a couple of reasons where we think an owner of the original book might consider getting a copy of the Ruby edition. The first reason is if you're not too familiar with Java and found the original book hard to follow because of that unfamiliarity. If so we hope you find a Ruby-focused book easier to work with. The second reason is if you're leading a Ruby team that has people who would struggle with the original book's Java focus. In that case a Ruby book would be a better tool to help pass on your understanding of refactoring.

Building on the Foundations Laid by Others

Occasionally people referred to me (Martin) as something like, "The Father of Refactoring." I always cringe when they do this because, although my book has helped to popularize refactoring, it certainly isn't my creation. In particular I built my work on the foundations laid by some leading people in the Smalltalk community

Two of the leading developers of refactoring were Ward Cunningham and Kent Beck. They used it as a central part of their development process in the early days and adapted their development processes to take advantage of it. In particular it was my collaboration with Kent that really showed me the importance of refactoring, an inspiration that led directly to this book.

Ralph Johnson leads a group at the University of Illinois at Urbana-Champaign that is notable for its long series of practical contributions to object technology. Ralph has long been a champion of refactoring, and several of his students have worked on the topic. Bill Opdyke developed the first detailed written work on refactoring in his doctoral thesis. John Brant and Don Roberts developed the world's first automated refactoring tool: the Smalltalk Refactoring Browser.

Many people have developed ideas in refactoring since my book. In particular, tool development has exploded. Any serious IDE now needs a "refactoring" menu, and many people now treat refactoring as an essential part of their development tools. It's important to point out that you can refactor effectively without a tool—but it sure makes it easier!

Making the Ruby Edition

People often wonder about how a book gets made, particularly when there's several people involved.

Martin began the original *Refactoring* book in early 1997. He did it by making notes of refactorings he did while programming, so these notes could remind him how to do certain refactorings efficiently. (These turned into the mechanics section of the book.) The book was published in 1999 and has sold steadily—around 15,000 copies a year.

Jay approached Martin in 2006 about doing a Ruby version. Jay looked around for people to help, and Shane was soon contributing enough to be a full author. Martin hasn't done much on this edition as his writing attention has been on other projects, but we left his name on the cover since he essentially provided the first draft, much of which is still there.

Acknowledgments

Refactoring is and always has been my (Jay's) favorite book. It was the gateway book that opened my eyes to how I could become a better programmer. I like the original version, but I wanted to lower the barrier for the many Ruby adopters. In late 2006 I had the idea to write a Ruby version. I called Martin and asked how he felt about the idea, and to my surprise he was very supportive. Unfortunately, the project didn't kick off for several months. At one point, a friend even said, "Why don't we just sit down this weekend and do it?"

Around January 2007 we finally got started working on it. Despite reusing much of the content, this book still took a significant amount of effort from several people. It took much longer than a weekend, and would not be possible without the contributions of those who helped out.

Ali Aghareza contributed several sections and the majority of the images.

John Hume and Stephen Chu both contributed several sections.

Even though the book is very similar to the original, the level of quality has been greatly raised by those who reviewed it and made suggestions: Brian Guthrie, Chris Stevenson, Clinton Begin, Dave Astels, Dave Hoover, George Malamidis, Justin Gehtland, Ola Bini, Ricky Lui, Ryan Plate, and Steve Deobald. I'm sure there are others who I've forgotten; I apologize and offer my thanks.

Stuart Halloway also reviewed the book and pushed us to add even more new content. I believe the book is better thanks to his nudge.

—Jay and Shane

My big thanks here go to Jay and Shane for doing the work to make a Ruby edition happen. This is certainly the easiest book I've ever had my name on, all I had to do was sit back and let them do it—if only all writing was this easy!

—Martin

Martin Fowler
Melrose, Massachusetts
fowler@acm.org
http://www.martinfowler.com
http://www.refactoring.com

Jay Fields
New York, New York
jay@jayfields.com
http://www.jayfields.com

Shane Harvie
Melbourne, Australia
shane@shaneharvie.com
http://www.shaneharvie.com

About the Authors

Jay Fields is a software developer for DRW Trading and a frequent conference presenter. Jay has a passion for discovering and maturing innovative solutions. Jay's website is available at www.jayfields.com.

Shane Harvie has delivered software in Agile environments in the USA, India, and Australia. He works for DRW Trading in Chicago and blogs at www.shaneharvie.com.

Martin Fowler is chief scientist at ThoughtWorks and describes himself as "an author, speaker, consultant, and general loud-mouth on software development. I concentrate on designing enterprise software—looking at what makes a good design and what practices are needed to come up with good design. I've been a pioneer of object-oriented technology, refactoring, patterns, agile methodologies, domain modeling, the Unified Modeling Language (UML), and Extreme Programming. For the last decade I've worked at ThoughtWorks, a really rather good system delivery and consulting firm."

Chapter 1

Refactoring, a First Example

When I wrote the original edition of *Refactoring* I had to decide how to open the book. Traditionally technical books start with a general introduction that outlines things like history and broad principles. When someone does that at a conference, I get slightly sleepy. My mind starts wandering with a low-priority background process that polls the speaker until he or she gives an example. The examples wake me up because it is with examples that I can see what is going on. With principles it is too easy to make generalizations, too hard to figure out how to apply things. An example helps make things clear.

So I decided to start the book with an example of refactoring. Several reviewers saw it as an unusual and somewhat brave move. But I've never regretted it. I used the same example for many talks I gave on refactoring too—and found that an example made a very good introduction. Although the specifics in the example were specific, you can use the concrete example to illustrate many broader issues.

It's no surprise then, that we wanted to start off with an example for this Ruby version. I'm using exactly the same example as I did for Java, although Jay translated it into Ruby. I reworked the text considerably to introduce things I've learned when talking about this example over the years. If you're familiar with the book we hope you'll enjoy some of the new discussion. If this book is new to you you're probably hoping I'll start with the content.

As with any introductory example, however, there is a big problem. If I pick a large program, describing it and how it is refactored is too complicated for any reader to work through. (I tried and even a slightly complicated example ran to more than 100 pages.) However, if I pick a program that is small enough to be comprehensible, refactoring does not look like it is worthwhile.

Thus I'm in the classic bind of anyone who wants to describe techniques that are useful for real-world programs. Frankly it is not worth the effort to do the refactoring that I'm going to show you on a small program like the one I'm going to use. But if the code I'm showing you is part of a larger system, then the refactoring soon becomes important. So I have to ask you to look at this and imagine it in the context of a much larger system.

The Starting Point

The sample program is simple. It is a program to calculate and print a statement of a customer's charges at a video store. The program is told which movies a customer rented and for how long. It then calculates the charges, which depend on how long the movie is rented, and identifies the type of movie. There are three kinds of movies: regular, children's, and new releases. In addition to calculating charges, the statement also computes frequent renter points, which vary depending on whether the film is a new release.

Several classes represent various video elements. Here's a class diagram to show them (see Figure 1.1).

I'll show the code for each of these classes in turn.

Movie

Movie is just a simple data class.

```
class Movie
  REGULAR = 0
  NEW_RELEASE = 1
  CHILDRENS = 2

  attr_reader :title
  attr_accessor :price_code

  def initialize(title, price_code)
    @title, @price_code = title, price_code
  end
end
```

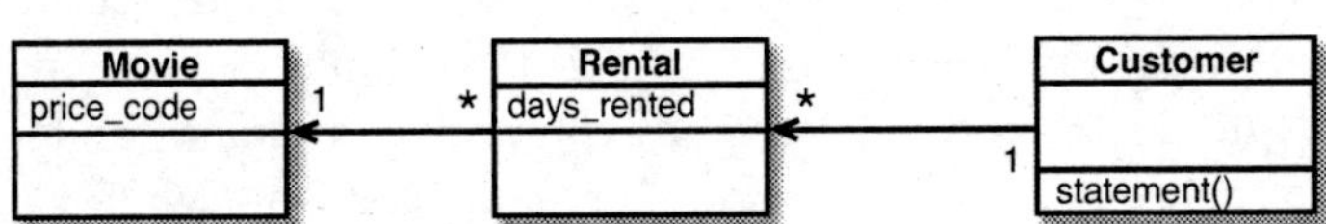

Figure 1.1 Class diagram of the starting point classes. Only the most important features are shown. The notation is Unified Modeling Language (UML) [Fowler, UML].

Rental

The rental class represents a customer renting a movie.

```
class Rental
  attr_reader :movie, :days_rented
```

```
  def initialize(movie, days_rented)
    @movie, @days_rented = movie, days_rented
  end
end
```

Customer

The customer class represents the customer of the store. Like the other classes it has data and accessors:

```
class Customer
  attr_reader :name

  def initialize(name)
    @name = name
    @rentals = []
  end

  def add_rental(arg)
    @rentals << arg
  end
```

Customer also has the method that produces a statement. Figure 1.2 shows the interactions for this method.

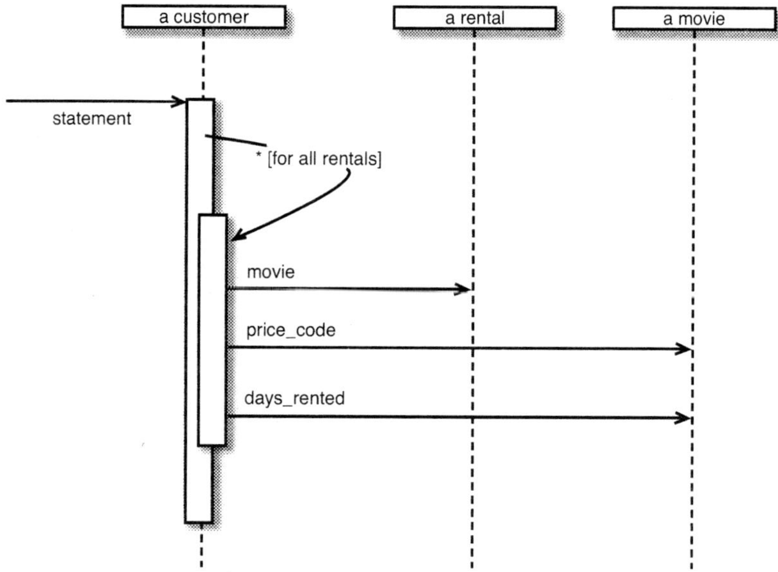

Figure 1.2 Interactions for the statement method.

The Starting Point

```
def statement
    total_amount, frequent_renter_points = 0, 0
    result = "Rental Record for #{@name}\n"
    @rentals.each do |element|
      this_amount = 0

      # determine amounts for each line
      case element.movie.price_code
      when Movie::REGULAR
        this_amount += 2
        this_amount += (element.days_rented - 2) * 1.5 if element.days_rented > 2
      when Movie::NEW_RELEASE
        this_amount += element.days_rented * 3
      when Movie::CHILDRENS
        this_amount += 1.5
        this_amount += (element.days_rented - 3) * 1.5 if element.days_rented > 3
      end

      # add frequent renter points
      frequent_renter_points += 1
      # add bonus for a two day new release rental
      if element.movie.price_code == Movie.NEW_RELEASE && element.days_rented > 1
          frequent_renter_points += 1
      end
      # show figures for this rental
      result += "\t" + element.movie.title + "\t" + this_amount.to_s + "\n"
      total_amount += this_amount
    end
    # add footer lines
    result += "Amount owed is #{total_amount}\n"
    result += "You earned #{frequent_renter_points} frequent renter points"
    result
  end
```

Comments on the Starting Program

What are your impressions about the design of this program? I would describe it as not well designed and certainly not object oriented. For a simple program like this, that does not really matter. There's nothing wrong with a quick and dirty simple program. But if this is a representative fragment of a more complex system, then I have some real problems with this program. That long statement routine in the Customer class does far too much. Many of the things that it does should really be done by the other classes.

Even so, the program works. Is this not just an aesthetic judgment, a dislike of ugly code? It is until we want to change the system. The interpreter doesn't care whether the code is ugly or clean. But when we change the system, there is a human involved, and humans do care. A poorly designed system is hard to change. Hard because it is hard to figure out where the changes are needed. If it is hard to figure out what to change, there is a strong chance that the programmer will make a mistake and introduce bugs.

In this case we have a couple of changes that the users would like to make. First they want a statement printed in HTML so that the statement can be Web enabled and more buzzword compliant. Consider the impact this change would have. As you look at the code you can see that it is impossible to reuse any of the behavior of the current statement method for an HTML statement. Your only recourse is to write a whole new method that duplicates much of the behavior of statement. Now, of course, this is not too onerous. You can just copy the statement method and make whatever changes you need.

But what happens when the charging rules change? You have to fix both statement and html_statement and ensure the fixes are consistent. The problem with copying and pasting code comes when you have to change it later. If you are writing a program that you don't expect to change, then cut and paste is fine. If the program is long lived and likely to change, then cut and paste is a menace.

This brings me to a second change. The users want to make changes to the way they classify movies, but they haven't yet decided on the change they are going to make. They have a number of changes in mind. These changes will affect both the way renters are charged for movies and the way that frequent renter points are calculated. As an experienced developer you are sure that whatever scheme the users come up with, the only guarantee you're going to have is that they will change it again within six months.

The statement method is where the changes have to be made to deal with changes in classification and charging rules. If, however, we copy the statement to an HTML statement, we need to ensure that any changes are completely consistent. Furthermore, as the rules grow in complexity it's going to be harder to figure out where to make the changes and harder to make them without making a mistake.

You may be tempted to make the fewest possible changes to the program; after all, it works fine. Remember the old engineering adage: "if it ain't broke, don't fix it." The program may not be broken, but it does hurt. It is making your life more difficult because you find it hard to make the changes your users want. This is where refactoring comes in.

Tip When you find you have to add a feature to a program, and the program's code is not structured in a convenient way to add the feature, first refactor the program to make it easy to add the feature, then add the feature.

The First Step in Refactoring

Whenever I do refactoring, the first step is always the same. I need to build a solid set of tests for that section of code. The tests are essential because even though I follow refactorings structured to avoid most of the opportunities for introducing bugs, I'm still human and still make mistakes. Thus I need solid tests.

Because the statement result produces a string, I create a few customers, give each customer a few rentals of various kinds of films, and generate the statement strings. I then do a string comparison between the new string and some reference strings that I have hand checked. I set up all of these tests so I can run them using Test::Unit. The tests take only a few seconds to run, and as you will see, I run them often.

An important part of the tests is the way they report their results. They either print "X tests, X assertions, 0 failures, 0 errors" meaning that all the strings are identical to the reference strings, or they print a list of failures: lines that turned out differently. The tests are thus self-checking. It is vital to make tests self-checking. If you don't, you end up spending time hand checking some numbers from the test against some numbers on a desk pad, and that slows you down.

When I wrote the original version of this book, testing like this was still a rarity. Many people were first introduced to this style of testing through that book. Since then, this kind of testing has spread widely through software development. We're happy that this approach has become a core style to both the

Ruby and Rails communities. You're not going to be taken seriously as a Ruby developer unless you use Test::Unit or Rspec to write tests as you write code.

As we do the refactoring, we will lean on the tests. I'm going to rely on the tests to tell me whether I introduce a bug. It is essential for refactoring that you have good tests. It's worth spending the time to build the tests, because the tests give you the security you need to change the program later. This is such an important part of refactoring that I go into more detail on testing in Chapter 4, "Building Tests."

Tip Before you start refactoring, check that you have a solid suite of tests. These tests must be self-checking.

Decomposing and Redistributing the Statement Method

The obvious first target of my attention is the overly long statement method. When I look at a long method like that, I am looking to decompose the method into smaller pieces. Smaller pieces of code tend to make things more manageable. They are easier to work with and move around.

The first phase of the refactorings in this chapter show how I split up the long method and move the pieces to better classes. My aim is to make it easier to write an HTML statement method with much less duplication of code.

My first step is to find a logical clump of code and use Extract Method. An obvious piece here is the case statement. This looks like it would make a good chunk to extract into its own method.

When I extract a method, as in any refactoring, I need to know what can go wrong. If I do the extraction badly, I could introduce a bug into the program. So before I do the refactoring I need to figure out how to do it safely. I've done this refactoring a few times before, so I've written down the safe steps in the catalog.

First I need to look in the fragment for any variables that are local in scope to the method we are looking at; the local variables and parameters. This segment of code uses two: `rental` and `this_amount`. Of these, `rental` is not modified by the code, but `this_amount` is modified. Any nonmodified variable I can pass in as a parameter. Modified variables need more care. If there is only one, I can return it. The temp is initialized to 0 each time around the loop and is not altered until the case gets to it. So I can just assign the result.

The next two pages show the code before and after refactoring. The before code is on the left, the resulting code on the right. The code I'm extracting from the original and any changes in the new code that I don't think are immediately obvious are in boldface type. As I continue with this chapter, I'll continue with this left-right convention.

```
def statement
  total_amount, frequent_renter_points = 0, 0
  result = "Rental Record for #{@name}\n"
  @rentals.each do |element|
    this_amount = 0

    # determine amounts for each line
    case element.movie.price_code
    when Movie::REGULAR
      this_amount += 2
      this_amount += (element.days_rented - 2) * 1.5 if element.days_rented > 2
    when Movie::NEW_RELEASE
      this_amount += element.days_rented * 3
    when Movie::CHILDRENS
      this_amount += 1.5
      this_amount += (element.days_rented - 3) * 1.5 if element.days_rented > 3
    end

    # add frequent renter points
    frequent_renter_points += 1
    # add bonus for a two day new release rental
    if element.movie.price_code == Movie.NEW_RELEASE &&
             element.days_rented > 1
        frequent_renter_points += 1
    end

    # show figures for this rental
    result += "\t" + each.movie.title + "\t" + this_amount.to_s + "\n"
    total_amount += this_amount
  end
  # add footer lines
  result += "Amount owed is #{total_amount}\n"
  result += "You earned #{frequent_renter_points} frequent renter points"
  result
end
```

```
def statement
  total_amount, frequent_renter_points = 0, 0
  result = "Rental Record for #{@name}\n"
  @rentals.each do |element|
    this_amount = amount_for(element)

    # add frequent renter points
    frequent_renter_points += 1
    # add bonus for a two day new release rental
    if element.movie.price_code == Movie.NEW_RELEASE &&
             element.days_rented > 1
        frequent_renter_points += 1
    end

    # show figures for this rental
    result += "\t" + each.movie.title + "\t" + this_amount.to_s + "\n"
    total_amount += this_amount
  end
  # add footer lines
  result += "Amount owed is #{total_amount}\n"
  result += "You earned #{frequent_renter_points} frequent renter points"
  result
end

def amount_for(element)
  this_amount = 0
  case element.movie.price_code
  when Movie::REGULAR
    this_amount += 2
    this_amount += (element.days_rented - 2) * 1.5 if element.days_rented > 2
  when Movie::NEW_RELEASE
    this_amount += element.days_rented * 3
  when Movie::CHILDRENS
    this_amount += 1.5
    this_amount += (element.days_rented - 3) * 1.5 if element.days_rented > 3
  end
end
```

Whenever I make a change like this, I test. When I wrote the original version of this book, I actually had the tests fail at this point. There I am, writing a book on refactoring, and I screw up the very first refactoring I show in the book. It wasn't my proudest moment. (The actual error isn't something you can see in Ruby as it was a subtle type error that wasn't caught by Java's type checking system.) While I felt bad at the time, it was actually a great illustration of why frequent testing is vital as these kind of errors can be difficult to track down if you make a lot of changes. But because I test after every tiny step, I don't have to look far to find where the error is. So whenever I give a (Java) talk on this I always replay that error to show the point. The key to testing is running tests after every small change so when you mess up you don't have to look in many places to find the problem. Comparing the failing version of code to a previous working version (which I call Diff Debugging) is a useful technique, particularly so when the diffs are small. Because each change is so small, any errors are easy to find. You don't spend a long time debugging, even if you are as careless as I am.

Tip Refactoring changes the programs in small steps. If you make a mistake, it is easy to find the bug.

Extract Method is a common refactoring task to do, it can also be a bit intricate since you have to look at these local variables. For programmers in many languages these days, this effort has been reduced to near-zero by automated refactoring tools. Such a tool can analyze the method, do the kind of analysis we see in the previous example, and leave the programmer with only having to choose the name of the new method. The first such refactoring tool was written for Smalltalk; these kinds of tools are now commonly used in Java and C#. As I write this Ruby tools are steadily becoming available.

Now that I've broken the original method down into chunks, I can work on them separately. I don't like some of the variable names in `amount_for`, and this is a good place to change them.

Here's the original code:

```
def amount_for(element)
  this_amount = 0
  case element.movie.price_code
  when Movie::REGULAR
    this_amount += 2
    this_amount += (element.days_rented - 2) * 1.5 if element.days_rented > 2
  when Movie::NEW_RELEASE
    this_amount += element.days_rented * 3
  when Movie::CHILDRENS
    this_amount += 1.5
    this_amount += (element.days_rented - 3) * 1.5 if element.days_rented > 3
  end
  this_amount
end
```

Here is the renamed code:

```
def amount_for(rental)
  result = 0
  case rental.movie.price_code
  when Movie::REGULAR
    result += 2
    result += (rental.days_rented - 2) * 1.5 if rental.days_rented > 2
  when Movie::NEW_RELEASE
    result += rental.days_rented * 3
  when Movie::CHILDRENS
    result += 1.5
    result += (rental.days_rented - 3) * 1.5 if rental.days_rented > 3
  end
  result
end
```

Once I've done the renaming, I test to ensure I haven't broken anything.

Is renaming worth the effort? Absolutely. Good code should communicate what it is doing clearly, and variable names are a key to clear code. Never be afraid to change the names of things to improve clarity. With good find and replace tools, it is usually not difficult (and automated refactoring tools can make it even easier). Testing highlights anything you miss. Remember this tip:

Tip Any fool can write code that a computer can understand. Good programmers write code that humans can understand.

Code that communicates its purpose is very important. I often refactor just when I'm reading some code. That way as I gain understanding about the program, I embed that understanding into the code for later so I don't forget what I learned.

Decomposing and Redistributing the Statement Method

Moving the Amount Calculation

As I look at amount_for, I can see that it uses information from the rental, but does not use information from the customer.

```
class Customer
  def amount_for(rental)
    result = 0
    case rental.movie.price_code
    when Movie::REGULAR
      result += 2
      result += (rental.days_rented - 2) * 1.5 if rental.days_rented > 2
    when Movie::NEW_RELEASE
      result += rental.days_rented * 3
    when Movie::CHILDRENS
      result += 1.5
      result += (rental.days_rented - 3) * 1.5 if rental.days_rented > 3
    end
    result
  end
end
```

This immediately raises my suspicions that the method is on the wrong object. In most cases a method should be on the object whose data it uses; thus the method should be moved to the rental. To do this I use Move Method. With this you first copy the code over to rental and adjust it to fit in its new home, as follows:

```
class Rental
  def charge
    result = 0
    case movie.price_code
    when Movie::REGULAR
      result += 2
      result += (days_rented - 2) * 1.5 if days_rented > 2
    when Movie::NEW_RELEASE
      result += days_rented * 3
    when Movie::CHILDRENS
      result += 1.5
      result += (days_rented - 3) * 1.5 if days_rented > 3
    end
    result
  end
end
```

In this case fitting into its new home means removing the parameter. I also renamed the method as I did the move.

I can now test to see whether this method works. To do this I replace the body of Customer.amount_for to delegate to the new method.

```
class Customer
  def amount_for(rental)
    rental.charge
  end
end
```

I can now test to see whether I've broken anything.

The next step is to find every reference to the old method and adjust the reference to use the new method, as follows:

```
class Customer
  def statement
    total_amount, frequent_renter_points = 0, 0
    result = "Rental Record for #{@name}\n"
    @rentals.each do |element|
      this_amount = amount_for(element)

      # add frequent renter points
      frequent_renter_points += 1
      # add bonus for a two day new release rental
      if element.movie.price_code == Movie.NEW_RELEASE &&
               element.days_rented > 1
         frequent_renter_points += 1
      end

      # show figures for this rental
      result += "\t" + each.movie.title + "\t" + this_amount.to_s + "\n"
      total_amount += this_amount
    end
    # add footer lines
    result += "Amount owed is #{total_amount}\n"
    result += "You earned #{frequent_renter_points} frequent renter points"
    result
  end
end
```

In this case this step is easy because we just created the method, and it is in only one place. In general, however, you need to search across all the classes that might be using that method:

```
class Customer
  def statement
    total_amount, frequent_renter_points = 0, 0
    result = "Rental Record for #{@name}\n"
    @rentals.each do |element|
      this_amount = element.charge

      # add frequent renter points
      frequent_renter_points += 1
      # add bonus for a two day new release rental
      if element.movie.price_code == Movie.NEW_RELEASE &&
               element.days_rented > 1
          frequent_renter_points += 1
      end

      # show figures for this rental
      result += "\t" + each.movie.title + "\t" + this_amount.to_s + "\n"
      total_amount += this_amount
    end
    # add footer lines
    result += "Amount owed is #{total_amount}\n"
    result += "You earned #{frequent_renter_points} frequent renter points"
    result
  end
end
```

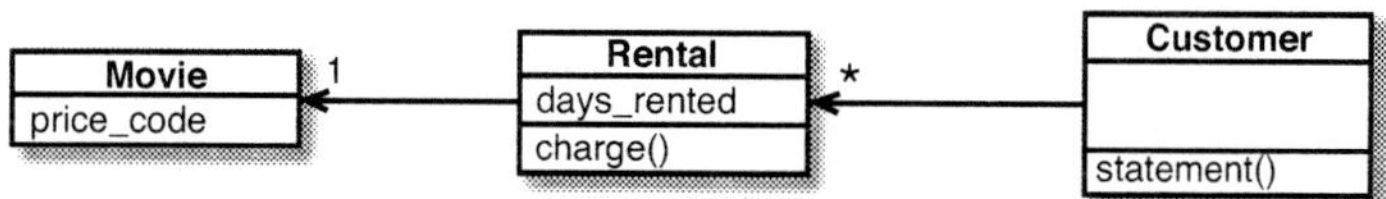

Figure 1.3 State of classes after moving the charge method.

Decomposing and Redistributing the Statement Method

When I've made the change (see Figure 1.3) the next thing is to remove the old method. The tests should tell me whether I missed or broke anything.

Sometimes I leave the old method to delegate to the new method. This is useful if it is a public method and I don't want to change the interface of the other class.

There is certainly some more I would like to do to `Rental.charge` but I will leave it for the moment and return to `Customer.statement`.

```
class Customer
  def statement
    total_amount, frequent_renter_points = 0, 0
    result = "Rental Record for #{@name}\n"
    @rentals.each do |element|
      this_amount = element.charge

      # add frequent renter points
      frequent_renter_points += 1
      # add bonus for a two day new release rental
      if element.movie.price_code == Movie.NEW_RELEASE &&
               element.days_rented > 1
         frequent_renter_points += 1
      end

      # show figures for this rental
      result += "\t" + each.movie.title + "\t" + this_amount.to_s + "\n"
      total_amount += this_amount
    end
    # add footer lines
    result += "Amount owed is #{total_amount}\n"
    result += "You earned #{frequent_renter_points} frequent renter points"
    result
  end
end
```

The next thing that strikes me is that this_amount is now redundant. It is set to the result of element.charge and not changed afterward. Thus I can eliminate this_amount by using Replace Temp with Query:

```
class Customer
  def statement
    total_amount, frequent_renter_points = 0, 0
    result = "Rental Record for #{@name}\n"
    @rentals.each do |element|

      # add frequent renter points
      frequent_renter_points += 1
      # add bonus for a two day new release rental
      if element.movie.price_code == Movie.NEW_RELEASE &&
               element.days_rented > 1
         frequent_renter_points += 1
      end

      # show figures for this rental
      result += "\t" + each.movie.title + "\t" + element.charge.to_s + "\n"
      total_amount += element.charge
    end
    # add footer lines
    result += "Amount owed is #{total_amount}\n"
    result += "You earned #{frequent_renter_points} frequent renter points"
    result
  end
end
```

Once I've made that change I test to make sure I haven't broken anything.

Whenever I've gone through this example in a talk, this refactoring leads to angst from at least some people in the audience. The biggest source of angst is performance. By removing the temporary variable I'm calling the charge method twice instead of once. Some people would avoid making this change solely for that reason. However this kind of thinking about performance isn't a good way to get good performance (see the section in Chapter 2 named "Refactoring and Performance"). While refactoring you should focus on clarity, and then later focus on performance as a separate activity. Almost all the time extra method calls won't matter; in the rare cases they do, they can be dealt with later. Indeed by refactoring you often get opportunities to make better performance improvements.

The bigger danger area in this refactoring is that you have to be sure that the `charge` method is idempotent. Usually a method like this is a query method and thus has no side effects. In this case you can call it as often as you like without changing anything. Good tests would expose this fault if it's there.

Decomposing and Redistributing the Statement Method

When breaking down large methods I find this refactoring useful. Temps are often a problem in that they cause a lot of parameters to be passed around when they don't have to be. You can easily lose track of what they are there for. By getting rid of them you can focus more clearly on what the code's trying to do rather than how to shuffle data around.

Extracting Frequent Renter Points

The next step is to do a similar thing for the frequent renter points. The rules vary with the kind of tape, although there is less variation than with charging. It seems reasonable to put the responsibility on the rental. First we need to use Extract Method on the frequent renter points part of the code (in boldface type):

```
class Customer
  def statement
    total_amount, frequent_renter_points = 0, 0
    result = "Rental Record for #{@name}\n"
    @rentals.each do |element|

      # add frequent renter points
      frequent_renter_points += 1
      # add bonus for a two day new release rental
      if element.movie.price_code == Movie.NEW_RELEASE &&
              element.days_rented > 1
         frequent_renter_points += 1
      end

      # show figures for this rental
      result += "\t" + each.movie.title + "\t" + element.charge.to_s + "\n"
      total_amount += element.charge
    end
    # add footer lines
    result += "Amount owed is #{total_amount}\n"
    result += "You earned #{frequent_renter_points} frequent renter points"
    result
  end
end
```

Again we look at the use of locally scoped variables. Again element is used and can be passed in as a parameter. The other temp used is frequent_renter_points. In this case frequent_renter_points does have a value beforehand. The body of the extracted method doesn't read the value, however, so we don't need to pass it in as a parameter as long as we use an appending assignment.

I did the extraction and tested and then did a move and tested again. With refactoring, small steps are the best; that way less tends to go wrong.

```
class Customer
  def statement
    total_amount, frequent_renter_points = 0, 0
    result = "Rental Record for #{@name}\n"
    @rentals.each do |element|
      frequent_renter_points += element.frequent_renter_points

      # show figures for this rental
      result += "\t" + each.movie.title + "\t" + element.charge.to_s + "\n"
      total_amount += element.charge
    end
    # add footer lines
    result += "Amount owed is #{total_amount}\n"
    result += "You earned #{frequent_renter_points} frequent renter points"
    result
  end
end

class Rental
  def frequent_renter_points
    (movie.price_code == Movie.NEW_RELEASE && days_rented > 1) ? 2 : 1
  end
end
```

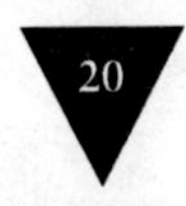

I'll summarize the changes I just made with some before-and-after Unified Modeling Language (UML) diagrams (see Figures 1.4 through 1.7). Again the diagrams on the left are before the change; those on the right are after the change.

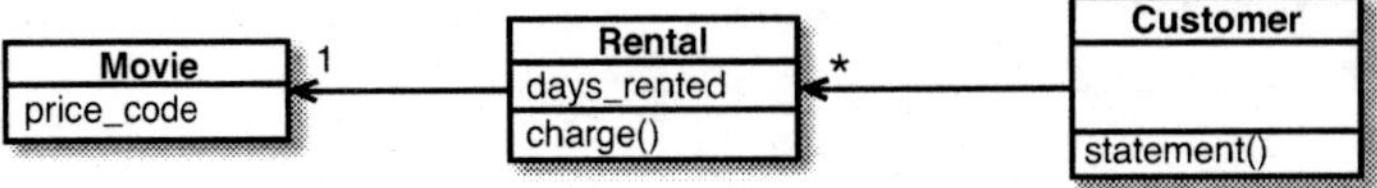

Figure 1.4 Class diagram before extraction and movement of the frequent renter points calculation.

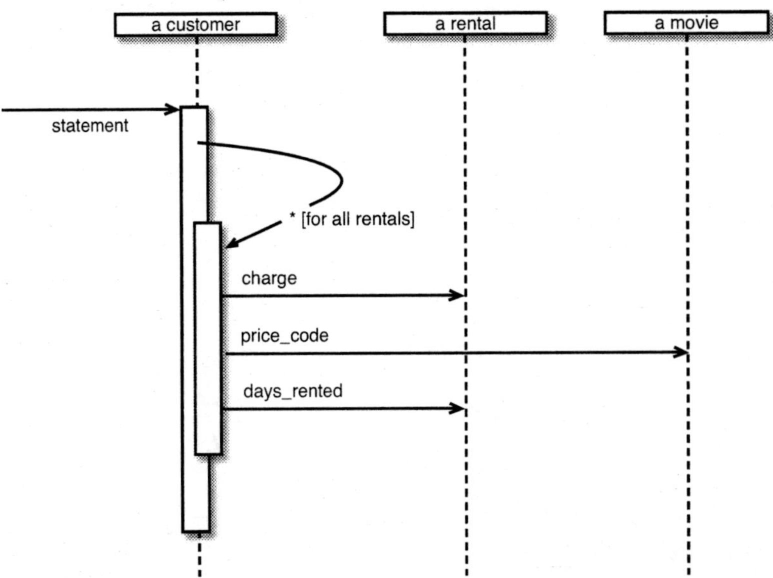

Figure 1.5 Sequence diagrams before extraction and movement of the frequent renter points calculation.

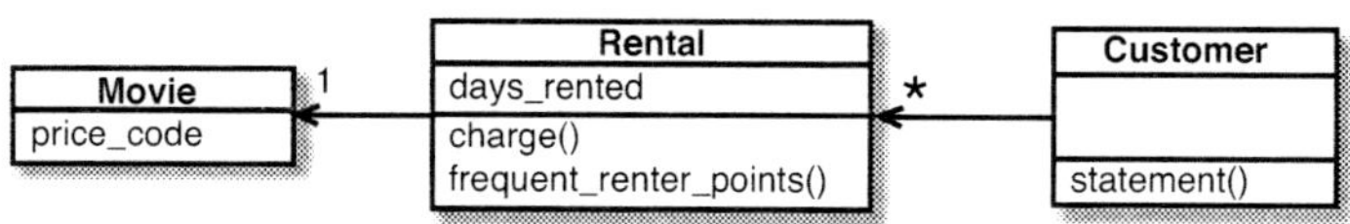

Figure 1.6 Class diagram after extraction and movement of the frequent renter points calculation.

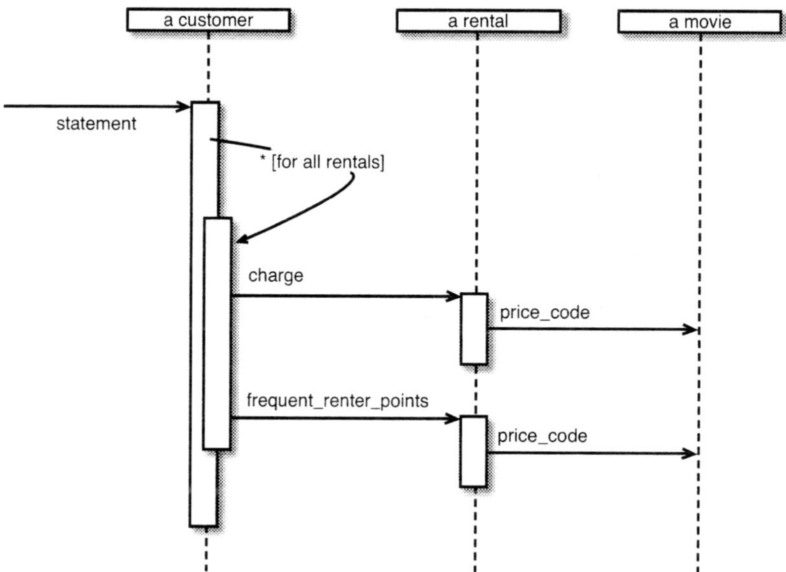

Figure 1.7 Sequence diagram after extraction and movement of the frequent renter points calculation.

Removing Temps

As I suggested before, temporary variables can be a problem. They are useful only within their own routine, and thus they encourage long, complex routines. In this case we have two temporary variables, both of which are being used to get a total from the rentals attached to the customer. Both the ASCII and HTML versions require these totals. I like to use Replace Temp with Query to replace `total_amount` and `frequent_renter_points` with query methods. Queries are accessible to any method in the class and thus encourage a cleaner design without long, complex methods:

```
class Customer
  def statement
    total_amount, frequent_renter_points = 0, 0
    result = "Rental Record for #{@name}\n"
    @rentals.each do |element|
      frequent_renter_points += element.frequent_renter_points

      # show figures for this rental
      result += "\t" + each.movie.title + "\t" + element.charge.to_s + "\n"
      total_amount += element.charge
    end
    # add footer lines
    result += "Amount owed is #{total_amount}\n"
    result += "You earned #{frequent_renter_points} frequent renter points"
    result
  end
end
```

I began by replacing total_amount with a total_charge method on customer:

```
class Customer
  def statement
    frequent_renter_points = 0
    result = "Rental Record for #{@name}\n"
    @rentals.each do |element|
      frequent_renter_points += element.frequent_renter_points

      # show figures for this rental
      result += "\t" + each.movie.title + "\t" + element.charge.to_s + "\n"
    end
    # add footer lines
    result += "Amount owed is #{total_charge}\n"
    result += "You earned #{frequent_renter_points} frequent renter points"
    result
  end

  private

  def total_charge
    result = 0
    @rentals.each do |element|
      result += element.charge
    end
    result
  end
end
```

This isn't the simplest case of Replace Temp with Query since total_amount was assigned to within the loop, so I have to copy the loop into the query method.

The total_charge method is short:

```
Customer
  def total_charge
    result = 0
    @rentals.each do |element|
      result += element.charge
    end
    result
  end
end
```

However, it can be made even more concise by applying Collection Closure Method and using inject.

```
class Customer
  def total_charge
    @rentals.inject(0) { |sum, rental| sum + rental.charge }
  end
end
```

After testing that refactoring, I did the same for frequent_renter_points:

```
class Customer
  def statement
    frequent_renter_points = 0
    result = "Rental Record for #{@name}\n"
    @rentals.each do |element|
      frequent_renter_points += element.frequent_renter_points

      # show figures for this rental
      result += "\t" + each.movie.title + "\t" + element.charge.to_s + "\n"
    end
    # add footer lines
    result += "Amount owed is #{total_charge}\n"
    result += "You earned #{frequent_renter_points} frequent renter points"
    result
  end
end
```

```
class Customer
  def statement
    result = "Rental Record for #{@name}\n"
    @rentals.each do |element|
      # show figures for this rental
      result += "\t" + each.movie.title + "\t" + element.charge.to_s + "\n"
    end
    # add footer lines
    result += "Amount owed is #{total_charge}\n"
    result += "You earned #{total_frequent_renter_points} frequent renter points"
    result
  end

  private

  def total_frequent_renter_points
    @rentals.inject(0) { |sum, rental| sum + rental.frequent_renter_points }
  end
end
```

Decomposing and Redistributing the Statement Method

Figures 1.8 through 1.11 show the change for these refactorings in the class diagrams and thc interaction diagram for the statement method.

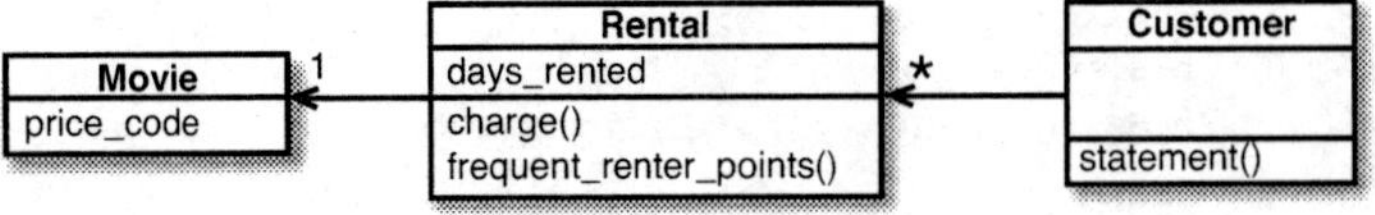

Figure 1.8 Class diagram before extraction of the totals.

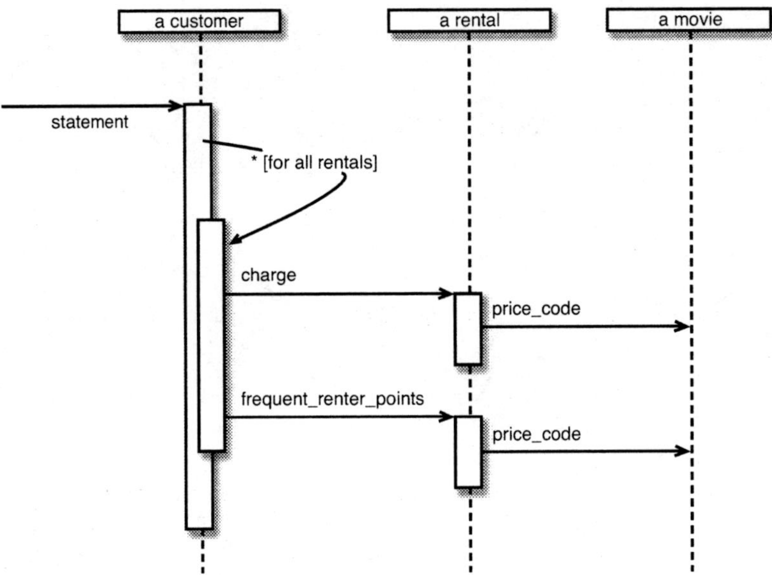

Figure 1.9 Sequence diagram before extraction of the totals.

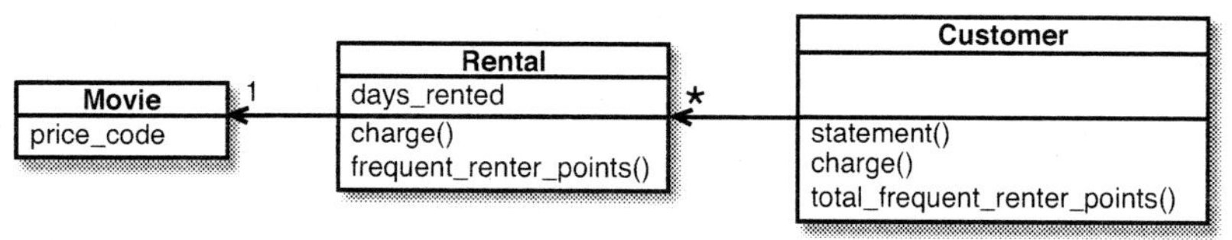

Figure 1.10 Class diagram after extraction of the totals.

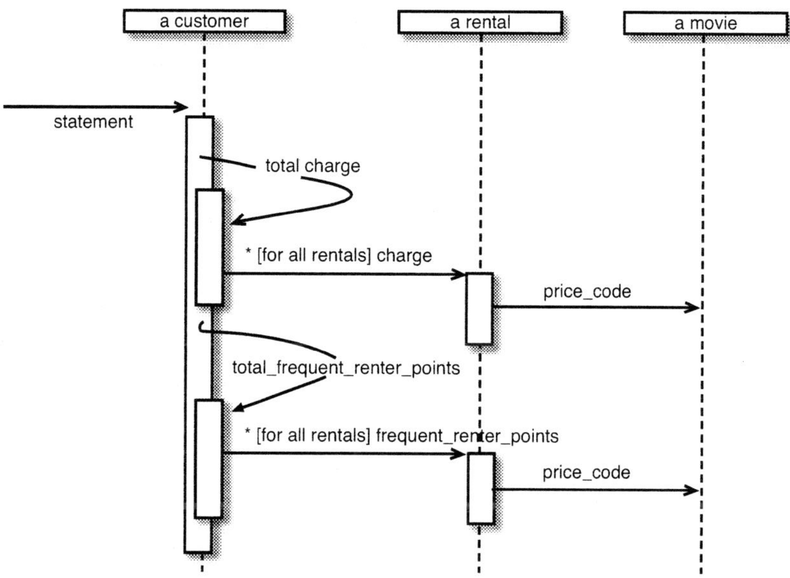

Figure 1.11 Sequence diagram after extraction of the totals.

As with Replace Temp With Query, this change can cause performance worries to inexperienced programmers. The same advice applies; make the code clean first and then use a profiler to deal with performance issues.

These queries are now available for any code written in the customer class. They can easily be added to the public interface of the class should other parts of the system need this information. Without queries like these, other methods have to deal with knowing about the rentals and building the enumerations. In a complex system, that leads to much more code to write and maintain.

You can see the difference immediately with the `html_statement`. I am now at the point where I take off my refactoring hat and put on my adding function hat. I can write `html_statement` as follows and add appropriate tests:

```
class Customer
  def html_statement
    result = "<h1>Rentals for <em>#{@name}</em></h1><p>\n"
    @rentals.each do |element|
      # show figures for this rental
      result += "\t" + each.movie.title + ": " + element.charge.to_s + "<br>\n"
    end
    # add footer lines
    result += "<p>You owe <em>#{total_charge}</em><p>\n"
    result += "On this rental you earned " +
          "<em>#{total_frequent_renter_points}</em> " +
          "frequent renter points<p>"
    result
  end
end
```

By extracting the calculations I can create the `html_statement` method and reuse all of the calculation code that was in the original `statement` method. I didn't copy and paste, so if the calculation rules change I have only one place in the code to go to. Any other kind of statement will be really quick and easy to prepare. The refactoring did not take long. I spent most of the time figuring out what the code did, and I would have had to do that anyway.

Some code is copied from the ASCII version, mainly due to setting up the loop. Further refactoring could clean that up. Extracting methods for header, footer, and detail line are one route I could take. You can see how to do this in the example for Form Template Method. Further work could lead to using string formatting statements instead of the concatenation, the Builder library to produce the HTML, or a templating system like ERB.

But now the users are clamoring again. They are getting ready to change the classification of the movies in the store. It's still not clear what changes they want to make, but it sounds like new classifications will be introduced, and the existing ones could well be changed. The charges and frequent renter point allocations for these classifications are to be decided. At the moment, making these kind of changes is awkward. I have to get into the charge and frequent renter point methods and alter the conditional code to make changes to film classifications. Back on with the refactoring hat.

Replacing the Conditional Logic on Price Code with Polymorphism

The first part of this problem is that case statement. It is a bad idea to do a case based on an attribute of another object. If you must use a case statement, it should be on your own data, not on someone else's.

```
class Rental
  def charge
    result = 0
    case movie.price_code
    when Movie::REGULAR
      result += 2
      result += (days_rented - 2) * 1.5 if days_rented > 2
    when Movie::NEW_RELEASE
      result += days_rented * 3
    when Movie::CHILDRENS
      result += 1.5
      result += (days_rented - 3) * 1.5 if days_rented > 3
    end
    result
  end
end
```

This implies that the charge method should move onto movie:

```
class Movie
  def charge(days_rented)
    result = 0
    case price_code
    when REGULAR
      result += 2
      result += (days_rented - 2) * 1.5 if days_rented > 2
    when NEW_RELEASE
      result += days_rented * 3
    when CHILDRENS
      result += 1.5
      result += (days_rented - 3) * 1.5 if days_rented > 3
    end
    result
  end
end
```

For this to work I had to pass in the length of the rental, which of course is data from the rental. The method effectively uses two pieces of data, the length of the rental and the type of the movie. Why do I prefer to pass the length of rental to the movie rather than the movie type to the rental? It's because the proposed changes are all about adding new types. Type information generally tends to be more volatile. If I change the movie type, I want the least ripple effect, so I prefer to calculate the charge within the movie.

I added the method into movie and then changed the charge on rental to use the new method (see Figures 1.12 and 1.13):

```
class Rental
  def charge
    movie.charge(days_rented)
  end
end
```

Once I've moved the charge method, I do the same with the frequent renter point calculation. That keeps both things that vary with the type together on the class that has the type:

```
class Rental
  def frequent_renter_points
    (movie.price_code == Movie::NEW_RELEASE && days_rented > 1) ? 2 : 1
  end
end
```

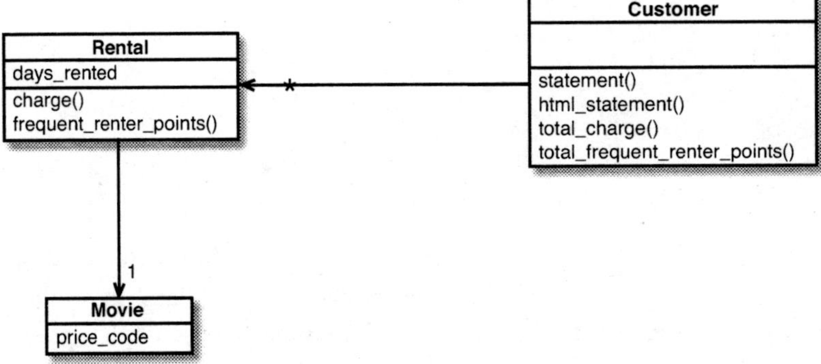

Figure 1.12 Class diagram before moving methods to movie.

```
class Rental
  def frequent_renter_points
    movie.frequent_renter_points(days_rented)
  end
end

class Movie
  def frequent_renter_points(days_rented)
    (price_code == NEW_RELEASE && days_rented > 1) ? 2 : 1
  end
end
```

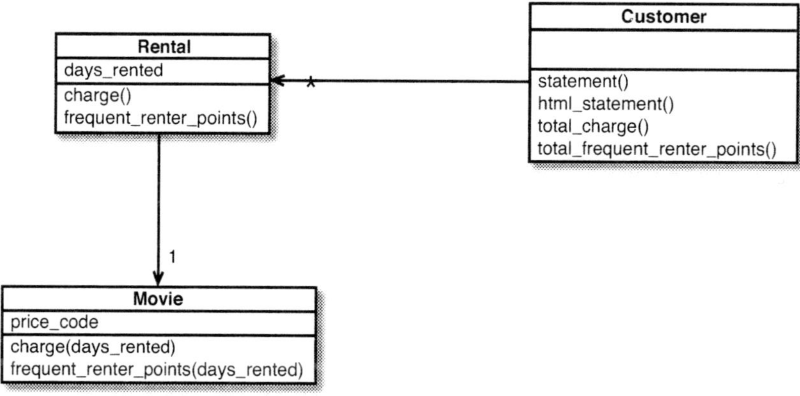

Figure 1.13 Class diagram after moving methods to movie.

Replacing the Conditional Logic on Price Code with Polymorphism

At Last...Inheritance

We have several types of movie that have different ways of answering the same question. This sounds like a job for subclasses. We can have three subclasses of movie, each of which can have its own version of charge (see Figure 1.14).

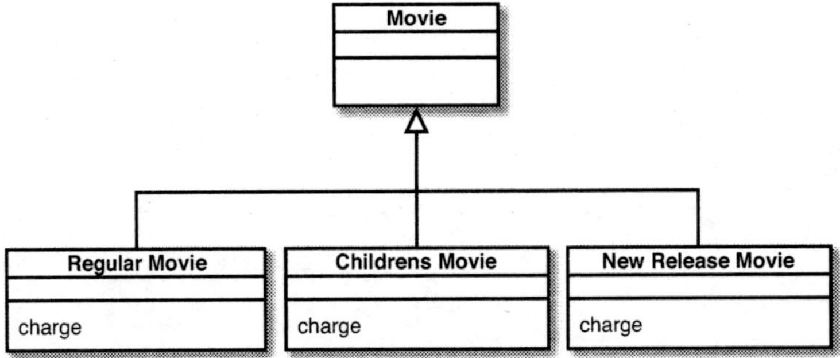

Figure 1.14 Using inheritance on movie.

This allows me to replace the case statement by using polymorphism. Sadly it has one slight flaw: It doesn't work. A movie can change its classification during its lifetime. An object cannot change its class during its lifetime. All is not lost, however. We can remove the case statement with the state pattern [Gang of Four].

With the state pattern the classes look like Figure 1.15. By adding the indirection we can change the price whenever we need to.

If you are familiar with the Gang of Four patterns, you may wonder, "Is this a state, or is it a strategy?" Does the price class represent an algorithm for calculating the price (in which case I prefer to call it `Pricer` or), or does it represent a state of the movie (Star Trek X is a new release)? At this stage the choice of pattern (and name) reflects how you want to think about the structure. At the moment I'm thinking about this as a state of movie. If I later decide a strategy communicates my intention better, I will refactor to do this by changing the names.

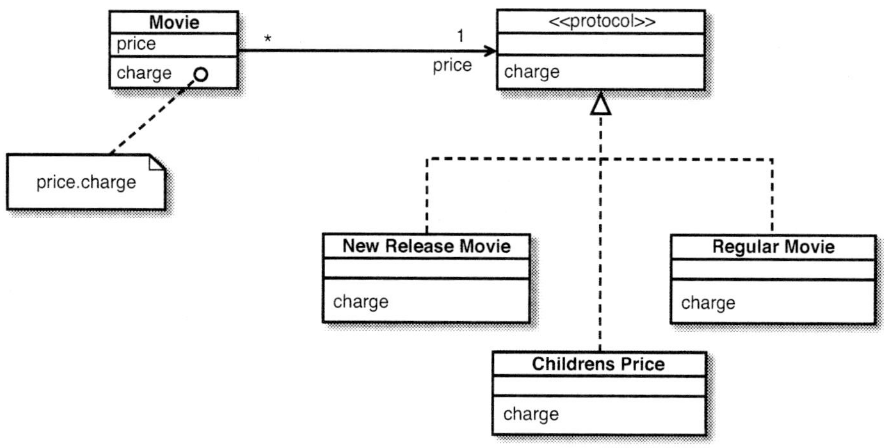

Figure 1.15 Using the state pattern on movie.*

---

*To show this in UML, I've made a «protocol» stereotype. This doesn't correspond to a class, or any explicit Ruby construct, but to the expectation the movie has of its price. UML does not have an accepted way to handle dynamic typed polymorphism like this.

The refactoring I'm going to use here is Replace Type Code with State/Strategy. The first step is to use Self Encapsulate Field on the type code to ensure that all uses of the type code go through getting and setting methods. Because most of the code came from other classes, most methods already use the getting method. However, the constructor does access the price code:

```
class Movie
  attr_accessor :price_code

  def initialize(title, price_code)
    @title, @price_code = title, price_code
  end
end
```

I introduce a custom setter method (because it's going to do something more interesting soon), and call it from the constructor.

```
class Movie
  attr_reader :price_code

  def price_code=(value)
    @price_code = value
  end

  def initialize(title, the_price_code)
    @title, self.price_code = title, the_price_code
  end
end
```

I test to make sure I didn't break anything. Now I add the new classes that add the type code behavior.

```
class RegularPrice

end

class NewReleasePrice

end

class ChildrensPrice

end
```

Now I do the interesting thing with the custom price code setter:

```
class Movie...

  def price_code=(value)
    @price_code = value
  end
```

I set a new instance variable called price to an instance of the appropriate type class.

```
class Movie...

  def price_code=(value)
    @price_code = value
    @price = case price_code
      when REGULAR: RegularPrice.new
      when NEW_RELEASE: NewReleasePrice.new
      when CHILDRENS: ChildrensPrice.new
    end
  end
end
```

You may notice the irony here. I'm putting in polymorphism to get rid of conditional logic, and the first thing I do is put a case in. The point is that once I'm done this will be the only case left. Depending on what else is going on I may be able to eliminate this one too.

Replacing the Conditional Logic on Price Code with Polymorphism

Next I choose one of the methods that needs to behave polymorphically. I start with charge.

```
class Movie
  def charge(days_rented)
    result = 0
    case price_code
    when REGULAR
      result += 2
      result += (days_rented - 2) * 1.5 if days_rented > 2
    when NEW_RELEASE
      result += days_rented * 3
    when CHILDRENS
      result += 1.5
      result += (days_rented - 3) * 1.5 if days_rented > 3
    end
    result
  end
end
```

I need to implement the charge method on one of the new price objects.

```
class RegularPrice
  def charge(days_rented)
    result = 2
    result += (days_rented - 2) * 1.5 if days_rented > 2
    result
  end
end
```

I call the new method from Movie's charge method. I need to pass in days_rented.

```
class Movie...
 def charge(days_rented)
   result = 0
   case price_code
   when REGULAR
     return @price.charge(days_rented)
   when NEW_RELEASE
     result += days_rented * 3
   when CHILDRENS
     result += 1.5
     result += (days_rented - 3) * 1.5 if days_rented > 3
   end
   result
 end
```

All going well, my tests should pass. I can then do the same for the other type classes.

```
class Movie...
 def charge(days_rented)
   result = 0
   case price_code
   when REGULAR
     return @price.charge(days_rented)
   when NEW_RELEASE
     result += days_rented * 3
   when CHILDRENS
     result += 1.5
     result += (days_rented - 3) * 1.5 if days_rented > 3
   end
   result
 end
```

```
class NewReleasePrice

  def charge(days_rented)
    days_rented * 3
  end

end

class ChildrensPrice

  def charge(days_rented)
    result = 1.5
    result += (days_rented - 3) * 1.5 if days_rented > 3
    result
  end
end
```

I turn Movie's charge method into a simple delegator when I'm done.

```
class Movie

  def charge(days_rented)
    @price.charge(days_rented)
  end
```

The next method to tackle is `frequent_renter_points`.

```
class Movie
  def frequent_renter_points(days_rented)
    (price_code == NEW_RELEASE && days_rented > 1) ? 2 : 1
  end
end
```

We want `frequent_renter_points` to be the same for `ChildrensPrice` and `RegularPrice`, but be different for `NewReleasePrice`. I use Extract Module and include the module into `RegularPrice` and `ChildrensPrice`. I then implement the special `frequent_renter_points` on `NewReleasePrice`.

```
module DefaultPrice
  def frequent_renter_points(days_rented)
    1
  end
end

class RegularPrice...
  include Price

end

class NewReleasePrice...

  def frequent_renter_points(days_rented)
    days_rented > 1 ? 2 : 1
  end
end

class ChildrensPrice...
  include Price

end
```

Like `charge`, `frequent_renter_points` on `Movie` now becomes a simple delegator.

```
class Movie...

  def frequent_renter_points(days_rented)
    @price.frequent_renter_points(days_rented)
  end
end
```

Replacing the Conditional Logic on Price Code with Polymorphism

As a final step, I can remove the case statement from the `price_code` setter method.

```
# calling code
movie = Movie.new("The Watchmen", Movie::NEW_RELEASE)
# and later...
movie.price_code = Movie::REGULAR

class Movie...

  def price_code=(value)
    @price_code = value
    @price = case price_code
      when REGULAR: RegularPrice.new
      when NEW_RELEASE: NewReleasePrice.new
      when CHILDRENS: ChildrensPrice.new
    end
  end
end
```

I can make the callers pass in an instance of the type themselves.

```
# calling code
movie = Movie.new("The Watchmen", NewReleasePrice.new)
# and later...
movie.price = RegularPrice.new

class Movie
  attr_writer :price
```

Putting in the state pattern was quite an effort. Was it worth it? The gain is that if I change any of price's behavior, add new prices, or add extra price-dependent behavior, the change will be much easier to make. The rest of the application does not know about the use of the state pattern. For the tiny amount of behavior I currently have, it is not a big deal. In a more complex system with a dozen or so price-dependent methods, this would make a big difference. All these changes were small steps. It seems slow to write it this way, but not once did I have to open the debugger, so the process actually flowed quite quickly. It took me much longer to write this section of the book than it did to change the code.

I've now completed the second major refactoring. It is going to be much easier to change the classification structure of movies, and to alter the rules for charging and the frequent renter point system. Figures 1.16 and 1.17 show how the state pattern works with price information.

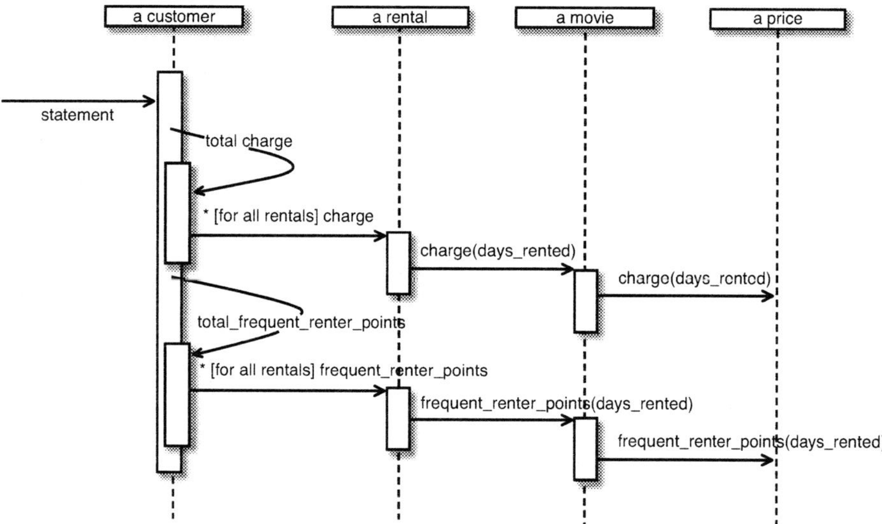

Figure 1.16 Interactions using the state pattern.

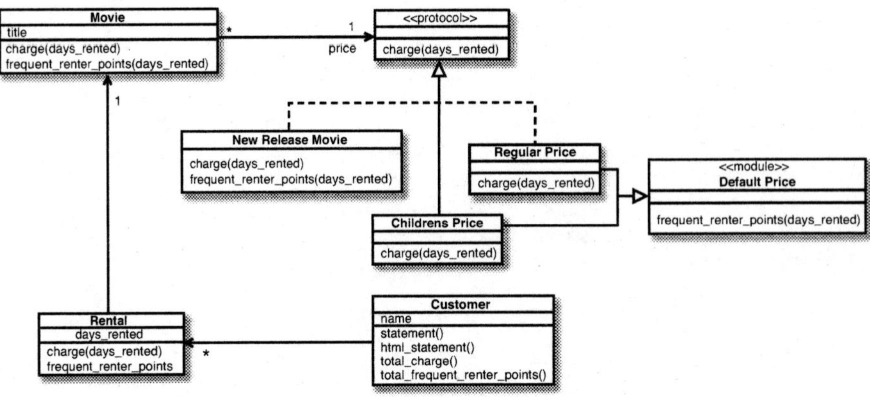

Figure 1.17 Class diagram after addition of the state pattern.

Final Thoughts

This is a simple example, yet I hope it gives you the feeling of what refactoring is like. I used several refactorings, including Extract Method, Move Method, and Replace Type Code with State/Strategy. All these lead to better-distributed responsibilities and code that is easier to maintain. It does look rather different from procedural style code, and that takes some getting used to. But once you are used to it, it is hard to go back to procedural programs.

The most important lesson from this example is the rhythm of refactoring: test, small change, test, small change, test, small change. It is that rhythm that allows refactoring to move quickly and safely.

If you're with me this far, you should now understand what refactoring is all about. We can now move on to some background, principles, and theory (although not too much!)

Chapter 2

Principles in Refactoring

The example in Chapter 1, "Refactoring, a First Example," should give you a good feel for what refactoring is all about. Now it's time to step back and look at the key principles of refactoring and at some of the issues you need to think about in using refactoring.

Where Did Refactoring Come From?

I've not succeeded in pinning down the real birth of the term refactoring. Good programmers certainly have spent at least some time cleaning up their code. They do this because they have learned that clean code is easier to change than complex and messy code, and good programmers know that they rarely write clean code the first time around.

Refactoring goes beyond this. In this book I'm advocating refactoring as a key element in the whole process of software development. Two of the first people to recognize the importance of refactoring were Ward Cunningham and Kent Beck, who worked with Smalltalk from the 1980s onward. Smalltalk is an environment that even then was particularly hospitable to refactoring. It is a dynamic environment that allows you quickly to write highly functional software. Smalltalk has a short compile-link-execute cycle, which makes it easy to change things quickly. It is also object oriented and thus provides powerful tools for minimizing the impact of change behind well-defined interfaces. Ward and Kent worked hard at developing a software development process geared to working with this kind of environment. (Kent used this style as inspiration for his book eXtreme Programming eXplained [Beck, XP].) They realized that refactoring was important in improving their productivity and ever since have been working with refactoring, applying it to serious software projects, and refining the process.

Ward and Kent's ideas have always been a strong influence on the Smalltalk community, and the notion of refactoring has become an important element in the Smalltalk culture. Ralph Johnson and Don Roberts, both of the University of Illinois, were also pioneers in Smalltalk refactoring. Ralph is famous as one of the Gang of Four [Gang of Four], and explored how refactoring can help develop an efficient and flexible framework.

Bill Opdyke was one of Ralph's doctoral students and is particularly interested in frameworks. He saw the potential value of refactoring and saw that it could be applied to much more than Smalltalk. His background was in telephone switch development, in which a great deal of complexity accrues over time, and changes are difficult to make. Bill's doctoral research looked at refactoring from a tool builder's perspective. Bill investigated the refactorings that would be useful for C++ framework development and researched the necessary semantics-preserving refactorings, how to prove they were semantics preserving, and how a tool could implement these ideas.

I remember meeting Bill at the OOPSLA conference in 1992. We sat in a café and discussed some of the work I'd done in building a conceptual framework for health care. Bill told me about his research, and I remember thinking, "Interesting, but not really that important." Boy was I wrong!

And me? I'd always been inclined to clean code, but I'd never considered it to be that important. Then I worked on a project with Kent and saw the way he used refactoring. I saw the difference it made in productivity and quality. That experience convinced me that refactoring was an important technique. I was frustrated, however, because there was no book that I could give to a working programmer, and none of the experts mentioned previously had any plans to write such a book. So, with their help, we wrote the first edition of *Refactoring*. Now, with Jay and Shane, we've been able to update the book with our learnings over the past nine years and add material that applies to Ruby, and dynamic languages in general.

Defining Refactoring

I'm always a little leery of definitions because everyone has his or her own, but when you write a book you get to choose your own definitions. In this case I'm basing my definitions on the work done by Ralph Johnson's group and assorted associates.

The first thing to say about this is that the word *refactoring* has two definitions depending on context. You might find this annoying (I certainly do), but it serves as yet another example of the realities of working with natural language.

The first definition is the noun form.

Tip Refactoring (noun): A change made to the internal structure of software to make it easier to understand and cheaper to modify without changing its observable behavior.

You can find examples of refactorings in the catalog, such as Extract Method and Replace Hash with Object. As such, a refactoring is usually a small change to the software, although one refactoring can involve others. For example, Extract Class usually involves Move Method and Move Field.

The other usage of refactoring is the verb form.

Tip Refactor (verb): To restructure software by applying a series of refactorings without changing its observable behavior.

So you might spend a few hours refactoring, during which you might apply a couple of dozen individual refactorings.

I've been asked, "Is refactoring just cleaning up code?" In a way the answer is yes, but I think refactoring goes further because it provides a technique for cleaning up code in a more efficient and controlled manner. Since I've been using refactoring, I've noticed that I clean code far more effectively than I did before. This is because I know which refactorings to use, I know how to use them in a manner that minimizes bugs, and I test at every possible opportunity.

I should amplify a couple of points in my definitions. First, the purpose of refactoring is to make the software easier to understand and modify. You can make many changes in software that make little or no change in the observable behavior. Only changes that make the software easier to understand are refactorings. A good contrast is performance optimization. Like refactoring, performance optimization does not usually change the behavior of a component (other than its speed); it only alters the internal structure. However, the purpose is different. Performance optimization often makes code harder to understand, but you need to do it to get the performance you need.

The second thing I want to highlight is that refactoring does not change the observable behavior of the software. The software still carries out the same function that it did before. Any user, whether an end user or another programmer, cannot tell that things have changed.

The Two Hats

This second point leads to Kent Beck's metaphor of two hats. When you use refactoring to develop software, you divide your time between two distinct activities: adding function and refactoring. When you add function, you shouldn't be changing existing code; you are just adding new capabilities. You can measure your progress by adding tests and getting the tests to work. When you refactor, you make a point of not adding function; you only restructure the code. You don't add any tests (unless you find a case you missed earlier); you only restructure the code. Additionally, you only change tests when you absolutely need to in order to cope with a change in an interface.

As you develop software, you probably find yourself swapping hats frequently. You start by trying to add a new function, and you realize this would be much easier if the code were structured differently. So you swap hats and refactor for a while. Once the code is better structured, you swap hats and add the new function. Once you get the new function working, you realize you coded it in a way that's awkward to understand, so you swap hats again and refactor. All this might take only ten minutes, but during this time you should always be aware of which hat you're wearing.

Why Should You Refactor?

I don't want to proclaim refactoring as the cure for all software ills. It is no "silver bullet." Yet it is a valuable tool, a pair of silver pliers that helps you keep a good grip on your code. Refactoring is a tool that can, and should, be used for several purposes.

Refactoring Improves the Design of Software

Without refactoring, the design of the program will decay. As people change code—whether changes to realize short-term goals or changes made without a full comprehension of the design of the code—the code loses its structure. It becomes harder to see the design by reading the code. Refactoring is rather like tidying up the code. Work is done to remove bits that aren't really in the right place. Loss of the structure of code has a cumulative effect. The harder it is to see the design in the code, the harder it is to preserve it, and the more rapidly it decays. Regular refactoring helps code retain its shape.

Poorly designed code usually takes more code to do the same things, often because the code literally does the same thing in several places. Thus an important aspect of improving design is to eliminate duplicate code. The importance of this lies in future modifications to the code. Reducing the amount of code won't make the system run any faster, because the effect on the footprint of the programs rarely is significant. Reducing the amount of code does, however, make a big difference in modification of the code. The more code there is, the harder it is to modify correctly. There's more code to understand. You change this bit of code here, but the system doesn't do what you expect because you didn't change that bit over there that does much the same thing in a slightly different context. By eliminating the duplicates, you ensure that the code says everything once and only once, which is the essence of good design.

Refactoring Makes Software Easier to Understand

Programming is in many ways a conversation with a computer. You write code that tells the computer what to do, and it responds by doing exactly what you tell it. In time you close the gap between what you want it to do and what you tell it to do. Programming in this mode is all about saying exactly what you want. But there is another user of your source code. Someone will try to read your code in a few months' time to make some changes. We easily forget that extra user of the code, yet that user is actually the most important. Who cares if the computer takes a few more cycles to execute something? It does matter if it takes a programmer a week to make a change that would have taken only an hour if she had understood your code.

The trouble is that when you are trying to get the program to work, you are not thinking about that future developer. It takes a change of rhythm to make changes that make the code easier to understand. Refactoring helps you to make your code more readable. When refactoring you have code that works but is not ideally structured. A little time spent refactoring can make the code better communicate its purpose. Programming in this mode is all about saying exactly what you mean.

I'm not necessarily being altruistic about this. Often this future developer is me. Here refactoring is particularly important. I'm a very lazy programmer. One form of my laziness is that I never remember things about the code I write. Indeed, I deliberately try not remember anything I can look up, because I'm afraid my brain will get full. I make a point of trying to put everything I should remember into the code so I don't have to remember it.

This understandability works another way, too. I use refactoring to help me understand unfamiliar code. When I look at unfamiliar code, I have to try to understand what it does. I look at a couple of lines and say to myself, oh yes, that's what this bit of code is doing. With refactoring I don't stop at the mental note. I actually change the code to better reflect my understanding, and then I test that understanding by rerunning the code to see if it still works.

Early on I do refactoring like this on little details. As the code gets clearer, I find I can see things about the design that I could not see before. Had I not changed the code, I probably never would have seen these things, because I'm just not clever enough to visualize all this in my head. Ralph Johnson describes these early refactorings as wiping the dirt off a window so you can see beyond. When I'm studying code I find refactoring leads me to higher levels of understanding that otherwise I would miss.

Refactoring Helps You Find Bugs

Help in understanding the code also helps me spot bugs. I admit I'm not terribly good at finding bugs. Some people can read a lump of code and see bugs; I cannot. However, I find that if I refactor code, I work deeply on understanding what the code does, and I put that new understanding right back into the code. By clarifying the structure of the program, I clarify certain assumptions I've made, to the point at which even I can't avoid spotting the bugs.

It reminds me of a statement Kent Beck often makes about himself, "I'm not a great programmer; I'm just a good programmer with great habits." Refactoring helps me be much more effective at writing robust code.

Refactoring Helps You Program Faster

In the end, all the earlier points come down to this: Refactoring helps you develop code more quickly.

This sounds counterintuitive. When I talk about refactoring, people can easily see that it improves quality. Improving design, improving readability, reducing bugs, all these improve quality. But doesn't all this reduce the speed of development?

I strongly believe that a good design is essential for rapid software development. Indeed, the whole point of having a good design is to allow rapid development. Without a good design, you can progress quickly for a while, but soon the poor design starts to slow you down. You spend time finding and fixing bugs instead of adding new function. Changes take longer as you try to understand the system and find the duplicate code. New features need more coding as you patch over a patch that patches a patch on the original code base.

A good design is essential to maintaining speed in software development. Refactoring helps you develop software more rapidly, because it stops the design of the system from decaying. It can even improve a design.

When Should You Refactor?

When I talk about refactoring, I'm often asked about how it should be scheduled. Should we allocate two weeks every couple of months to refactoring?

In almost all cases, I'm opposed to setting aside time for refactoring. In my view refactoring is not an activity you set aside time to do. Refactoring is something you do all the time in little bursts. You don't decide to refactor, you refactor because you want to do something else, and refactoring helps you do that other thing.

The Rule of Three

Here's a guideline Don Roberts gave me: The first time you do something, you just do it. The second time you do something similar, you wince at the duplication, but you do the duplicate thing anyway. The third time you do something similar, you refactor.

Tip Three strikes and you refactor.

Refactor When You Add Function

The most common time to refactor is when I want to add a new feature to some software. Often the first reason to refactor here is to help me understand some code I need to modify. This code may have been written by someone else, or I may have written it. Whenever I have to think to understand what the code is doing, I ask myself if I can refactor the code to make that understanding more immediately apparent. Then I refactor it. This is partly for the next time I pass by here, but mostly it's because I can understand more things if I clarify the code as I'm going along.

The other driver of refactoring here is a design that does not help me add a feature easily. I look at the design and say to myself, "If only I'd designed the code this way, adding this feature would be easy." In this case I don't fret over my past misdeeds—I fix them by refactoring. I do this partly to make future enhancements easy, but mostly I do it because I've found it's the fastest way. Refactoring is a quick and smooth process. Once I've refactored, adding the feature can go much more quickly and smoothly.

Sometimes a new framework is released or a new technique is found that may replace a portion of your application. Developers are often eager to both remove existing pain points and experiment with new solutions. Refactoring when you add function always needs Return on Investment (ROI) consideration; however, there is often hidden ROI. For example, replacing a section of your code with a framework means there is less code for the existing team and new members to understand. Of course, this must be weighed against the fact that the framework likely isn't bulletproof. However, when using a framework you can not only utilize your team to diagnose problems, you can also utilize the community that uses the framework. Another hidden ROI for utilizing new frameworks or ideas is that you may fail when attempting to put it in your code base; however, failure is often as important as success. If you never try the framework (or technique) you will never know where it applies and where it doesn't. Today's failure may result in a deeper understanding of the framework that may lead to a great gain in the future when it is utilized in a successful way.

Refactor When You Need to Fix a Bug

In fixing bugs much of the use of refactoring comes from making code more understandable. As I look at the code trying to understand it, I refactor to help improve my understanding. Often I find that this active process of working with the code helps in finding the bug. One way to look at it is that if you do get a bug report, it's a sign you need refactoring, because the code was not clear enough for you to see there was a bug.

Refactor As You Do a Code Review

Some organizations do regular code reviews; those that don't would do better if they did. Code reviews help spread knowledge through a development team. Reviews help more experienced developers pass knowledge to less experienced people. They help more people understand more aspects of a large software system. They are also important in writing clear code. My code may look clear to me but not to my team. That's inevitable—it's hard for people to put themselves in the shoes of someone unfamiliar with the things they are working on. Reviews also give the opportunity for more people to suggest useful ideas. I can only think of so many good ideas in a week. Having other people contribute makes my life easier, so I always look for many reviews.

I've found that refactoring helps me review someone else's code. Before I started using refactoring, I could read the code, understand some degree of it, and make suggestions. Now when I come up with ideas, I consider whether they can be easily implemented then and there with refactoring. If so, I refactor. When I do it a few times, I can see more clearly what the code looks like with the suggestions in place. I don't have to imagine what it would be like, I can see what it is like. As a result, I can come up with a second level of ideas that I would never have realized had I not refactored.

Refactoring also helps the code review have more concrete results. Not only are there suggestions, but also many suggestions are implemented there and then. You end up with much more of a sense of accomplishment from the exercise.

To make this process work, you have to have small review groups. My experience suggests having one reviewer and the original author work on the code together. The reviewer suggests changes, and they both decide whether the changes can be easily refactored in. If so, they make the changes.

With larger design reviews it is often better to obtain several opinions in a larger group. Showing code often is not the best device for this. I prefer UML diagrams and walking through scenarios with Class-Responsibility-Collaboration (CRC) cards. So I do design reviews with groups and code reviews with individual reviewers.

This idea of active code review is taken to its limit with the extreme programming [Beck, XP] practice of pair programming. With this technique all serious development is done with two developers at one machine. In effect it's a continuous code review folded into the development process, and the refactoring that takes place is folded in as well.

Refactoring for Greater Understanding (aka, Refactor to the Same Thing)

A senior developer once joined a team I was leading, halfway through the project. When he joined he saw things that he didn't agree with and suggested that we refactor the code toward a better domain model. Anxious to learn from the senior developer, I paired with him over the next few days while we made various changes to the domain model. Unfortunately, many of the changes that the senior developer suggested could not be implemented due to additional constraints imposed by required features. In the end, the code was refactored to be slightly better; however, the largest benefit was the deep understanding that the senior developer gained from the refactoring. From that point forward he delivered value at the level you would expect from a team member who has been on the project from day one. The project lost two development days toward new features; however, it gained a fully productive senior developer only two days after joining the project. That developer's contribution in the following months greatly outweighed the original slowdown.

I see refactoring for greater understanding fairly often; however, I don't think it's a bad thing. When developers have a deeper understanding of the code base they can be more effective at adding to it and suggesting how to improve it.

Why Refactoring Works

Kent Beck

Programs have two kinds of value: What they can do for you today and what they can do for you tomorrow. Most times when programming, we are focused on what we want the program to do today. Whether we are fixing a bug or adding a feature, we are making today's program more valuable by making it more capable.

You can't program long without realizing that what the system does today is only a part of the story. If you can get today's work done today, but you do it in such a way that you can't possibly get tomorrow's work done tomorrow, then you lose. Notice, though, that you know what you need to do today, but you're not quite sure about tomorrow. Maybe you'll do this, maybe that, maybe something you haven't imagined yet.

I know enough to do today's work. I don't know enough to do tomorrow's. But if I only work for today, I won't be able to work tomorrow at all.

Refactoring is one way out of the bind. When you find that yesterday's decision doesn't make sense today, you change the decision. Now you can do today's work. Tomorrow, some of your understanding as of today will seem naive, so you'll change that, too.

What makes programs hard to work with? I can think of four things:

- Programs that are hard to read are hard to modify.
- Programs that have duplicated logic are hard to modify.
- Programs that require additional behavior that requires you to change running code are hard to modify.
- Programs with complex conditional logic are hard to modify.

So, we want programs that are easy to read, that have all logic specified in one and only one place, that do not allow changes to endanger existing behavior, and that allow conditional logic to be expressed as simply as possible.

Refactoring is the process of taking a running program and adding to its value, not by changing its behavior but by giving it more of these qualities that enable us to continue developing at speed.

What Do I Tell My Manager?

How to tell a manager about refactoring is one of the most common questions I've been asked. If the manager is technically savvy, introducing the subject may not be that hard. If the manager is genuinely quality oriented, then the thing to stress is the quality aspect. Here using refactoring in the review process is a good way to work things. Many studies show that technical reviews are an important way to reduce bugs and thus speed up development. Take a look at any book on reviews, inspections, or the software development process for the latest citations. These should convince most managers of the value of reviews. It is then a short step to introduce refactoring as a way of getting review comments into the code.

Of course, many people say they are driven by quality but are more driven by schedule. In these cases I give my more controversial advice: Don't tell!

Subversive? I don't think so. Software developers are professionals. Our job is to build effective software as rapidly as we can. My experience is that refactoring is a big aid to building software quickly. If I need to add a new function and the design does not suit the change, I find it's quicker to refactor first and then add the function. If I need to fix a bug, I need to understand how the software works and I find refactoring is the fastest way to do this. A schedule-driven manager wants me to do things the fastest way I can; how I do it is my business. The fastest way is to refactor; therefore I refactor.

Indirection and Refactoring

Kent Beck

Computer science is the discipline that believes all problems can be solved with one more layer of indirection. —Dennis DeBruler

Given software engineers' infatuation with indirection, it may not surprise you to learn that most refactoring introduces more indirection into a program.

Refactoring tends to break big objects and big methods into several smaller ones.

Indirection is a two-edged sword, however. Every time you break one thing into two pieces, you have more things to manage. It also can make a program harder to read as an object delegates to an object delegating to an object. So you'd like to minimize indirection.

Indirection and Refactoring

Not so fast, buddy. Indirection can pay for itself. Here are some of the ways:

- To enable sharing of logic. For example, a submethod invoked in two different places or a method in a superclass shared by all subclasses.
- To explain intention and implementation separately. Choosing the name of each class and the name of each method gives you an opportunity to explain what you intend. The internals of the class or method explain how the intention is realized. If the internals also are written in terms of intention in yet smaller pieces, you can write code that communicates most of the important information about its own structure.
- To isolate change. I use an object in two different places. I want to change the behavior in one of the two cases. If I change the object, I risk changing both. So I first make a subclass and refer to it in the case that is changing. Now I can modify the subclass without risking an inadvertent change to the other case.
- To encode conditional logic. Objects have a fabulous mechanism, polymorphic messages, to flexibly but clearly express conditional logic. By changing explicit conditionals to messages, you can often reduce duplication, add clarity, and increase flexibility all at the same time.

Here is the refactoring game: Maintaining the current behavior of the system, how can you make your system more valuable, either by increasing its quality or by reducing its cost?

The most common variant of the game is to look at your program. Identify a place where it is missing one or more of the benefits of indirection. Put in that indirection without changing the existing behavior. Now you have a more valuable program because it has more qualities that we will appreciate tomorrow.

Contrast this with careful up-front design. Speculative design is an attempt to put all the good qualities into the system before any code is written. Then the code can just be hung on the sturdy skeleton. The problem with this process is that it is too easy to guess wrong. With refactoring, you are never in danger of being completely wrong. The program always behaves at the end as it did at the beginning. In addition, you have the opportunity to add valuable qualities to the code.

There is a second, rarer refactoring game. Identify indirection that isn't paying for itself and take it out. Often this takes the form of intermediate methods that used to serve a purpose but no longer do. Or it could be a component that you expected to be shared or polymorphic but turned out to be used in only one place. When you find parasitic indirection, take it out. Again, you will have a more valuable program, not because there is more of one of the four qualities listed earlier but because it costs less indirection to get the same amount from the qualities.

Problems with Refactoring

When you learn a new technique that greatly improves your productivity, it is hard to see when it does not apply. Usually you learn it within a specific context, often just a single project. It is hard to see what causes the technique to be less effective, even harmful. When writing the original book, refactoring was a relatively new practice, and it was difficult to identify potential problems. Now, refactoring is a mature practice, and we can speak more confidently about the benefits and potential pitfalls.

Changing Interfaces

One of the important things about objects is that they allow you to change the implementation of a software module separately from changing the interface. You can safely change the internals of an object without anyone else's worrying about it, but the interface is important—change that and anything can happen.

Something disturbing about refactoring is that many of the refactorings do change an interface. Something as simple as Rename Method is all about changing an interface. So what does this do to the treasured notion of encapsulation?

There is no problem changing a method name if you have access to all the code that calls that method. Even if the method is public, as long as you can reach and change all the callers, you can rename the method. There is a problem only if the interface is being used by code that you cannot find and change. When this happens, I say that the interface becomes a published interface (a step beyond a public interface). Once you publish an interface, you can no longer safely change it and just edit the callers. You need a somewhat more complicated process.

This notion changes the question. Now the problem is: What do you do about refactorings that change published interfaces?

In short, if a refactoring changes a published interface, you have to retain both the old interface and the new one, at least until your users have had a chance to react to the change. Fortunately, this is not too awkward. You can usually arrange things so that the old interface still works. Try to do this so that the old interface calls the new interface. In this way when you change the name of a method, keep the old one, and just let it call the new one. Don't copy the method body—that leads you down the path to damnation by way of duplicated code. You should also create some type of deprecation facility; that way your callers will know that something is up (See the "Refactor with Deprecation" section of "Replace Array with Object" in Chapter 8 for details).

Protecting interfaces usually is doable, but it is a pain. You have to build and maintain these extra methods, at least for a time. The methods complicate the interface, making it harder to use. There is an alternative: Don't publish the interface. Now I'm not talking about a total ban here, clearly you have to have published interfaces. If you are building APIs for outside consumption, as Sun does, then you have to have published interfaces. I say this because I often see development groups using published interfaces far too much. I've seen a team of three people operate in such a way that each person published interfaces to the other two. This led to all sorts of gyrations to maintain interfaces when it would have been easier to go into the code base and make the edits. Organizations with an overly strong notion of code ownership tend to behave this way. Using published interfaces is useful, but it comes with a cost. So don't publish interfaces unless you really need to. This may mean modifying your code ownership rules to allow people to change other people's code to support an interface change. Often it is a good idea to do this with pair programming.

Tip Don't publish interfaces prematurely. Modify your code ownership policies to smooth refactoring.

Databases

One problem area for refactoring is databases. Many business applications are tightly coupled to the database schema that support them. That's one reason that the database is difficult to change. Another reason is data migration. Even if you have carefully layered your system to minimize the dependencies between the database schema and the object model, changing the database schema forces you to migrate the data, which can be a long and fraught task. The addition of a rigorous one-click deployment process with database migrations as part of that process certainly helps. Write your migrations to modify the schema and migrate the data. Use temporary tables if you need to preserve the data while you modify the schema. Write tests for your migrations.

The migration task can still take a very long time, and in some systems regular modification of the schema may not be feasible. One way to deal with this problem is to place a separate layer of software between your object model and your database model. That way you can isolate the changes to the two different models. As you update one model, you don't need to update the other. You just update the intermediate layer. Such a layer adds complexity but gives you a lot of flexibility. Even without refactoring it is very important in situations in which you have multiple databases or a complex database model that you don't have control over.

You don't have to start with a separate layer. You can create the layer as you notice parts of your object model becoming volatile. This way you get the greatest leverage for your changes.

For more information on Refactoring databases see Pramod Sadalage and Scott Ambler's book *Refactoring Databases* [Sadalage].

Design Changes That Are Difficult to Refactor

Can you refactor your way out of any design mistake, or are some design decisions so central that you cannot count on refactoring to change your mind later? In the vast majority of situations, refactoring will see you through. Certain architectural decisions, such as the choice of framework or choice of integration technology are harder to refactor away from, but certainly possible. In one project we wanted to move to a message-oriented architecture to improve performance and decouple components of the system, but the business was reluctant to pay for a wholesale change. So when it came time to introduce a new set of features, we implemented them using the message-oriented architecture. We were able to stand up the required infrastructure for these relatively simple features, and as modifications were requested of the old features, we refactored them one-by-one to use the new architecture. It took time, but in the end we were successful, and the business was able to receive new features throughout the entire process.

That said, choice of framework and integration architecture should not be made lightly. But once these decisions are made, proceed forward with confidence that by applying refactoring techniques, mistakes made today can easily be reversed tomorrow. As you consider design alternatives, ask yourself how difficult it would be to refactor from one design into another. If it seems easy, don't worry too much about the choice, and pick the simplest design, even if it does not cover all the potential requirements. However, if you cannot see a simple way to refactor, then put more effort into the design. You should find such situations are in the minority.

When Shouldn't You Refactor?

There are times when you should not refactor at all. The principle example is when you should rewrite from scratch instead. There are times when the existing code is such a mess that although you could refactor it, it would be easier to start from the beginning. This decision is not an easy one to make, and I admit that I don't really have good guidelines for it.

A clear sign of the need to rewrite is when the current code just does not work. You may discover this only by trying to test it and discovering that the code is so full of bugs that you cannot stabilize it. Remember, code has to work mostly correctly before you refactor.

A compromise route is to refactor a large piece of software into components with strong encapsulation. Then you can make a refactor-versus-rebuild decision for one component at a time. Perform Extract Class and Move Method on coherent pieces of behavior. If the behavior is not tested, write tests for it.

Another time you should avoid refactoring is when you are close to a deadline. At that point the productivity gain from refactoring would appear after the deadline and thus be too late. Ward Cunningham has a good way to think of this. He describes unfinished refactoring as going into debt. Most companies need some debt to function efficiently. However, with debt comes interest payments, that is, the extra cost of maintenance and extension caused by overly complex code. You can bear some interest payments, but if the payments become too great, you will be overwhelmed. It is important to manage your debt, paying parts of it off by means of refactoring.

Other than when you are very close to a deadline, however, you should not put off refactoring because you haven't got time. Experience with several projects has shown that a bout of refactoring results in increased productivity. Not having enough time usually is a sign that you need to do some refactoring.

The most costly refactoring is refactoring for academic purposes. Refactoring for academic purposes is in direct conflict with delivering working software. In your career you will likely find many lines of code that you do not agree with; however, disagreeing with implementation is not a good enough reason to refactor code. If the code currently hinders your ability to deliver software (or will in the future), you can refactor, but changing code because you philosophically disagree is simply wrong.

For example, if you believe that state-based testing is the only way to test, that isn't a good enough reason to alter the existing tests that utilize mocks. If those tests become a maintenance problem, that's another issue, but simply disliking mocks does not give you the right to remove them. Creating a beautiful code base should always be a priority; however, creating working software is the number one priority. To make matters worse, when you refactor for academic purposes you do not always improve the quality of the code, thus you don't increase your ability to deliver new features.

Slowing delivery generally upsets the business sponsors and project managers. Refactoring is a good thing and everyone should be on board with it. If you can't prove to the business and the project manager that a refactoring is worth doing, you might be refactoring for academic purposes.

Refactoring and Design

Refactoring has a special role as a complement to design. When I first learned to program, I just wrote the program and muddled my way through it. In time I learned that thinking about the design in advance helped me avoid costly rework, and I got more into this style of up-front design. Many people consider design to be the key piece and programming just mechanics. The analogy is, design is an engineering drawing and code is the construction work. But software is different from physical machines. It is much more malleable, and it is all about thinking. As Alistair Cockburn, codeveloper of the Agile Manifesto puts it, "With design I can think very fast, but my thinking is full of little holes."

One argument is that refactoring can be an alternative to up-front design. In this scenario you don't do any design at all. You just code the first approach that comes into your head, get it working, and then refactor it into shape. Actually, this approach can work. I've seen people do this and come out with a well-designed piece of software. Those who support extreme programming [Beck, XP] often are portrayed as advocating this approach.

Although doing only refactoring does work, it is not the most efficient way to work. Even the extreme programmers do some design first. They will try out various ideas with CRC cards or the like until they have a plausible first solution. Only after generating a plausible first shot will they code and then refactor. The point is that refactoring changes the role of up-front design. If you don't refactor, there is a lot of pressure in getting that up-front design right. The sense is that any changes to the design later are going to be expensive. Thus you put more time and effort into the up-front design to avoid the need for such changes.

With refactoring the emphasis changes. You still do up-front design, but now you don't try to find the perfect solution. Instead all you want is a reasonable solution. You know that as you build the functionality, as you understand more about the problem, you may realize that the best solution is different from the one you originally came up with. With refactoring this is not a problem, for it no longer is expensive to make the changes.

Refactoring and Design

An important result of this change in emphasis is a greater movement toward simplicity of design. Before I used refactoring, I always looked for flexible solutions. With any requirement I would wonder how that requirement would change during the life of the system. Because design changes were expensive, I would look to build a design that would stand up to the changes I could foresee. The problem with building a flexible solution is that flexibility costs. Flexible solutions are more complex than simple ones. The resulting software is more difficult to maintain in general, although it is easier to flex in the direction I had in mind. Even there, however, you have to understand how to flex the design. For one or two aspects this is no big deal, but changes occur throughout the system. Building flexibility in all these places makes the overall system a lot more complex and expensive to maintain. The big frustration, of course, is that all this flexibility is not needed. Some of it is, but it's impossible to predict which pieces those are. To gain flexibility, you are forced to put in a lot more flexibility than you actually need.

With refactoring you approach the risks of change differently. You still think about potential changes; you still consider flexible solutions. But instead of implementing these flexible solutions, you ask yourself, "How difficult is it going to be to refactor a simple solution into the flexible solution?" If, as happens most of the time, the answer is "pretty easy," you just implement the simple solution.

Refactoring can lead to simpler designs without sacrificing flexibility. This makes the design process easier and less stressful. Once you have a broad sense of things that refactor easily, you don't even think of the flexible solutions. You have the confidence to refactor if the time comes. You build the simplest thing that can possibly work. As for the flexible, complex design, most of the time you aren't going to need it.

It Takes A While to Create Nothing

Ron Jeffries

The Chrysler Comprehensive Compensation pay process was running too slowly. Although we were still in development, it began to bother us, because it was slowing down the tests.

Kent Beck, Martin Fowler, and I decided we'd fix it up. While I waited for us to get together, I was speculating, on the basis of my extensive knowledge of the system, about what was probably slowing it down. I thought of several possibilities and chatted with folks about the changes that were probably necessary. We came up with some really good ideas about what would make the system go faster.

Then we measured performance using Kent's profiler. None of the possibilities I had thought of had anything to do with the problem. Instead, we found that the system was spending half its time creating instances of date. Even more interesting was that all the instances had the same couple of values.

When we looked at the date-creation logic, we saw some opportunities for optimizing how these dates were created. They were all going through a string conversion even though no external inputs were involved. The code was just using string conversion for convenience of typing. Maybe we could optimize that.

Then we looked at how these dates were being used. It turned out that the huge bulk of them were all creating instances of date range, an object with a "from date" and a "to date." Looking around a little more, we realized that most of these date ranges were empty!

As we worked with date range, we used the convention that any date range that ended before it started was empty. It's a good convention and fits in well with how the class works. Soon after we started using this convention, we realized that just creating a date range that starts after it ends wasn't clear code, so we extracted that behavior into a factory method for empty date ranges.

We had made that change to make the code clearer, but we received an unexpected payoff. We created a constant empty date range and adjusted the factory method to return that object instead of creating it every time. That change doubled the speed of the system, enough for the tests to be bearable. It took us about five minutes.

I had speculated with various members of the team (Kent and Martin deny participating in the speculation) on what was likely wrong with the code we knew very well. We had even sketched some designs for improvements without first measuring what was going on.

We were completely wrong. Aside from having a really interesting conversation, we were doing no good at all.

The lesson is: Even if you know exactly what is going on in your system, measure performance; don't speculate. You'll learn something, and nine times out of ten, it won't be that you were right!

Refactoring and Performance

A common concern with refactoring is the effect it has on the performance of a program. To make the software easier to understand, you often make changes that will cause the program to run more slowly. This is an important issue. I'm not one of the school of thought that ignores performance in favor of design purity or in hopes of faster hardware. Software has been rejected for being too slow, and faster machines merely move the goalposts. Refactoring certainly will make software go more slowly, but it also makes the software more amenable to performance tuning. The secret to fast software, in all but hard real-time contexts, is to write tunable software first and then to tune it for sufficient speed.

I've seen three general approaches to writing fast software. The most serious of these is time budgeting, used often in hard real-time systems. In this situation, as you decompose the design you give each component a budget for resources—time and footprint. That component must not exceed its budget, although a mechanism for exchanging budgeted times is allowed. Such a mechanism focuses hard attention on hard performance times. It is essential for systems such as heart pacemakers, in which late data is always bad data. This technique is overkill for other kinds of systems, such as the corporate information systems with which I usually work.

The second approach is the constant attention approach. With this approach every programmer, all the time, does whatever he or she can to keep performance high. This is a common approach and has intuitive attraction, but it does not work very well. Changes that improve performance usually make the program harder to work with. This slows development. This would be a cost worth paying if the resulting software were quicker, but usually it is not. The performance improvements are spread all around the program, and each improvement is made with a narrow perspective of the program's behavior.

The interesting thing about performance is that if you analyze most programs, you find that they waste most of their time in a small fraction of the code. If you optimize all the code equally, you end up with 90 percent of the optimizations wasted, because you are optimizing code that isn't run much. The time spent making the program fast, the time lost because of lack of clarity, is all wasted time.

The third approach to performance improvement takes advantage of this 90 percent statistic. In this approach you build your program in a well-factored manner without paying attention to performance until you begin a performance optimization stage, usually fairly late in development. During the performance optimization stage, you follow a specific process to tune the program.

You begin by running the program under a profiler that monitors the program and tells you where it is consuming time and space. This way you can find that small part of the program where the performance hot spots lie. Then you focus on those performance hot spots and use the same optimizations you would use if you were using the constant attention approach. But because you are focusing your attention on a hot spot, you are having much more effect for less work. Even so you remain cautious. As in refactoring you make the changes in small steps. After each step you test and rerun the profiler. If you haven't improved performance, you back out the change. You continue the process of finding and removing hot spots until you get the performance that satisfies your users. McConnel [McConnel] gives more information on this technique in his book Code Complete: A Practical Handbook of Software Construction.

Having a well-factored program helps with this style of optimization in two ways. First, it gives you time to spend on performance tuning. Because you have well-factored code, you can add function more quickly. This gives you more time to focus on performance. (Profiling ensures you focus that time on the right place.) Second, with a well-factored program you have finer granularity for your performance analysis. Your profiler leads you to smaller parts of the code, which are easier to tune. Because the code is clearer, you have a better understanding of your options and of what kind of tuning will work.

I've found that refactoring helps me write fast software. It slows the software in the short term while I'm refactoring, but it makes the software easier to tune during optimization. I end up well ahead.

Optimizing a Payroll System

Rich Garzaniti

We had been developing the Chrysler Comprehensive Compensation System for quite a while before we started to move it to GemStone. Naturally, when we did that, we found that the program wasn't fast enough. We brought in Jim Haungs, a master GemSmith, to help us optimize the system.

After a little time with the team to learn how the system worked, Jim used GemStone's ProfMonitor feature to write a profiling tool that plugged into our functional tests. The tool displayed the numbers of objects that were being created and where they were being created.

To our surprise, the biggest offender turned out to be the creation of strings. The biggest of the big was repeated creation of 12,000-byte strings. This was a particular problem because the string was so big that GemStone's usual garbage-collection facilities wouldn't deal with it. Because of the size, GemStone was paging the string to disk every time it was created. It turned out the strings were being built way down in our IO framework, and they were being built three at a time for every output record!

Our first fix was to cache a single 12,000-byte string, which solved most of the problem. Later, we changed the framework to write directly to a file stream, which eliminated the creation of even the one string.

Once the huge string was out of the way, Jim's profiler found similar problems with some smaller strings: 800 bytes, 500 bytes, and so on. Converting these to use the file stream facility solved them as well.

With these techniques we steadily improved the performance of the system. During development it looked like it would take more than 1,000 hours to run the payroll. When we actually got ready to start, it took 40 hours. After a month we got it down to around 18; when we launched we were at 12. After a year of running and enhancing the system for a new group of employees, it was down to 9 hours.

Our biggest improvement was to run the program in multiple threads on a multiprocessor machine. The system wasn't designed with threads in mind, but because it was so well factored, it took us only three days to run in multiple threads. Now the payroll takes a couple of hours to run.

Before Jim provided a tool that measured the system in actual operation, we had good ideas about what was wrong. But it was a long time before our good ideas were the ones that needed to be implemented. The real measurements pointed in a different direction and made a much bigger difference.

Chapter 3

Bad Smells in Code

If it stinks, change it.

Grandma Beck, discussing child-rearing philosophy

By now you have a good idea of how refactoring works. But just because you know how doesn't mean you know when. Deciding when to start refactoring, and when to stop, is just as important to refactoring as knowing how to operate the mechanics of a refactoring.

Now comes the dilemma. It is easy to explain how to delete an instance variable or create a hierarchy. These are simple matters. Trying to explain when you should do these things is not so cut-and-dried. Rather than appealing to some vague notion of programming aesthetics (which frankly is what we consultants usually do), I wanted something a bit more solid.

I was mulling over this tricky issue when I visited Kent Beck in Zurich. Perhaps he was under the influence of the odors of his newborn daughter at the time, but he had come up with the notion describing the "when" of refactoring in terms of smells. "Smells," you say, "and that is supposed to be better than vague aesthetics?" Well, yes. We look at lots of code, written for projects that span the gamut from wildly successful to nearly dead. In doing so, we have learned to look for certain structures in the code that suggest (sometimes they scream for) the possibility of refactoring. (We are switching over to "we" in this chapter to reflect the fact that Kent and I wrote this chapter jointly. You can tell the difference because the funny jokes are mine and the others are his.)

One thing we won't try to do here is give you precise criteria for when a refactoring is overdue. In our experience no set of metrics rivals informed human intuition. What we will do is give you indications that there is trouble that can be solved by a refactoring. You will have to develop your own sense of how many instance variables are too many instance variables and how many lines of code in a method are too many lines.

You should use this chapter and the table on the inside back cover as a way to give you inspiration when you're not sure what refactorings to do. Read the chapter (or skim the table) to try to identify what it is you're smelling, and then go to the refactorings we suggest to see whether they will help you. You may not find the exact smell you can detect, but hopefully it should point you in the right direction.

Duplicated Code

Number one in the stink parade is duplicated code. If you see the same code structure in more than one place, you can be sure that your program will be better if you find a way to unify them.

The simplest duplicated code problem is when you have the same expression in two methods of the same class. Then all you have to do is Extract Method and invoke the code from both places.

Another common duplication problem is when you have the same expression in two sibling subclasses. You can eliminate this duplication by using Extract Method in both classes and then Pull Up Method. If the code is similar but not the same, you need to use Extract Method to separate the similar bits from the different bits. You may then find you can use Form Template Method. If the methods do the same thing with a different algorithm, you can choose the clearer of the two algorithms and use Substitute Algorithm. If the duplication is in the middle of the method, use Extract Surrounding Method.

If you have duplicated code in two unrelated classes, consider using Extract Class or Extract Module in one class and then use the new component in the other. Another possibility is that the method really belongs only in one of the classes and should be invoked by the other class or that the method belongs in a third class that should be referred to by both of the original classes. You have to decide where the method makes sense and ensure it is there and nowhere else.

Long Method

The object programs that live best and longest are those with short methods. Programmers new to objects often feel that no computation ever takes place, that object programs are endless sequences of delegation. When you have lived with such a program for a few years, however, you learn just how valuable all those little methods are. All of the payoffs of indirection—explanation, sharing, and choosing—are supported by little methods (see the section "Indirection and Refactoring" in Chapter 2, "Principles in Refactoring.")

Since the early days of programming people have realized that the longer a procedure is, the more difficult it is to understand. Older languages carried an overhead in subroutine calls, which deterred people from small methods. Modern Object Oriented languages have pretty much eliminated that overhead for in-process calls. There is still an overhead to the reader of the code because you have to switch context to see what the subprocedure does. Development environments that allow you to see two methods at once help to eliminate this step, but the real key to making it easy to understand small methods is good naming. If you have a good name for a method you don't need to look at the body.

The net effect is that you should be much more aggressive about decomposing methods. A heuristic we follow is that whenever we feel the need to comment something, we write a method instead. Such a method contains the code that was commented but is named after the intention of the code rather than how it does it. We may do this on a group of lines or on as little as a single line of code. We do this even if the method call is longer than the code it replaces, provided the method name explains the purpose of the code. The key here is not method length but the semantic distance between what the method does and how it does it.

Ninety-nine percent of the time, all you have to do to shorten a method is Extract Method. Find parts of the method that seem to go nicely together and make a new method.

If you have a method with many parameters and temporary variables, these elements get in the way of extracting methods. If you try to use Extract Method, you end up passing so many of the parameters and temporary variables as parameters to the extracted method that the result is scarcely more readable than the original. You can often use Replace Temp with Query or Replace Temp with Chain to eliminate the temps. Long lists of parameters can be slimmed down with Introduce Parameter Object and Preserve Whole Object.

If you've tried that, and you still have too many temps and parameters, it's time to get out the heavy artillery: Replace Method with Method Object.

How do you identify the clumps of code to extract? A good technique is to look for comments. They often signal this kind of semantic distance. A block of code with a comment that tells you what it is doing can be replaced by a method whose name is based on the comment. Even a single line is worth extracting if it needs explanation.

Conditionals and loops also give signs for extractions. Use Decompose Conditional to deal with conditional expressions. Replace loops with Collection

Closure Methods and consider using Extract Method on the call to the closure method and the closure itself.

Large Class

When a class is trying to do too much, it often shows up as too many instance variables. When a class has too many instance variables, duplicated code cannot be far behind.

Long Parameter List

You can Extract Class to bundle a number of the variables. Choose variables to go together in the component that makes sense for each. For example, `deposit_amount` and `deposit_currency` are likely to belong together in a component. More generally, common prefixes or suffixes for some subset of the variables in a class suggest the opportunity for a component. If the component makes sense as a subclass, you'll find Extract Subclass often is easier. Another option if the component doesn't make sense as a delegate is Extract Module.

Sometimes a class does not use all of its instance variables all of the time. If so, you may be able to Extract Class, Extract Module, or Extract Subclass many times.

As with a class with too many instance variables, a class with too much code is prime breeding ground for duplicated code, chaos, and death. The simplest solution (have we mentioned that we like simple solutions?) is to eliminate redundancy in the class itself. If you have five hundred-line methods with a lot of duplicate code, you may be able to turn them into five ten-line methods with another ten two-line methods extracted from the original.

As with a class with a huge wad of variables, the usual solution for a class with too much code is either to Extract Class, Extract Module, or Extract Subclass. A useful trick is to determine how clients use the class and to use Extract Module for each of these uses. That may give you ideas on how you can further break up the class.

Long Parameter List

In our early programming days we were taught to pass in as parameters everything needed by a routine. This was understandable because the alternative was global data, and global data is evil and usually painful. Objects change this situation because if you don't have something you need, you can always ask another object to get it for you. Thus with objects you don't pass in everything the method needs; instead you pass enough so that the method can get to everything it needs. A lot of what a method needs is available on the method's host class. In object-oriented programs parameter lists tend to be much smaller than in traditional programs.

This is good because long parameter lists are hard to understand, because they become inconsistent and difficult to use, and because you are forever changing them as you need more data. Most changes are removed by passing objects because you are much more likely to need to make only a couple of requests to get at a new piece of data.

Use Replace Parameter with Method when you can get the data in one parameter by making a request of an object you already know about. This object might be an instance variable or it might be another parameter. Use Preserve Whole Object to take a bunch of data gleaned from an object and replace it with the object itself. If you have several data items with no logical object, use Introduce Parameter Object to clump them together, or Introduce Named Parameter to improve the fluency.

There is one important exception to making these changes. This is when you explicitly do not want to create a dependency from the called object to the larger object. In those cases, unpacking data and sending it along as parameters is reasonable, but pay attention to the pain involved. If the parameter list is too long or changes too often, you need to rethink your dependency structure.

Divergent Change

We structure our software to make change easier; after all, software is meant to be soft. When we make a change we want to be able to jump to a single clear point in the system and make the change. When you can't do this you are smelling one of two closely related pungencies.

Divergent change occurs when one class is commonly changed in different ways for different reasons. If you look at a class and say, "Well, I will have to change these three methods every time I get a new database; I have to change these four methods every time there is a new financial instrument," you likely have a situation in which two objects are better than one. That way each object is changed only as a result of one kind of change. Of course, you often discover this only after you've added a few databases or financial instruments. Any change to handle a variation should change a single class or module, and all the typing in the new class/module should express the variation. To clean this up you identify everything that changes for a particular cause and use Extract Class to put them all together.

Shotgun Surgery

Shotgun surgery is similar to divergent change but is the opposite. You whiff this when every time you make a kind of change, you have to make a lot of little changes to a lot of different classes. When the changes are all over the place, they are hard to find, and it's easy to miss an important change.

In this case you want to use Move Method and Move Field to put all the changes into a single class. If no current class looks like a good candidate, create one. Often you can use Inline Class to bring a whole bunch of behavior together. You get a small dose of divergent change, but you can easily deal with that.

Divergent change is one class that suffers many kinds of changes, and shotgun surgery is one change that alters many classes. Either way you want to arrange things so that, ideally, there is a one-to-one link between common changes and classes.

Feature Envy

The whole point of objects is that they are a technique to package data with the processes used on that data. A classic smell is a method that seems more interested in a class other than the one it actually is in. The most common focus of the envy is the data. We've lost count of the times we've seen a method that invokes half a dozen getting methods on another object to calculate some value. Fortunately the cure is obvious, the method clearly wants to be elsewhere, so you use Move Method to get it there. Sometimes only part of the method suffers from envy; in that case use Extract Method on the jealous bit and Move Method to give it a dream home.

Of course not all cases are cut-and-dried. Often a method uses features of several classes, so which one should it live with? The heuristic we use is to determine which class has most of the data and put the method with that data. This step is often made easier if Extract Method is used to break the method into pieces that go into different places.

Of course there are several sophisticated patterns that break this rule. From the Gang of Four [Gang of Four] Strategy and Visitor immediately leap to mind. Kent Beck's Self-Delegation pattern from his Smalltalk Best Practices book [Beck] is another. You use these to combat the divergent change smell. The fundamental rule of thumb is to put things together that change together. Data and the behavior that references that data usually change together, but there are exceptions. When the exceptions occur, we move the behavior to keep changes in one place. Strategy and Visitor allow you to change behavior easily, because they isolate the small amount of behavior that needs to be overridden, at the cost of further indirection.

Data Clumps

Data items tend to be like children; they enjoy hanging around in groups together. Often you'll see the same three or four data items together in many places: instance variables in a couple of classes, and parameters in many method signatures. Bunches of data that hang around together really ought to be made into their own object. The first step is to look for where the clumps appear as instance variables. Use Extract Class on the instance variables to turn the clumps into an object. Then turn your attention to method signatures using Introduce Parameter Object or Preserve Whole Object to slim them down. The immediate benefit is that you can shrink a lot of parameter lists and simplify method calling. Don't worry about data clumps that use only some of the attributes of the new object. As long as you are replacing two or more instance variables with the new object, you'll come out ahead.

A good test is to consider deleting one of the data values: If you did this, would the others make any sense? If they don't, it's a sure sign that you have an object that's dying to be born.

Reducing instance variable lists and parameter lists will certainly remove a few bad smells, but once you have the objects, you get the opportunity to make a nice perfume. You can now look for cases of feature envy, which suggest behavior that can be moved into your new classes. Before long these classes will be productive members of society.

Primitive Obsession

Most programming environments have two kinds of data. Record types allow you to structure data into meaningful groups. Primitive types are your building blocks. Records always carry a certain amount of overhead: They may mean tables in a database, or they may be awkward to create when you want them for only one or two things.

One of the valuable things about objects is that they blur or even break the line between primitive and larger classes. You can easily write little classes that are indistinguishable from the built-in types of the language. Ruby makes everything an object, but for the sake of this discussion, we're designating built-in types such as Fixnum and String as primitives.

People new to objects are usually reluctant to use small objects for small tasks, such as money classes that combine number and currency, and special strings such as telephone numbers and ZIP codes. You can move out of the cave into the centrally heated world of objects by using Replace Data Value with Object on individual data values. If you have conditionals that depend on a type code, use Replace Type Code with Polymorphism, Replace Type Code with Module Extension, or Replace Type Code with State/Strategy.

If you have a group of instance variables that should go together, use Extract Class. If you see these primitives in parameter lists, try a civilizing dose of Introduce Parameter Object. If you find yourself picking apart an array, use Replace Array with Object.

Case Statements

One of the most obvious symptoms of object-oriented code is its comparative lack of case statements. The problem with case statements is essentially that of duplication. Often you find the same case statement scattered about a program in different places. If you add a new clause to the case, you have to find all these case statements and change them. The object-oriented notion of polymorphism gives you an elegant way to deal with this problem.

Most times when you see a case statement you should consider polymorphism. The issue is where the polymorphism should occur. Often the case statement matches on a type code. You want the method or class that hosts the type code value. So use Extract Method to extract the case statement and then Move Method to get it onto the class where the polymorphism is needed. At that point you have to decide whether to Replace Type Code with Polymorphism, Replace Type Code with Module Extension, or Replace Type Code with State/Strategy.

If you only have a few cases that affect a single method, and you don't expect them to change, then polymorphism is overkill. In this case Replace Parameter with Explicit Methods is a good option. If one of your conditional cases is a null, try Introduce Null Object.

Parallel Inheritance Hierarchies

Parallel inheritance hierarchies is really a special case of shotgun surgery. In this case, every time you make a subclass of one class, you also have to make a subclass of another. You can recognize this smell because the prefixes of the class names in one hierarchy are the same as the prefixes in another hierarchy.

The general strategy for eliminating the duplication is to make sure that instances of one hierarchy refer to instances of the other. If you use Move Method and Move Field, the hierarchy on the referring class disappears.

Lazy Class

Each class you create costs money to maintain and understand. A class that isn't doing enough to pay for itself should be eliminated. Often this might be a class that used to pay its way but has been downsized with refactoring. Or it might be a class that was added because of changes that were planned but not made. Either way, you let the class die with dignity. If you have subclasses or modules that aren't doing enough, try to use Collapse Hierarchy. Nearly useless components should be subjected to Inline Class or Inline Module.

Speculative Generality

Speculative generality is a smell to which we are very sensitive. You get it when people say, "Oh, I think we need the ability to do this kind of thing someday" and thus want all sorts of hooks and special cases to handle things that aren't required. The result often is harder to understand and maintain. If all this machinery were being used, it would be worth it. But if it isn't, it isn't. The machinery just gets in the way, so get rid of it.

If you have classes or modules that aren't doing much, use Collapse Hierarchy. Unnecessary delegation can be removed with Inline Class. Methods with unused parameters should be subject to Remove Parameter. Methods named with odd names should be brought down to earth with Rename Method.

Speculative generality can be spotted when the only users of a method, a code branch, or an entire class are test cases. If you find this type of code, delete it and the test case that exercises it. If you have a method or class that is a helper for a test case that exercises legitimate functionality, you have to leave it in, of course.

Temporary Field

Sometimes you see an object in which an instance variable is set only in certain circumstances. Such code is difficult to understand, because you expect an object to need all of its variables. Trying to understand why a variable is there when it doesn't seem to be used can drive you nuts.

Use Extract Class to create a home for the poor orphan variables. Put all the code that concerns the variables into the component. You may also be able to eliminate conditional code by using Introduce Null Object to create an alternative component for when the variables aren't valid.

A common case of temporary field occurs when a complicated algorithm needs several variables. Because the implementer didn't want to pass around a huge parameter list (who does?), he put them in instance variables. But the instance variables are valid only during the algorithm; in other contexts they are just plain confusing. In this case you can use Extract Class with these variables and the methods that require them. The new object is a Method Object [Beck].

Message Chains

You see message chains when a client asks one object for another object, which the client then asks for yet another object, which the client then asks for yet another object, and so on. You may see these as a long line of get_this methods, or as a sequence of temps. Navigating this way means the client is coupled to the structure of the navigation. Any change to the intermediate relationships causes the client to have to change.

The move to use here is Hide Delegate. In principle you can apply Hide Delegate to potentially every object in the chain, but doing this often turns every intermediate object into a middle man. Often a better alternative is to see what the resulting object is used for. See whether you can use Extract Method to take a piece of the code that uses it and then Move Method to push it down the chain. If several clients of one of the objects in the chain want to navigate the rest of the way, add a method to do that.

Some people consider any method chain to be a terrible thing. We are known for our calm, reasoned moderation. Well, at least in this case we are.

Middle Man

One of the prime features of objects is encapsulation—hiding internal details from the rest of the world. Encapsulation often comes with delegation. You ask a director whether she is free for a meeting; she delegates the message to her diary and gives you an answer. All well and good. There is no need to know whether the director uses a diary, an electronic gizmo, or a secretary to keep track of her appointments.

However, this can go too far. You look at a class's interface and find half the methods are delegating to this other class. After a while it is time to use Remove Middle Man and talk to the object that really knows what's going on. If only a few methods aren't doing much, use Inline Method to inline them into the caller. If there is additional behavior, you can use Replace Delegation with Hierarchy to turn the real object into a module and include it in the middle man. That allows you to extend behavior without chasing all that delegation.

Inappropriate Intimacy

Sometimes classes become far too intimate and spend too much time delving into each other's private parts. We may not be prudes when it comes to people, but we think our classes should follow strict, puritan rules.

Overly intimate classes need to be broken up as lovers were in ancient days. Use Move Method and Move Field to separate the pieces to reduce the intimacy. See whether you can arrange a Change Bidirectional Association to Unidirectional. If the classes do have common interests, use Extract Class to put the commonality in a safe place and make honest classes of them. Or use Hide Delegate to let another class act as go-between.

Inheritance often can lead to over-intimacy. Subclasses are always going to know more about their parents than their parents would like them to know. If it's time to leave home, apply Replace Inheritance with Delegation.

Alternative Classes with Different Interfaces

Use Rename Method on any methods that do the same thing but have different signatures for what they do. Often this doesn't go far enough. In these cases the classes aren't yet doing enough. Keep using Move Method to move behavior to the classes until the protocols are the same. If you have to redundantly move code to accomplish this, you may be able to use Extract Module or Introduce Inheritance to atone.

Incomplete Library Class

Reuse is often touted as the purpose of objects. We think reuse is overrated (we just use). However, we can't deny that much of our programming skill is based on library classes so that nobody can tell whether we've forgotten our sort algorithms.

Builders of library classes are rarely omniscient. We don't blame them for that; after all, we can rarely figure out a design until we've mostly built it, so library builders have a really tough job.

In other languages extending an existing library class can be impossible or messy. However, Ruby's open classes make this easy to fix using Move Method to move the behavior needed directly to the library class.

Data Class

These are classes that have attributes, and nothing else. Such classes are dumb data holders and are almost certainly being manipulated in far too much detail by other classes. Use Remove Setting Method on any instance variable that should not be changed. If you have collection instance variables, check to see whether they are properly encapsulated and apply Encapsulate Collection if they aren't.

Look for where these getting and setting methods are used by other classes. Try to use Move Method to move behavior into the data class. If you can't move a whole method, use Extract Method to create a method that can be moved. After a while you can start using Hide Method on the getters and setters.

Data classes are like children. They are okay as a starting point, but to participate as a grownup object, they need to take some responsibility.

Refused Bequest

Subclasses get to inherit the methods and data of their parents. But what if they don't want or need what they are given? They are given all these great gifts and pick just a few to play with.

The traditional story is that this means the hierarchy is wrong. You need to create a new sibling class and use Push Down Method to push all the unused methods to the sibling. That way the parent holds only what is common.

You'll guess from our snide use of "traditional" that we aren't going to advise this, at least not all the time. We do subclassing to reuse a bit of behavior all the time, and we find it a perfectly good way of doing business. There is a smell, we can't deny it, but usually it isn't a strong smell. So we say that if the refused bequest is causing confusion and problems, follow the traditional advice. However, don't feel you have to do it all the time. Nine times out of ten this smell is too faint to be worth cleaning.

The smell of refused bequest is much stronger if the subclass is reusing behavior but does not want to support the public methods of the superclass. We don't mind refusing implementations, but refusing public methods gets us on our high horses. In this case, however, don't fiddle with the hierarchy; you want to gut it by applying Replace Inheritance with Delegation.

Comments

Don't worry, we aren't saying that people shouldn't write comments. In our olfactory analogy, comments aren't a bad smell; indeed they are a sweet smell. The reason we mention comments here is that comments often are used as a deodorant. It's surprising how often you look at thickly commented code and notice that the comments are there because the code is bad.

Comments lead us to bad code that has all the rotten whiffs we've discussed in the rest of this chapter. Our first action is to remove the bad smells by refactoring. When we're finished, we often find that the comments are superfluous.

If you need a comment to explain what a block of code does, try Extract Method. If the method is already extracted but you still need a comment to explain what it does, use Rename Method. If you need to state some rules about the required state of the system, use Introduce Assertion.

Tip When you feel the need to write a comment, first try to refactor the code so that any comment becomes superfluous.

A good time to use a comment is when you don't know what to do. In addition to describing what is going on, comments can indicate areas in which you aren't sure. A comment is a good place to say why you did something. This kind of information helps future modifiers, especially forgetful ones.

Metaprogramming Madness

While in most cases Ruby's dynamic nature provides great benefits, it can be misused. Some metaprogramming techniques can result in obfuscated code. The `method_missing` hook, for example, often results in code that is difficult to understand. It can be a powerful tool if an object's interface cannot be determined at coding time, but unless it's absolutely necessary I use Replace Dynamic Receptor with Dynamic Method Definition or even a simple Extract Method to remove the `method_missing` definition. If the `method_missing` definition is truly needed, I might use Isolate Dynamic Receptor to separate concerns.

Disjointed API

Libraries are often written with flexibility as the number one priority. The author needs to build in this flexibility so that her library can be used by many different people in many different ways. This flexibility often presents itself as a relatively fine-grained, disjointed API, with many configuration options.

More often than not, an individual project will not take advantage of all the configuration options. The same configuration options will be used over and over. If this is the case, use Introduce Gateway to interact with the API in a simplified way.

Introduce Expression Builder can be applied to both internal and external APIs to interact with the public interface in a more fluent manner.

Repetitive Boilerplate

One of the easiest ways to remove duplication is Extract Method. Extract the method and call it from multiple places. Some kinds of methods become so commonplace that we can go even further. Take for example `attr_reader` in Ruby. Implementing attribute readers is so common in object-oriented languages that the author of Ruby decided to provide a succinct way to declare them. Introduce Class Annotation involves annotating a class by calling a class method from the class definition in the same way that `attr_reader` is called. Most code isn't simple enough to declare in this way, but when the purpose of the code can be captured clearly in a declarative statement, Introduce Class Annotation can clarify the intention of your code.

Chapter 4

Building Tests

When Martin originally wrote *Refactoring*, tests were anything but mainstream. However, even back then he knew: If you want to refactor, the essential precondition is having solid tests. Even if you are fortunate enough to have a tool that can automate the refactorings, you still need tests.

Since the days of the original Refactoring book, creating self-testing code has become a much more common activity. And, while this book isn't about testing, if you want to refactor, you must have tests.

The Value of Self-Testing Code

If you look at how most programmers who do not write self-testing code spend their time, you'll find that writing code actually is quite a small fraction. Some time is spent figuring out what ought to be going on, some time is spent designing, but most time is spent debugging. Those programmers can tell a story of a bug that took a whole day (or more) to find. Fixing the bug is usually pretty quick, but finding it is a nightmare. Some stand by this style of development; however, I've found life to be much easier if I have a test suite to lean on.

The event that started Martin on the road to self-testing code was a talk at OOPSLA in 1992. Someone (I think it was Dave Thomas, coauthor of *The Pragmatic Programmer*) said offhandedly, "Classes should contain their own tests." And thus were the early days of self-testing code.

Since those days, it's become a standard to follow the Red/Green/Refactor movement. In short, you write a failing test, make it pass, and then refactor the code to the best of your ability. This process is done many times a day, at least once with each new feature added. As you add features to the system, you build a regression suite that verifies that an application runs as expected. When developing in this manner you can complete large refactorings and have the confidence that you haven't broken existing features of the system. The result is a tremendous productivity gain. Additionally, I find I hardly ever spend more than a few minutes debugging per day.

Of course, it is not so easy to persuade others to follow this route. Tests themselves are a lot of extra code to write. Unless you have actually experienced the way it speeds programming, self-testing does not seem to make sense. This is not helped by the fact that many people have never learned to write tests or even to think about tests.

As the Red/Green/Refactor movement advocates, one of the most useful times to write tests is before you start programming. When you need to add a feature, begin by writing the test. This isn't as backward as it sounds. By writing the test you are asking yourself what needs to be done to add the function. Writing the test also concentrates on the interface rather than the implementation (which is always a good thing). It also means you have a clear point at which you are done coding—when the test works.

This notion of frequent testing is an important part of extreme programming [Beck, XP]. The name conjures up notions of programmers who are fast and loose hackers. But extreme programmers are dedicated testers. They want to develop software as fast as possible, and they know that tests help you to go as fast as you possibly can.

That's enough of the polemic. Although I believe everyone would benefit by writing self-testing code, it is not the point of this book. This book is about refactoring. Refactoring requires tests. If you want to refactor, you have to write tests. This chapter gives you a start in doing this for Ruby. This is not a testing book, so I'm not going to go into much detail. But with testing I've found that a remarkably small amount can have surprisingly big benefits.

As with everything else in this book, I describe the testing approach using examples. When I develop code, I write the tests as I go. But often when I'm working with people on refactoring, we have a body of non-self-testing code to work on. So first we have to make the code self-testing before we refactor.

The standard Ruby idiom for testing is to build separate test classes that work in a framework to make testing easier. The most popular framework is Test::Unit, and it is part of the Ruby standard library.

The Test::Unit Testing Framework

A number of testing frameworks are available in Ruby. The original was Test::Unit, an open-source testing framework developed by Nathaniel Talbott. The framework is simple, yet it allows you to do all the key things you need for testing. In this chapter we use this framework to develop tests for some IO classes. We considered using RSpec for the test examples (another popular testing framework), but decided against it because we felt that test/unit examples resulted in a lower barrier of entry for the readers.

To begin, I'm going to write some tests for Ruby's `File` class. I wouldn't normally write tests for a language class—I'd hope that the author of the language has taken care of that—but it will serve as a good example. To begin I create a `FileTest` class. Any class that contains tests must subclass the `TestCase` class from the testing framework. The framework uses the composite pattern [Gang of Four] and groups all the tests into a suite (see Figure 4.1) . This makes it easy to run all the tests as one suite automatically.

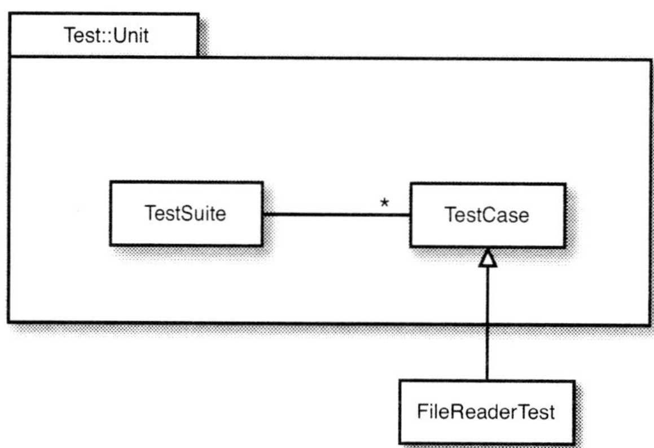

Figure 4.1 The composite structure of tests.

My first job is to set up the test data. Because I'm reading a file I need to set up a test file, as follows:

```
Bradman 99.94 52 80 10 6996 334 29
Pollock 60.97 23 41 4 2256 274 7
Headley 60.83 22 40 4 2256 270* 10
Sutcliffe 60.73 54 84 9 4555 194 16
```

Now that I have the test fixture in place, I can start writing tests. The first is to test the read method. To do this I read the entire file and then check that the fourth character is the character I expect.

```
require 'test/unit'

def test_read_4th_character
  contents = File.read('data.txt')
  assert_equal 'd', contents[3,1]
end
```

The automatic test is the `assert_equal` method. If the expected value is equal to the actual value, all is well. Otherwise we signal an error. I show how the framework does that later.

To execute the test, simply use Ruby to run the file.

```
ruby file_test.rb
```

You can take a look at the Test::Unit source code to figure out how it does it. I just treat it as magic.

It's easy to run a group of tests simply by requiring each test case.

```
Dir['**/*_test.rb'].each { |test| require test }
```

The preceding code creates the test suite and when I run it I see:

```
Loaded suite -
Started
.
Finished in 0.000359 seconds.

1 tests, 1 assertions, 0 failures, 0 errors
```


Test::Unit prints a period for each test that runs (so you can see progress). It tells you how long the tests have taken to run. It then says the number of tests, assertions, failures, and errors. I can run a thousand tests, and if all goes well, I'll see that. This simple feedback is essential to self-testing code. Without it you'll never run the tests often enough. With it you can run masses of tests and see the results immediately.

What happens if something goes wrong? I'll demonstrate by putting in a deliberate bug, as follows:

```
def test_read_4th_content_is_2
  contents = File.read('data.txt')
  assert_equal '2', contents[3,1]
end
```

The result looks like this:

```
Loaded suite -
Started
F
Finished in 0.006046 seconds.

1) Failure:
test_read(F) [-:6]:
<"2"> expected but was
<"d">.

1 tests, 1 assertions, 1 failures, 0 errors
```

Again I'll mention that when I'm writing tests, I start by making them fail. With existing code I either change it to make it fail (if I can touch the code) or put an incorrect expected value in the assertion. I do this because I like to prove to myself that the test does actually run and the test is actually testing what it's supposed to (which is why I prefer changing the tested code if I can). This may be paranoia, but you can really confuse yourself when tests are testing something other than what you think they are testing.

In addition to catching failures (assertions coming out false), the framework also catches errors (unexpected exceptions). If I attempt to open a file that doesn't exist, I should get an exception. I can test this with:

```
def test_read_causes_error_when_file_not_found
  contents = File.read('datas.txt')
  assert_equal '2', contents[3,1]
end
```

If I run this I get:

```
Loaded suite -
Started
E
Finished in 0.000362 seconds.

1) Error:
test_read(Tes):
Errno::ENOENT: No such file or directory - datas.txt
-:3:in `read'
-:3:in `test_read'

1 tests, 0 assertions, 0 failures, 1 errors
```

It is useful to differentiate failures and errors, because they tend to turn up differently and the debugging process is different.

Developer and Quality Assurance Tests

This framework is used for developer tests, so I should mention the difference between developer tests and quality assurance (QA) tests. The tests I'm talking about are developer tests. I write them to improve my productivity as a programmer. Making the quality assurance department happy is just a side effect.

Quality assurance tests are a different animal. They are written to ensure the software as a whole works. They provide quality assurance to the customer and don't care about programmer productivity. They should be developed by a different team, one who delights in finding bugs. This team uses heavyweight tools and techniques to help them do this.

Functional tests typically treat the whole system as a black box as much as possible. In a GUI-based system, they operate through the GUI. In a file or database update program, the tests just look at how the data is changed for certain inputs.

When quality assurance testers, or users, find a bug in the software, at least two things are needed to fix it. Of course you have to change the production code to remove the bug. But you should also add a developer test that exposes the bug. Indeed, when I get a bug report, I begin by writing a developer test that causes the bug to surface. I write more than one test if I need to narrow the scope of the bug, or if there may be related failures. I use the developer tests to help pin down the bug and to ensure that a similar bug doesn't get past my developer tests again.

Tip When you get a bug report, start by writing a unit test that exposes the bug.

The Test::Unit framework is designed for writing developer tests. Quality assurance tests often are performed with other tools. GUI-based test tools are good examples. Often, however, you write your own application-specific test tools that make it easier to manage test-cases than do GUI scripts alone. You can perform quality assurance tests with Test::Unit, but it's usually not the most efficient way. For refactoring purposes, I count on the developer tests—the programmer's friend.

Adding More Tests

Now we should continue adding more tests. The style I follow is to look at all the things the class should do and test each one of them for any conditions that might cause the class to fail. This is not the same as "test every public method," which some programmers advocate. Testing should be risk driven; remember, you are trying to find bugs now or in the future. So I don't test accessors that just read and write. Because they are so simple, I'm not likely to find a bug there.

This is important because trying to write too many tests usually leads to not writing enough. I've often read books on testing, and my reaction has been to shy away from the mountain of stuff I have to do to test. This is counterproductive, because it makes you think that to test you have to do a lot of work. You get many benefits from testing even if you do only a little testing. The key is to test the areas that you are most worried about going wrong. That way you get the most benefit for your testing effort.

Tip It is better to write and run incomplete tests than not to run complete tests.

At the moment I'm looking at the read method. What else should it do? One thing it says is that it can return a specified length. Let's test it.

```
def test_read_with_a_length_specified
  contents = File.read('data.txt', 15)
  assert_equal 'Bradman 99.', contents
end
```


Running the test file causes each of its tests (the two test-cases) to run. It's important to write isolated tests that do not depend on each other. There's no guarantee on what order the test runner will run the tests. You wouldn't want to get test failures where the code was actually correct, but your test depended on a previous test running.

Test::Unit identifies each test by finding all the methods that begin with the "`test_`" prefix. Following this convention means that each test I write is automatically added to the suite.

Tip Think of the boundary conditions under which things might go wrong and concentrate your tests there.

Part of looking for boundaries is looking for special conditions that can cause the test to fail. For files, empty files are always a good choice:

```
def test_read_empty_file_returns_empty_string
  File.open('empty_data.txt', 'w') { }
  contents = File.read('empty_data.txt')
  assert_equal "", contents
end
```

What happens if you attempt to read a length larger than the length of the file? The entire file should be returned with no error. I can easily add another test to ensure that:

```
def test_read_an_out_of_bounds_length_causes_no_error
  File.open('simple_data.txt', 'w') { |file| file << "simple file" }
  contents = File.read('simple_data.txt', 100)
  assert_equal "simple file", contents
end
```

Notice how I'm playing the part of an enemy to code. I'm actively thinking about how I can break it. I find that state of mind to be both productive and fun. It indulges the mean-spirited part of my psyche.

When you are doing tests, don't forget to check that expected errors occur properly. If you try to read a file that doesn't exist, you should get an exception. This too should be tested:


```
def test_read_raises_error_when_file_not_found
  begin
    File.read('datas.txt')
  rescue
    rescued = true
  end
  assert_equal true, rescued
end
```

In fact, testing that exceptions are correctly raised is common enough that Test::Unit has an `assert_raises` method designed for exactly that.

```
def test_read_raises_error_when_file_not_found
  assert_raises Errno::ENOENT do
    File.read('datas.txt')
  end
end
```

Tip Don't forget to test that exceptions are raised when things are expected to go wrong.

Fleshing out the tests continues along these lines. It takes a while to go through the public methods of some classes to do this, but in the process you get to really understand the interface of the class. In particular, it helps to think about error conditions and boundary conditions. That's another advantage for writing tests as you write code, or even before you write the production code.

When do you stop? I'm sure you have heard many times that you cannot prove a program has no bugs by testing. That's true but does not affect the ability of testing to speed up programming. I've seen various proposals for rules to ensure you have tested every combination of everything. It's worth taking a look at these, but don't let them get to you. There is a point of diminishing returns with testing, and there is the danger that by trying to write too many tests, you become discouraged and end up not writing any. You should concentrate on where the risk is. Look at the code and see where it becomes complex. Look at the function and consider the likely areas of error. Your tests will not find every bug, but as you refactor you will understand the program better and thus find more bugs. Although I always start refactoring with a test suite, I invariably add to it as I go along.

Tip Don't let the fear that testing can't catch all bugs stop you from writing the tests that will catch most bugs.

One of the tricky things about objects is that the inheritance and polymorphism can make testing harder, because there are many combinations to test. If you have three classes that collaborate and each has three subclasses, you have nine alternatives but twenty-seven combinations. I don't always try to test all the combinations possible, but I do try to test each alternative. It boils down to the risk in the combinations. If the alternatives are reasonably independent of each other, I'm not likely to try each combination. There's always a risk that I'll miss something, but it is better to spend a reasonable time to catch most bugs than to spend ages trying to catch them all.

A difference between test code and production code is that it is okay to copy and edit test code. When dealing with combinations and alternatives, I often do that. I begin by writing a test for a "regular pay event" scenario, next I write a test for a "seniority" scenario, finally I create a test for a "disabled before the end of the year" scenario. After those tests are passing I create test scenarios without "seniority" and "disabled before the end of the year," and so on. With simple alternatives like that on top of a reasonable test structure, I can generate tests quickly.

I hope I have given you a feel for writing tests. I can say a lot more on this topic, but that would obscure the key message. Build a good bug detector and run it frequently. It is a wonderful tool for any development and is a precondition for refactoring.

Chapter 5

Toward a Catalog of Refactorings

Chapters 5 to 12 form an initial catalog of refactorings. They've grown from the notes I've made in refactoring over the last few years. This catalog is by no means comprehensive or watertight, but it should provide a solid starting point for your own refactoring work.

Format of the Refactorings

As I describe the refactorings in this and other chapters, I use a standard format. Each refactoring has five parts, as follows:

- I begin with a **name**. The name is important to building a vocabulary of refactorings. This is the name I use elsewhere in the book.
- I follow the name with a short **summary** of the situation in which you need the refactoring and a summary of what the refactoring does. This helps you find a refactoring more quickly.
- The **motivation** describes why the refactoring should be done and describes circumstances in which it shouldn't be done.
- The **mechanics** are a concise, step-by-step description of how to carry out the refactoring.
- The **examples** show a simple use of the refactoring to illustrate how it works.

The summary includes a short statement of the problem that the refactoring helps you with, a short description of what you do, and a sketch that shows you a simple before and after example. Sometimes I use code for the sketch and sometimes Unified Modeling Language (UML), depending on which seems to best convey the essence of the refactoring. (All UML diagrams in this book are drawn from the implementation perspective [Fowler, UML].) If you've seen the refactoring before, the sketch should give you a good idea what the refactoring is about. If not you'll probably need to work through the example to get a better idea.

The mechanics come from my own notes to remember how to do the refactoring when I haven't done it for a while. As such they are somewhat terse, usually without explanations of why the steps are done that way. I give more expansive explanations in the example. This way the mechanics are short notes you can refer to easily when you know the refactoring but need to look up the steps (at least this is how I use them). You'll probably need to read the example when you first do the refactoring.

I've written the mechanics in such a way that each step of each refactoring is as small as possible. I emphasize the safe way of doing the refactoring, which is to take small steps and test after every one. At work I usually take larger steps than some of the baby steps described, but if I run into a bug, I back out the step and take the smaller steps. The steps include a number of references to special cases. The steps thus also function as a checklist; I often forget these things myself.

The examples are of the laughably simple textbook kind. My aim with the example is to help explain the basic refactoring with minimal distractions, so I hope you'll forgive the simplicity. (They are certainly not examples of good business object design.) I'm sure you'll be able to apply them to your rather more complex situations. Some simple refactorings don't have examples because I didn't think an example would add much.

In particular, remember that the examples are included only to illustrate the one refactoring under discussion. In most cases, there are still problems with the code at the end, but fixing these problems requires other refactorings. In a few cases in which refactorings often go together, I carry examples from one refactoring to another. In most cases I leave the code as it is after the single refactoring. I do this to make each refactoring self-contained, because the primary role of the catalog is as a reference.

Don't take any of these examples as suggestions for how to design employee or order objects. These examples are there only to illustrate the refactorings, nothing more.

I use boldface code to highlight changed code where it is buried among code that has not been changed and may be difficult to spot. I do not use boldface type for all changed code, because too much defeats the purpose.

Finding References

Many of the refactorings call for you to find all references to a method, an instance variable, or a class. When you do this, enlist the computer to help you. By using the computer you reduce your chances of missing a reference and can usually do the search much more quickly than you would if you were simply to eyeball the code.

Most languages treat computer programs as text files. Your best help here is a suitable text search. Many programming environments allow you to text search a single file or a group of files. The access control of the feature you are looking for will tell you the range of files you need to look for.

Don't just search and replace blindly. Inspect each reference to ensure it really refers to the thing you are replacing. You can be clever with your search pattern, but I always check mentally to ensure I am making the right replacement. If you can use the same method name on different classes or methods of different signatures on the same class, there are too many chances you will get it wrong.

Chapter 6

Composing Methods

A large part of my refactoring is composing methods to package code properly. Almost all the time the problems come from methods that are too long. Long methods are troublesome because they often contain a lot of information, which gets buried by the complex logic that usually gets dragged in. The key refactoring is Extract Method, which takes a clump of code and turns it into its own method. Inline Method is essentially the opposite. You take a method call and replace it with the body of the code. I need Inline Method when I've done multiple extractions and realize some of the resulting methods are no longer pulling their weight or if I need to reorganize the way I've broken down methods.

The biggest problem with Extract Method is dealing with local variables, and temps are one of the main sources of this issue. When I'm working on a method, I like Replace Temp with Query to get rid of any temporary variables that I can remove. If the temp is used for many things, I use Split Temporary Variable first to make the temp easier to replace.

Sometimes, however, the temporary variables are just too tangled to replace. I need Replace Method with Method Object. This allows me to break up even the most tangled method, at the cost of introducing a new class for the job.

Parameters are less of a problem than temps, provided you don't assign to them. If you do, you need Remove Assignments to Parameters.

Once the method is broken down, I can understand how it works much better. I may also find that the algorithm can be improved to make it clearer. I then use Substitute Algorithm to introduce the clearer algorithm.

To improve the fluency of code I use Introduce Named Parameter. If I find later that the fluency the named parameter brings is no longer worth the complexity on the receiver, I can remove it with Remove Named Parameter.

When a default parameter becomes unused, I need to remove it using Remove Unused Default Parameter.

Extract Method

You have a code fragment that can be grouped together.

Turn the fragment into a method whose name explains the purpose of the method.

```
def print_owing(amount)
  print_banner
  puts "name: #{@name}"
  puts "amount: #{amount}"
end
```

```
def print_owing(amount)
  print_banner
  print_details amount
end

def print_details(amount)
  puts "name: #{@name}"
  puts "amount: #{amount}"
end
```


Motivation

Extract Method is one of the most common refactorings I do. I look at a method that is too long or look at code that needs a comment to understand its purpose. I then turn that fragment of code into its own method.

I prefer short, well-named methods for several reasons. First, it increases the chances that other methods can use a method when the method is finely grained. Second, it allows the higher-level methods to read more like a series of comments. Overriding also is easier when the methods are finely grained.

It does take a little getting used to if you are used to seeing larger methods. And small methods really work only when you have good names, so you need to pay attention to naming. People sometimes ask me what length I look for in a method. To me length is not the issue. The key is the semantic distance between the method name and the method body. If extracting improves clarity, do it, even if the name is longer than the code you have extracted.

Mechanics

1. Create a new method, and name it after the intention of the method (name it by what it does, not by how it does it).

   ⟹ *If the code you want to extract is very simple, such as a single message or function call, you should extract it if the name of the new method reveals the intention of the code in a better way. If you can't come up with a more meaningful name, don't extract the code.*

2. Copy the extracted code from the source method into the new target method.

3. Scan the extracted code for references to any variables that are local in scope to the source method. These are local variables and parameters to the method.

4. See whether any temporary variables are used only within this extracted code. If so, declare them in the target method as temporary variables.

5. Look to see whether any of these local-scope variables are modified by the extracted code. If one variable is modified, see whether you can treat the extracted code as a query and assign the result to the variable concerned. If this is awkward, or if there is more than one such variable, you can't extract the method as it stands. You may need to use Split Temporary Variable and try again. You can eliminate temporary variables with Replace Temp with Query (see the discussion in the examples).

6. Pass into the target method as parameters local-scope variables that are read from the extracted code.

7. Replace the extracted code in the source method with a call to the target method.

   ⟹ *If you moved any temporary variables over to the target method, look to see whether they were declared outside the extracted code. If so, you can now remove the declaration.*

8. Test.

Example: No Local Variables

In the simplest case, Extract Method is trivially easy. Take the following method:

```
def print_owing
  outstanding = 0.0

  # print banner
  puts "*************************"
  puts "***** Customer Owes *****"
  puts "*************************"

  # calculate outstanding
  @orders.each do |order|
    outstanding += order.amount
  end

  # print details
  puts "name: #{@name}"
  puts "amount: #{outstanding}"
end
```

Tip Comments often identify pieces of a method that can be extracted. Additionally, the comment itself can be a potential name for the extracted method. For example, in the preceding code the print banner functionality is a primary candidate for extraction.

It is easy to extract the code that prints the banner. I just cut, paste, and put in a call:

```
def print_owing
  outstanding = 0.0

  print_banner

  # calculate outstanding
  @orders.each do |order|
    outstanding += order.amount
  end

  # print details
  puts "name: #{@name}"
```

```
  puts "amount: #{outstanding}"
end

def print_banner
  # print banner
  puts "*************************"
  puts "***** Customer Owes *****"
  puts "*************************"
end
```

Example: Using Local Variables

So what's the problem? The problem is local variables: parameters passed into the original method and temporaries declared within the original method. Local variables are only in scope in that method, so when I use Extract Method, these variables cause me extra work. In some cases they even prevent me from doing the refactoring at all.

The easiest case with local variables is when the variables are read but not changed. In this case I can just pass them in as a parameter. So if I have the following method:

```
def print_owing
  outstanding = 0.0

  print_banner

  # calculate outstanding
  @orders.each do |order|
    outstanding += order.amount
  end

  # print details
  puts "name: #{@name}"
  puts "amount: #{outstanding}"
end

def print_banner
  # print banner
  puts "*************************"
  puts "***** Customer Owes *****"
  puts "*************************"
end
```

I can extract the printing of details with a method with one parameter:

```
def print_owing
  outstanding = 0.0

  print_banner

  # calculate outstanding
  @orders.each do |order|
    outstanding += order.amount
  end

  print_details outstanding
end

def print_details(outstanding)
  puts "name: #{@name}"
  puts "amount: #{outstanding}"
end
```

Example: Reassigning a Local Variable

It's the assignment to local variables that becomes complicated. In this case we're only talking about temps. If you see an assignment to a parameter, you should immediately use Remove Assignments to Parameters.

For temps that are assigned to, there are two cases. The simpler case is that in which the variable is a temporary variable used only within the extracted code. When that happens, you can move the temp into the extracted code. The other case is use of the variable outside the code. If the variable is not used after the code is extracted, you can make the change in just the extracted code. If it is used afterward, you need to make the extracted code return the changed value of the variable. I can illustrate this with the following method:

```
def print_owing
  outstanding = 0.0

  print_banner

  # calculate outstanding
  @orders.each do |order|
    outstanding += order.amount
  end
```

```
  print_details outstanding
end
```

Now I extract the calculation:

```
def print_owing
  print_banner
  outstanding = calculate_outstanding
  print_details outstanding
end

def calculate_outstanding
  outstanding = 0.0
  @orders.each do |order|
    outstanding += order.amount
  end
  outstanding
end
```

Once I've tested for the extraction, I use the inject Collection Closure Method on Array:

```
def calculate_outstanding
  @orders.inject(0.0) { |result, order| result + order.amount }
end
```

In this case the outstanding variable is initialized only to an obvious initial value, so I can initialize it only within the extracted method. If something more involved happens to the variable, I have to pass in the previous value as a parameter. The initial code for this variation might look like this:


```
def print_owing(previous_amount)
  outstanding = previous_amount * 1.2

  print_banner

  # calculate outstanding
  @orders.each do |order|
    outstanding += order.amount
  end

  print_details outstanding
end
```

In this case the extraction would look like this:

```
def print_owing(previous_amount)
  outstanding = previous_amount * 1.2
  print_banner
  outstanding = calculate_outstanding(outstanding)
  print_details outstanding
end

def calculate_outstanding(initial_value)
  @orders.inject(initial_value) { |result, order| result + order.amount }
end
```

After I test this, I clear up the way the outstanding variable is initialized:

```
def print_owing(previous_amount)
  print_banner
  outstanding = calculate_outstanding(previous_amount * 1.2)
  print_details outstanding
end
```

At this point you may be wondering, "What happens if more than one variable needs to be returned?"

Though parallel assignment can be used to return multiple values, I prefer to use single return values as much as possible. In this case, I try to do multiple extractions with each extraction only returning one value.

Temporary variables often are so plentiful that they make extraction very awkward. In these cases I try to reduce the temps by using Replace Temp with Query. If whatever I do things are still awkward, I resort to Replace Method with Method Object. This refactoring doesn't care how many temporaries you have or what you do with them.

Inline Method

A method's body is just as clear as its name.

Put the method's body into the body of its callers and remove the method.

```
def get_rating
  more_than_five_late_deliveries ? 2 : 1
end

def more_than_five_late_deliveries
  @number_of_late_deliveries > 5
end
```

```
def get_rating
  @number_of_late_deliveries > 5 ? 2 : 1
end
```

Motivation

A theme of this book is to use short methods named to show their intention, because these methods lead to clearer and easier to read code. But sometimes you do come across a method in which the body is as clear as the name. Or you refactor the body of the code into something that is just as clear as the name. When this happens, you should then get rid of the method. Indirection can be helpful, but needless indirection is irritating.

Another time to use Inline Method is when you have a group of methods that seem badly factored. You can inline them all into one big method and then re-extract the methods. Kent Beck finds it is often good to do this before using Replace Method with Method Object. You inline the various calls made by the method that have behavior you want to have in the method object. It's easier to move one method than to move the method and its called methods.

I commonly use Inline Method when someone is using too much indirection, and it seems that every method does simple delegation to another method, and I get lost in all the delegation. In these cases some of the indirection is worthwhile, but not all of it. By trying to inline I can flush out the useful ones and eliminate the rest.

Mechanics

1. Check that the method is not polymorphic.

   ⟹ *Don't inline if subclasses override the method; they cannot override a method that isn't there.*

2. Find all calls to the method.

3. Replace each call with the method body.

4. Test.

5. Remove the method definition.

Written this way, Inline Method is simple. In general it isn't. I could write pages on how to handle recursion, multiple return points, inlining into another object when you don't have accessors, and the like. The reason I don't is that if you encounter these complexities, you shouldn't do this refactoring.

Inline Temp

You have a temp that is assigned to once with a simple expression, and the temp is getting in the way of other refactorings.

Replace all references to that temp with the expression.

```
base_price = an_order.base_price
return (base_price > 1000)
```

```
return (an_order.base_price > 1000)
```

Motivation

Most of the time Inline Temp is used as part of Replace Temp with Query, so the real motivation is there. The only time Inline Temp is used on its own is when you find a temp that is assigned the value of a method call. Often this temp isn't doing any harm and you can safely leave it there. If the temp is getting in the way of other refactorings, such as Extract Method, it's time to inline it.

Mechanics

1. Find all references to the temp and replace them with the right-hand side of the assignment.

2. Test after each change.

3. Remove the declaration and the assignment of the temp.

4. Test.

Replace Temp with Query

You are using a temporary variable to hold the result of an expression.

Extract the expression into a method. Replace all references to the temp with the expression. The new method can then be used in other methods.

```
base_price = @quantity * @item_price

if (base_price > 1000)
  base_price * 0.95
else
  base_price * 0.98
end
```

⇓

```
if (base_price > 1000)
  base_price * 0.95
else
  base_price * 0.98
end

def base_price
  @quantity * @item_price
end
```


Motivation

The problem with temps is that they are temporary and local. Because they can be seen only in the context of the method in which they are used, temps tend to encourage longer methods, because that's the only way you can reach the temp. By replacing the temp with a query method, any method in the class can get at the information. That helps a lot in coming up with cleaner code for the class.

Replace Temp with Query often is a vital step before Extract Method. Local variables make it difficult to extract, so replace as many variables as you can with queries.

The straightforward cases of this refactoring are those in which temps are assigned only to once and those in which the expression that generates the assignment is free of side effects. Other cases are trickier but possible. You may need to use Split Temporary Variable or Separate Query from Modifier first to make things easier. If the temp is used to collect a result (such as summing over a loop), you need to copy some logic into the query method.

Mechanics

Here is the simple case:

1. Extract the right-hand side of the assignment into a method.

   ⟹ *Initially mark the method as private. You may find more use for it later, but you can easily relax the protection then.*

   ⟹ *Ensure the extracted method is free of side effects—that is, it does not modify any object. If it is not free of side effects, use Separate Query from Modifier.*

2. Test.

3. Inline Temp on the temp.

Temps often are used to store summary information in loops. The entire loop can be extracted into a method; this removes several lines of noisy code. Sometimes a loop may be used to sum up multiple values, as in the `total_charge` method in the Decomposing and Redistributing the Statement Method section in Chapter 1. When this is the case, duplicate the loop for each temp so that you can replace each temp with a query. The loop should be simple, so there is little danger in duplicating the code.

You may be concerned about performance in this case. As with other performance issues, let it slide for the moment. Nine times out of ten, it won't matter. When it does matter, you will fix the problem during optimization. With your code better factored, you often find more powerful optimizations that you would have missed without refactoring. If worse comes to worst, it's easy to put the temp back.

Example

I start with a simple method:

```
def price
  base_price = @quantity * @item_price
  if base_price > 1000
    discount_factor = 0.95
  else
```

```
    discount_factor = 0.98
  end
  base_price * discount_factor
end
```

I replace the temps one at a time. First I extract the right-hand side of the assignment:

```
def price
  a_base_price = base_price
  if a_base_price > 1000
    discount_factor = 0.95
  else
    discount_factor = 0.98
  end
  a_base_price * discount_factor
end

def base_price
   @quantity * @item_price
end
```

I test; then I begin with Inline Temp. First I replace the first reference to the temp:

```
def price
  a_base_price = base_price
  if base_price > 1000
    discount_factor = 0.95
  else
    discount_factor = 0.98
  end
  a_base_price * discount_factor
end

def base_price
   @quantity * @item_price
end
```


Test and do the next (sounds like a caller at a line dance). Because it's the last, I also remove the temp assignment:

```
def price
  if base_price > 1000
    discount_factor = 0.95
  else
    discount_factor = 0.98
```

```
  end
  base_price * discount_factor
end

def base_price
  @quantity * @item_price
end
```

With that gone I can extract discount_factor in a similar way:

```
def price
  a_discount_factor = discount_factor
  base_price * a_discount_factor
end

def discount_factor
  base_price > 1000 ? 0.95 : 0.98
end
```

See how it would have been difficult to extract discount_factor if I had not replaced base_price with a query?

The price method ends up as follows:

```
def price
  base_price * discount_factor
end
```


Replace Temp with Chain

You are using a temporary variable to hold the result of an expression.

Change the methods to support chaining, thus removing the need for a temp.

```
mock = Mock.new
expectation = mock.expects(:a_method_name)
expectation.with("arguments")
expectation.returns([1, :array])
```

```
mock = Mock.new
mock.expects(:a_method_name).with("arguments").returns([1, :array])
```

Motivation

Calling methods on different lines gets the job done, but at times it makes sense to chain method calls together and provide a more fluent interface. In the previous example, assigning an expectation to a local variable is only necessary so that the arguments and return value can be specified. The solution utilizing Method Chaining removes the need for the local variable. Method Chaining can also improve maintainability by providing an interface that allows you to compose code that reads naturally.

At first glance, Replace Temp With Chain might seem to be in direct contrast to Hide Delegate. The important difference is that Hide Delegate should be used to hide the fact that an object of one type needs to delegate to an object of another type. It is about encapsulation—the calling object should not reach down through a series of subordinate objects to request information—it should tell the nearest object to do a job for it. Replace Temp With Chain, on the other hand, involves only one object. It's about improving the fluency of one object by allowing chaining of its method calls.

Mechanics

1. Return `self` from methods that you want to allow chaining from.

2. Test.

3. Remove the local variable and chain the method calls.

4. Test.

Example

Suppose you were designing a library for creating HTML elements. This library would likely contain a method that created a select drop-down and allowed you to add options to the select. The following code contains the `Select` class that could enable creating the example HTML and an example usage of the `Select` class.

```
class Select
  def options
    @options ||= []
  end
```

```
  def add_option(arg)
    options << arg
  end
end

select = Select.new
select.add_option(1999)
select.add_option(2000)
select.add_option(2001)
select.add_option(2002)
select # => #<Select:0x28708 @options=[1999, 2000, 2001, 2002]>
```

The first step in creating a Method Chained solution is to create a method that creates the Select instance and adds an option.

```
class Select
  def self.with_option(option)
    select = self.new
    select.options << option
    select
  end

  # ...
end

select = Select.with_option(1999)
select.add_option(2000)
select.add_option(2001)
select.add_option(2002)
select # => #<Select:0x28488 @options=[1999, 2000, 2001, 2002]>
```


Next, change the method that adds options to return self so that it can be chained.

```
class Select
  # ...

  def add_option(arg)
    options << arg
    self
  end
end

select = Select.with_option(1999).add_option(2000).add_option(2001).
         add_option(2002)
```

```
select # => #<Select:0x28578 @options=[1999, 2000, 2001, 2002]>
```

Finally, rename the add_option method to something that reads more fluently, such as "and".

```
class Select
  def self.with_option(option)
    select = self.new
    select.options << option
    select
  end

  def options
    @options ||= []
  end

  def and(arg)
    options << arg
    self
  end
end

select = Select.with_option(1999).and(2000).and(2001).and(2002)

select # => #<Select:0x28578 @options=[1999, 2000, 2001, 2002]>
```


Introduce Explaining Variable

You have a complicated expression.

Put the result of the expression, or parts of the expression, in a temporary variable with a name that explains the purpose.

```
if (platform.upcase.index("MAC") &&
    browser.upcase.index("IE") &&
    initialized? &&
    resize > 0
  )
  # do something
end
```

```
is_mac_os = platform.upcase.index("MAC")
is_ie_browser = browser.upcase.index("IE")
was_resized = resize > 0

if (is_mac_os && is_ie_browser && initialized? && was_resized)
  # do something
end
```

Motivation

Expressions can become complex and hard to read. In such situations temporary variables can be helpful to break down the expression into something more manageable.

Introduce Explaining Variable is particularly valuable with conditional logic in which it is useful to take each clause of a condition and explain what the condition means with a well-named temp. Another case is a long algorithm, in which each step in the computation can be explained with a temp.

Note In this, and the two refactorings that follow, we introduce temporary variables. It should be stated that temps should not be introduced lightly. Extraneous temporary variables are not a good thing: They can clutter method bodies and distract the reader, hindering their understanding of the code. So why do we introduce them? It turns out that in some circumstances, temporary variables can make code a little less ugly. But whenever I'm tempted to introduce a temporary variable, I ask myself if there's another option. In the case of Introduce Explaining Variable, I almost always prefer to use Extract Method if I can. A temp can only be used within the context of one method. A method is useful throughout the object and to other objects. There are times, however, when other local variables make it difficult to use Extract Method. That's when I bite the bullet and use a temp.

Mechanics

1. Assign a temporary variable to the result of part of the complex expression.

2. Replace the result part of the expression with the value of the temp.

   ⟹ *If the result part of the expression is repeated, you can replace the repeats one at a time.*

3. Test.

4. Repeat for other parts of the expression.

Example

I start with a simple calculation:

```
def price
  # price is base price - quantity discount + shipping
  return @quantity * @item_price -
    [0, @quantity - 500].max * @item_price * 0.05 +
    [@quantity * @item_price * 0.1, 100.0].min
end
```

Simple it may be, but I can make it easier to follow. First I identify the base price as the quantity times the item price. I can turn that part of the calculation into a temp:


```
def price
  # price is base price - quantity discount + shipping
  base_price = @quantity * @item_price
  return base_price -
    [0, @quantity - 500].max * @item_price * 0.05 +
    [@quantity * @item_price * 0.1, 100.0].min
end
```

Quantity times item price is also used later, so I can substitute with the temp there as well:

```
def price
  # price is base price - quantity discount + shipping
  base_price = @quantity * @item_price
  return base_price -
    [0, @quantity - 500].max * @item_price * 0.05 +
```

```
    [base_price * 0.1, 100.0].min
end
```

Next I take the quantity discount:

```
def price
  # price is base price - quantity discount + shipping
  base_price = @quantity * @item_price
  quantity_discount = [0, @quantity - 500].max * @item_price * 0.05
  return base_price -
    quantity_discount +
    [base_price * 0.1, 100.0].min
end
```

Finally, I finish with the shipping. As I do that, I can remove the comment, too, because now it doesn't say anything the code doesn't say:

```
def price
  base_price = @quantity * @item_price
  quantity_discount = [0, @quantity - 500].max * @item_price * 0.05
  shipping = [base_price * 0.1, 100.0].min
  return base_price - quantity_discount + shipping
end
```

Example with Extract Method

For this example I usually wouldn't have done the explaining temps; I would prefer to do that with Extract Method. I start again with

```
def price
  # price is base price - quantity discount + shipping
  return @quantity * @item_price -
    [0, @quantity - 500].max * @item_price * 0.05 +
    [@quantity * @item_price * 0.1, 100.0].min
end
```

but this time I extract a method for the base price:

```
def price
  # price is base price - quantity discount + shipping
  return base_price -
    [0, @quantity - 500].max * @item_price * 0.05 +
    [base_price * 0.1, 100.0].min
```

```
end

def base_price
  @quantity * @item_price
end
```

I continue one at a time. When I'm finished I get:

```
def price
  base_price - quantity_discount + shipping
end

def base_price
  @quantity * @item_price
end

def quantity_discount
   [0, @quantity - 500].max * @item_price * 0.05
end

def shipping
  [base_price * 0.1, 100.0].min
end
```

Split Temporary Variable

You have a temporary variable assigned to more than once, but it is not a loop variable nor a collecting temporary variable.

Make a separate temporary variable for each assignment.

```
temp = 2 * (@height + @width)
puts temp
temp = @height * @width
puts temp
```

```
perimeter = 2 * (@height + @width)
puts perimeter
area = @height * @width
puts area
```

Motivation

Temporary variables are made for various uses. Some of these uses naturally lead to the temps being assigned to several times. Loop variables [Beck] change for each run around a loop. Collecting temporary variables [Beck] collect together some value that is built up during the method.

Many other temporaries are used to hold the result of a long-winded bit of code for easy reference later. These kinds of variables should be set only once. That they are set more than once is a sign that they have more than one responsibility within the method. Any variable with more than one responsibility should be replaced with a temp for each responsibility. Using a temp for two different things is confusing for the reader.

Mechanics

1. Change the name of a temp at its first assignment.

   ⟹ *If the later assignments are of the form* `i = i + some_expression`, *that indicates that it is a collecting temporary variable, so don't split it. The operator for a collecting temporary variable usually is addition, string concatenation, writing to a stream, or adding to a collection.*

2. Change all references of the temp up to its second assignment.

3. Test.

4. Repeat in stages, each stage renaming at the assignment, and changing references until the next assignment.

Example

For this example I compute the distance traveled by a haggis. From a standing start, a haggis experiences an initial force. After a delayed period a secondary force kicks in to further accelerate the haggis. Using the common laws of motion, I can compute the distance traveled as follows:

```
def distance_traveled(time)
  acc = @primary_force / @mass
  primary_time = [time, @delay].min
  result = 0.5 * acc * primary_time * primary_time
  secondary_time = time - @delay
  if(secondary_time > 0)
    primary_vel = acc * @delay
    acc = (@prmary_force + @secondary_force) / @mass
    result += primary_vel * secondary_time + 5 * acc * secondary_time *
      secondary_time
  end
  result
end
```

A nice awkward little function. The interesting thing for our example is the way the variable acc is set twice. It has two responsibilities: one to hold the initial acceleration caused by the first force and another later to hold the acceleration with both forces. This I want to split.

I start at the beginning by changing the name of the temp. Then I change all references to the temp from that point up to the next assignment:

```
def distance_traveled(time)
  primary_acc = @primary_force / @mass
  primary_time = [time, @delay].min
  result = 0.5 * primary_acc * primary_time * primary_time
  secondary_time = time - @delay
  if(secondary_time > 0)
    primary_vel = primary_acc * @delay
    acc = (@prmary_force + @secondary_force) / @mass
    result += primary_vel * secondary_time + 5 * acc * secondary_time *
              secondary_time
  end
  result
end
```


I choose the new name to represent only the first use of the temp. My tests should pass.

I continue on the second assignment of the temp. This removes the original temp name completely, replacing it with a new temp named for the second use.

```
def distance_traveled(time)
  primary_acc = @primary_force / @mass
  primary_time = [time, @delay].min
  result = 0.5 * primary_acc * primary_time * primary_time
```

```
  secondary_time = time - @delay
  if(secondary_time > 0)
    primary_vel = primary_acc * @delay
    secondary_acc = (@prmary_force + @secondary_force) / @mass
    result += primary_vel * secondary_time + 5 * secondary_acc *
              secondary_time * secondary_time
  end
  result
end
```

I'm sure you can think of a lot more refactoring to be done here. Enjoy it. (I'm sure it's better than eating the haggis—do you know what they put in those things?)

Remove Assignments to Parameters

The code assigns to a parameter.

Use a temporary variable instead.

```
def discount(input_val, quantity, year_to_date)
  if input_val > 50
    input_val -= 2
  end
end
```


⇓

```
def discount(input_val, quantity, year_to_date)
  result = input_val
  if input_val > 50
    result -= 2
  end
end
```

Motivation

First let me make sure we are clear on the phrase "assigns to a parameter." If you pass an object named foo as a parameter to a method, assigning to the parameter means to change foo to refer to a different object. I have no problems with doing something to the object that was passed in; I do that all the time. I just object to changing foo to refer to another object entirely:

```
def a_method(foo)
  foo.modify_in_some_way # that's OK
  foo = another_object # trouble and despair will follow you
end
```

The reason I don't like this comes down to lack of clarity and to confusion between pass by value and pass by reference. Ruby uses pass by value exclusively (see later), and this discussion is based on that usage.

With pass by value, any change to the parameter is not reflected in the calling routine. Those who have used pass by reference will probably find this confusing.

The other area of confusion is within the body of the code itself. It is much clearer if you use only the parameter to represent what has been passed in, because that is a consistent usage.

In Ruby, don't assign to parameters, and if you see code that does, apply Remove Assignments to Parameters.

Of course this rule does not necessarily apply to other languages that use output parameters, although even with these languages I prefer to use output parameters as little as possible.

Mechanics

1. Create a temporary variable for the parameter.
2. Replace all references to the parameter, made after the assignment, to the temporary variable.
3. Change the assignment to assign to the temporary variable.
4. Test.

Example

I start with the following simple routine:

```
def discount(input_val, quantity, year_to_date)
  input_val -= 2 if input_val > 50
  input_val -= 1 if quantity > 100
```

```
  input_val -= 4 if year_to_date > 10000
  input_val
end
```

Replacing with a temp leads to:

```
def discount(input_val, quantity, year_to_date)
  result = inputval
  result -= 2 if input_val > 50
  result -= 1 if quantity > 100
  result -= 4 if year_to_date > 10000
  result
end
```

Use of pass by value often is a source of confusion in Ruby. Ruby strictly uses pass by value in all places, thus the following program:

```
x = 5
def triple(arg)
  arg = arg * 3
  puts "arg in triple: #{arg}"
end
triple x
puts "x after triple #{x}"
```

produces the following output:

```
arg in triple: 15
x after triple 5
```


The confusion arises because I can call methods on the object that modify its state:

```
class Ledger

  attr_reader :balance

  def initialize(balance)
    @balance = balance
  end

  def add(arg)
    @balance += arg
  end

end
```

```
class Product

  def self.add_price_by_updating(ledger, price)
    ledger.add(price)
    puts "ledger in add_price_by_updating: #{ledger.balance}"
  end

  def self.add_price_by_replacing(ledger, price)
    ledger = Ledger.new(ledger.balance + price)
    puts "ledger in add_price_by_replacing: #{ledger.balance}"
  end

end

l1 = Ledger.new(0)
Product.add_price_by_updating(l1, 5)
puts "l1 after add_price_by_updating: #{l1.balance}"

l2 = Ledger.new(0)
Product.add_price_by_replacing(l2, 5)
puts "l2 after add_price_by_replacing: #{l2.balance}"
```

It produces this output:

```
ledger in add_price_by_updating: 5
l1 after add_price_by_updating: 5
ledger in add_price_by_replacing: 5
l2 after add_price_by_replacing: 0
```


Essentially the object reference is passed by value. I can use the reference to call methods and make changes to the state that will be reflected further up the call stack. But if I assign to the reference, the fact that this reference has been passed by value means that this new assignment will not be reflected outside the scope of the method body.

Replace Method with Method Object

You have a long method that uses local variables in such a way that you cannot apply Extract Method.

Turn the method into its own object so that all the local variables become instance variables on that object. You can then decompose the method into other methods on the same object.

```
class Order

  def price
    primary_base_price = 0
    secondary_base_price = 0
    tertiary_base_price = 0
    # long computation
  end

end
```

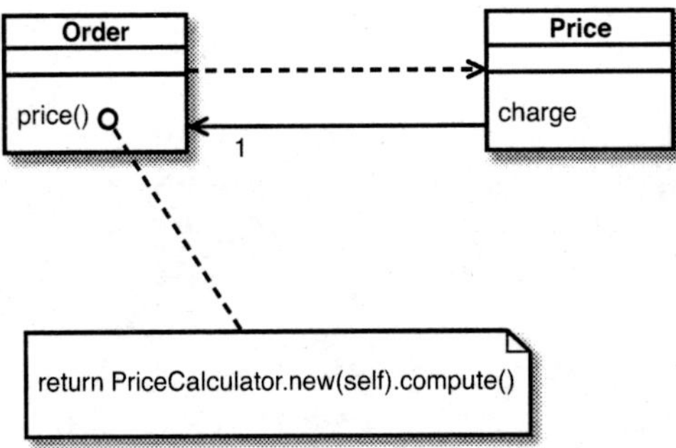

Replace Method with Method Object

Motivation

In this book I emphasize the beauty of small methods. By extracting pieces out of a large method, you make things much more comprehensible.

The difficulty in decomposing a method lies in local variables. If they are rampant, decomposition can be difficult. Using Replace Temp with Query helps to reduce this burden, but occasionally you may find you cannot break down a method that needs breaking. In this case you reach deep into the tool bag and get out your Method Object [Beck].

Applying Replace Method with Method Object turns all these local variables into attributes on the method object. You can then use Extract Method on this new object to create additional methods that break down the original method.

Mechanics

Stolen shamelessly from Kent Beck's Smalltalk Best Practices.

1. Create a new class, name it after the method.

2. Give the new class an attribute for the object that hosted the original method (the source object) and an attribute for each temporary variable and each parameter in the method.

3. Give the new class a constructor that takes the source object and each parameter.

4. Give the new class a method named "`compute`"

5. Copy the body of the original method into `compute`. Use the source object instance variable for any invocations of methods on the original object.

6. Test.

7. Replace the old method with one that creates the new object and calls compute.

Now comes the fun part. Because all the local variables are now attributes, you can freely decompose the method without having to pass any parameters.

Example

A proper example of this requires a long chapter, so I'm showing this refactoring for a method that doesn't need it. (Don't ask what the logic of this method is, I made it up as I went along.)

```
class Account

  def gamma(input_val, quantity, year_to_date)
    inportant_value1 = (input_val * quantity) + delta
    important_value2 = (input_val * year_to_date) + 100
    if (year_to_date - important_value1) > 100
      important_value2 -= 20
    end
    important_value3 = important_value2 * 7
    # and so on.
    important_value3 - 2 * important_value1
```

```
  end

end
```

To turn this into a method object, I begin by declaring a new class. I provide an attribute for the original object and an attribute for each parameter and temporary variable in the method.

```
class Gamma
  attr_reader :account,
              :input_val,
              :quantity,
              :year_to_date,
              :important_value1,
              :important_value2,
              :important_value3

end
```

I add a constructor:

```
def initialize(account, input_val_arg, quantity_arg, year_to_date_arg)
  @account = account
  @input_val = input_val_arg
  @quantity = quantity_arg
  @year_to_date = year_to_date_arg
end
```


Now I can move the original method over. I need to modify any calls of features of account to use the `@account` instance variable.

```
def compute
  @inportant_value1 = (input_val * quantity) + @account.delta
  @important_value2 = (input_val * year_to_date) + 100
  if (year_to_date - important_value1) > 100
    @important_value2 -= 20
  end
  @important_value3 = important_value2 * 7
  # and so on.
  @important_value3 - 2 * important_value1
end
```

I then modify the old method to delegate to the method object:

```
def gamma(input_val, quantity, year_to_date)
  Gamma.new(self, input_val, quantity, year_to_date).compute
end
```

That's the essential refactoring. The benefit is that I can now easily use Extract Method on the compute method without ever worrying about the argument's passing:

```
def compute
  @inportant_value1 = (input_val * quantity) + @account.delta
  @important_value2 = (input_val * year_to_date) + 100
  important_thing
  @important_value3 = important_value2 * 7
  # and so on.
  @important_value3 - 2 * important_value1
end

def important_thing
  if (year_to_date - important_value1) > 100
     @important_value2 -= 20
   end
end
```

Substitute Algorithm

You want to replace an algorithm with one that is clearer.

Replace the body of the method with the new algorithm.


```
def found_friends(people)
  friends = []
  people.each do |person|
    if(person == "Don")
      friends << "Don"
    end
    if(person == "John")
      friends << "John"
    end
    if(person == "Kent")
      friends << "Kent"
    end
  end
  return friends
end
```

```
def found_friends(people)
  people.select do |person|
    %w(Don John Kent).include? person
  end
end
```

Motivation

I've never tried to skin a cat. I'm told there are several ways to do it. I'm sure some are easier than others. So it is with algorithms. If you find a clearer way to do something, you should replace the complicated way with the clearer way. Refactoring can break down something complex into simpler pieces, but sometimes you just reach the point at which you have to remove the whole algorithm and replace it with something simpler. This occurs as you learn more about the problem and realize that there's an easier way to do it. It also happens if you start using a library that supplies features that duplicate your code.

Sometimes when you want to change the algorithm to do something slightly different, it is easier to substitute the algorithm first into something easier for the change you need to make.

When you have to take this step, make sure you have decomposed the method as much as you can. Substituting a large, complex algorithm is difficult; only by making it simple can you make the substitution tractable.

Mechanics

1. Prepare your alternative algorithm.

2. Run the new algorithm against your tests. If the results are the same, you're finished.

3. If the results aren't the same, use the old algorithm for comparison in testing and debugging.

   ⟹ *Run each test case with old and new algorithms and watch both results. That helps you see which test cases are causing trouble, and how.*

Replace Loop with Collection Closure Method

You are processing the elements of a collection in a loop.

Replace the loop with a collection closure method.

Motivation

In most mainstream programming languages you operate on collections using loops, grabbing each element one at a time and processing it. It turns out there are common patterns of processing that you do in loops, but these are difficult to extract into libraries unless your programming language has closures.

Two of Ruby's mentor languages are Lisp and Smalltalk, both of which have closures and library code to manipulate collections easily. Ruby has followed their lead and offers a really nice set of methods. The Enumberable module, included in Array and Hash, is a perfect example.

By replacing loops with the relevant collection closure methods you can make the code easier to follow. The collection closure method hides away the infrastructure code used to traverse the collection and create derived collections, allowing us to focus on business logic.

There are times when a more complex task requires a sequence of collection closure methods chained together.

Mechanics

1. Identify what the basic pattern of the loop is.

2. Replace the loop with the appropriate collection closure methods.

3. Test.

Examples

There are quite a few common cases when different collection closure methods are useful. Here I show the most common transformations.

```
managers = []
employees.each do |e|
  managers << e if e.manager?
end
```

```
managers = employees.select {|e| e.manager?}
```

The `reject` method reverses the test of the filter. In both cases the original collection isn't touched unless you use the destructive form (`select!` or `reject!`).

```
offices = []

employees.each {|e| offices << e.office}
```

```
offices = employees.collect {|e| e.office}
```

`collect` is aliased as "`map`". `collect` is the Smalltalk word, and `map` is the Lisp word, so the choice depends on whether you like parentheses or square brackets.

Often you'll find loops that include more than one task going on. In this case you can often replace them with a sequence of collection closure methods.

```
managerOffices = []

employees.each do |e|
  managerOffices << e.office if e.manager?
end
```

```
managerOffices = employees.select {|e| e.manager?}.
                           collect {|e| e.office}
```

It might be useful to think of this chaining as a series of pipes and filters. Here, we've piped the original collection through the `select` filter and onto the `collect` filter. Also note the way I've laid out the code here—listing each filter on its own line makes the transformations a little clearer. If you finish a line with a period, Ruby knows not to treat the end of line as a statement terminator.

When the series of pipes and filters becomes so complex that it's no longer easy to understand, you might want to consider writing a custom traversal method whose name explains the purpose of the traversal.

If you need to do something in a loop that produces a single value, such as a sum, consider using the `inject` method. This can take a bit more getting used to.

```
total = 0
employees.each {|e| total += e.salary}
```

```
total = employees.inject(0) {|sum, e| sum + e.salary}
```

Extract Surrounding Method

You have two methods that contain nearly identical code. The variance is in the middle of the method.

Extract the duplication into a method that accepts a block and yields back to the caller to execute the unique code.

```
def charge(amount, credit_card_number)
  begin
    connection = CreditCardServer.connect(...)
    connection.send(amount, credit_card_number)
  rescue IOError => e
    Logger.log "Could not submit order #{@order_number} to the server: #{e}"
    return nil
  ensure
    connection.close
  end
end
```

```
def charge(amount, credit_card_number)
  connect do |connection|
```

```
    connection.send(amount, credit_card_number)
  end
end

def connect
  begin
    connection = CreditCardServer.connect(...)
    yield connection
  rescue IOError => e
    Logger.log "Could not submit order #{@order_number} to the server: #{e}"
    return nil
  ensure
    connection.close
  end
end
```

Motivation

It's not hard to remove duplication when the offending code is at the top or bottom of a method: Just use Extract Method to move the duplication out of the way. But what happens when the unique code is in the middle of the method? You can use Form Template Method, but that involves introducing an inheritance hierarchy, which isn't always ideal.

Conveniently, Ruby's blocks allow us to extract the surrounding duplication and have the extracted method yield back to the calling code to execute the unique logic. As well as removing duplication, this refactoring can be used to hide away infrastructure code (for example, code for iterating over a collection or connecting to an external service), so that the business logic becomes more prominent.

Mechanics

1. Use Extract Method on one piece of duplication. Name it after the duplicated behavior.

   ⟹ *This will become our surrounding method.*

   ⟹ *For now the surrounding method will still perform the unique behavior.*

2. Test.

3. Modify the calling method to pass a block to the surrounding method. Copy the unique logic from the surrounding method into the block.

4. Replace the unique logic in the extracted method with the yield keyword.

5. Identify any variables in the surrounding method that are needed by the unique logic and pass them as parameters in the call to yield.

6. Test.

7. Modify any other methods that can use the new surrounding method.

Example

Let's say that we are modeling family trees, and we have a person class that has a self-referential one-to-many relationship to itself, called children (see Figure 6.1).

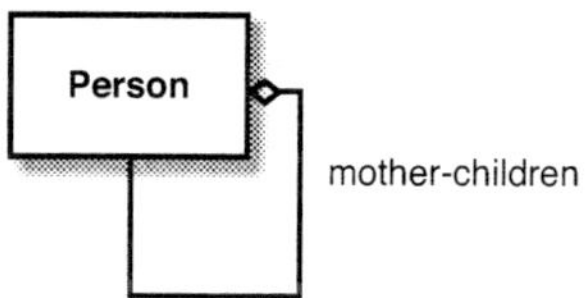

Figure 6.1 A mother can have many children.

For now, we only need to capture the mother of each child. Our person class looks like this:

```
class Person
  attr_reader :mother, :children, :name

  def initialize(name, date_of_birth, date_of_death=nil, mother=nil)
    @name, @mother = name, mother,
    @date_of_birth, @date_of_death = date_of_birth, date_of_death
    @children = []
    @mother.add_child(self) if @mother
  end

  def add_child(child)
    @children << child
  end
```

The person class has two methods that we're interested in: one for counting the number of living descendants, and one for counting the number of descendants with a particular name.

```
def number_of_living_descendants
  children.inject(0) do |count, child|
    count += 1 if child.alive?
    count + child.number_of_living_descendants
  end
end

def number_of_descendants_named(name)
  children.inject(0) do |count, child|
    count += 1 if child.name == name
    count + child.number_of_descendants_named(name)
  end
end

def alive?
  @date_of_death.nil?
end
```

Both of these methods iterate over the collection of children, recursively down the family tree. Recursion isn't trivial, and once I get it correct, I try to avoid duplication of the recursive logic. But the means to remove this duplication isn't always obvious. Extract Method can reduce duplication if you can parameterize the method in a way that allows its use in different situations. But in this case, the duplication is in the decision about whether to increment the count or not—and this decision can't be made without context as to the state of the person object that you are examining at each step of the iteration.

Fortunately, Ruby's blocks allow us to provide this context. We can yield the person object back to the caller at each iteration step, and the caller can decide whether we should count. The first step is to perform Extract Method on one of the duplicates. I start with the `number_of_descendants_named` method. I name the extracted method after the common behavior—the counting of descendants matching a certain criteria. This will become the surrounding method.

```
def number_of_descendants_named(name)
  count_descendants_matching(name)
end

protected
def count_descendants_matching(name)
  children.inject(0) do |count, child|
```

```
    count += 1 if child.name == name
    count + child.count_descendants_matching(name)
  end
end
```

Next, I make the calling method pass a block to the surrounding method, and push the logic that checks for a matching name up into the block. I need to yield the child back to the caller so that it can perform the check:

```
def number_of_descendants_named(name)
  count_descendants_matching { |descendant| descendant.name == name }
end

def count_descendants_matching(&block)
  children.inject(0) do |count, child|
    count += 1 if yield child
    count + child.count_descendants_matching(&block)
  end
end
```

And finally, I can modify the `number_of_living_descendants` method to use our new surrounding method.

```
def number_of_living_descendants
  count_descendants_matching { |descendant| descendant.alive? }
end
```

The duplication has been removed, and I have the added benefit of having kept the business logic (the logic determining whether to count the descendant) up in the public method. I've separated this business logic from the infrastructure logic required to iterate over the collection, which helps during maintenance.

Introduce Class Annotation

You have a method whose implementation steps are so common that they can safely be hidden away.

Declare the behavior by calling a class method from the class definition.

```
class SearchCriteria...

  def initialize(hash)
    @author_id = hash[:author_id]
    @publisher_id = hash[:publisher_id]
```

```
    @isbn = hash[:isbn]
  end
```

```
class SearchCriteria...

  hash_initializer :author_id, :publisher_id, :isbn
```

Motivation

Attribute readers and writers are so common in Object-Oriented programming languages that the author of Ruby decided to provide a succinct way to declare them. The `attr_accessor`, `attr_reader`, and `attr_writer` methods can be called from the definition of a class or module with a list of names of attributes. The implementation of an attribute accessor is so easy to understand that it can be hidden away and replaced with a class annotation. Most code isn't this simple, and hiding it away would serve only to obfuscate the solution. But when the purpose of the code can be captured clearly in a declarative statement, Introduce Class Annotation can clarify the intention of your code.

Mechanics

1. Decide on the signature of your class annotation. Declare it in the appropriate class.

2. Convert the original method to a class method. Make the appropriate changes so that the method works at class scope.

   ⟹ *Make sure the class method is declared before the class annotation is called; otherwise, you'll get an exception when the parser tries to execute the annotation.*

3. Test.

4. Consider using Extract Module on the class method to make the annotation more prominent in your class definition.

5. Test.

Example

For this example, we have a `SearchCriteria` class that takes a `Hash` of parameters and assigns them to instance variables.

```
class SearchCriteria...

  def initialize(hash)
    @author_id = hash[:author_id]
    @publisher_id = hash[:publisher_id]
    @isbn = hash[:isbn]
  end
```

Since we're dealing with `initialize` here, we'll use Rename Method as well as change the method to class scope, just to make things a little clearer. We want to define the `initialize` method dynamically so that we can handle any list of key-names.

```
class SearchCriteria

  def self.hash_initializer(*attribute_names)
    define_method(:initialize) do |*args|
      data = args.first || {}
      attribute_names.each do |attribute_name|
        instance_variable_set "@#{attribute_name}", data[attribute_name]
      end
    end
  end

  hash_initializer :author_id, :publisher_id, :isbn

end
```

The unfortunate thing here is that we're not really taking advantage of our succinct class annotation with the ugliness of the `hash_initializer` standing above it. Since we'll probably use `hash_initializer` in a lot of classes, it makes sense to extract it to a module and move it to class Class.

```
module CustomInitializers

  def hash_initializer(*attribute_names)
    define_method(:initialize) do |*args|
```

```
      data = args.first || {}
      attribute_names.each do |attribute_name|
        instance_variable_set "@#{attribute_name}", data[attribute_name]
      end
    end
  end

end

Class.send :include, CustomInitializers

class SearchCriteria...

  hash_initializer :author_id, :publisher_id, :isbn
```

Introduce Named Parameter

The parameters in a method call cannot easily be deduced from the name of the method you are calling.

Convert the parameter list into a Hash, and use the keys of the Hash as names for the parameters.


```
SearchCriteria.new(5, 8, "0201485672")
```

```
SearchCriteria.new(:author_id => 5, :publisher_id => 8, :isbn =>"0201485672")
```

Motivation

So much of object-oriented design depends on the effectiveness of the abstractions that you create. Let's say you have object A that delegates to object B, which in turn delegates to object C. It is much easier to understand the algorithm if each object can be synthesized in isolation by the reader. To provide for this, the clarity of the public interface of the object being delegated to is important. If object B's public interface represents a cohesive piece of behavior with a well-named class, well-named methods, and parameter lists that make sense given the name of the method, a reader is less likely to have to delve into the details of object B to understand object A. Without this clear abstraction around the behavior of object B, the reader will have to move back and forth between object A and object B (and perhaps object C as well), and understanding of the algorithm will be much more difficult.

Ruby's `Hash` object provides another way to improve the readability of a method. By replacing a list of parameters with a `Hash` of key-value pairs, with the key representing the name of the parameter and the value representing the parameter itself, the fluency of the calling code can be improved significantly. The reader of the calling code can see how the parameters might relate to one another and deduce how the method might use them. It's particularly useful for optional parameters—parameters that are only used in some of the calls can be extra hard to understand.

Mechanics

1. Choose the parameters that you want to name. If you are not naming all of the parameters, move the parameters that you want to name to the end of the parameter list.

   ⟹ *That way your calling code does not need to wrap the named parameters in curly braces.*

2. Test

3. Replace the parameters in the calling code with name/value pairs

4. Replace the parameters with a `Hash` object in the receiving method. Modify the receiving method to use the new `Hash`.

5. Test.

Example 1: Naming All of the Parameters

We start with a SearchCriteria object that is responsible for finding books. Its constructor takes an `author_id`, `publisher_id`, and `isbn`.

```
class SearchCriteria...

  attr_reader :author_id, :publisher_id, :isbn

  def initialize(author_id, publisher_id, isbn)
    @author_id = author_id
    @publisher_id = publisher_id
    @isbn = isbn
  end
```

Some client code might look like this:

```
criteria = SearchCriteria.new(5, 8, "0201485672")
```

Without looking at the class definition, it's hard to know what the parameters are. And without knowing what the parameters are, it's hard to infer how the SearchCriteria object might behave.

First we change the calling code to pass key-value pairs to the constructor.

```
criteria = SearchCriteria.new(
          :author_id => 5, :publisher_id => 8, :isbn =>"0201485672")
```

Next we change the initialize method to take a Hash, and initialize the instance variables with the values from the Hash.

```
class SearchCriteria...

  def initialize(params)
    @author_id = params[:author_id]
    @publisher_id = params[:publisher_id]
    @isbn = params[:isbn]
  end
```

Our calling code is a lot cleaner, but if a developer is looking at the class definition and wants to know the required parameters for the method, she needs to examine the method definition to find all that are used. For initialize methods such as this that simply assign instance variables of the same name as the keys in the Hash, I like to use Introduce Class Annotation to declare the initialize method.


```
class SearchCriteria...

  def initialize(hash)
    @author_id = hash[:author_id]
    @publisher_id = hash[:publisher_id]
    @isbn = hash[:isbn]
  end
```

becomes

```
class SearchCriteria...

  hash_initializer :author_id, :publisher_id, :isbn
```

To do this, we add a method to the Class class:

```
module CustomInitializers
```

```
  def hash_initializer(*attribute_names)
    define_method(:initialize) do |*args|
      data = args.first || {}
      attribute_names.each do |attribute_name|
        instance_variable_set "@#{attribute_name}", data[attribute_name]
      end
    end
  end

end

Class.send :include, CustomInitializers
```

And then we can use our `hash_initializer` method in any class definition.

Example 2: Naming Only the Optional Parameters

It can be useful to distinguish between optional and required parameters to better communicate the method's use to the developer trying to call the method. Take for example the following SQL-building code:

```
class Books...

  def self.find(selector, conditions="", *joins)
    sql = ["SELECT * FROM books"]
    joins.each do |join_table|
      sql << "LEFT OUTER JOIN #{join_table} ON"
      sql << "books.#{join_table.to_s.chap}_id"
      sql << " = #{join_table}.id"
    end
    sql << "WHERE #{conditions}" unless conditions.empty?
    sql << "LIMIT 1" if selector == :first

    connection.find(sql.join(" "))
  end
```

Both the `conditions` and `joins` parameters are optional, but the `selector` is required. The `selector` can be either `:all`, or `:first`. The former brings back all records that meet the given criteria, and the latter brings back only the first record that meets the criteria. Here are some clients of this code:

```
Books.find(:all)
Books.find(:all, "title like '%Voodoo Economics'")
Books.find(:all, "authors.name = 'Jenny James'", :authors)
Books.find(:first, "authors.name = 'Jenny James'", :authors)
```

While the conditions parameter might be reasonably intuitive to a developer who understands SQL, the joins parameter is not as clear. The following syntax better communicates the use of the parameters:

```
Books.find(:all)
Books.find(:all, :conditions => "title like '%Voodoo Economics'")
Books.find(:all, :conditions => "authors.name = 'Jenny James'",
                 :joins =>[:authors])
Books.find(:first, :conditions => "authors.name = 'Jenny James'",
                   :joins =>[:authors])
```

Since the parameters we want to name are already at the end of the parameter list, we don't need to move them.

We convert the conditions and joins parameters to a Hash, and modify the method definition accordingly.

```
class Books...

  def self.find(selector, hash={})
    hash[:joins] ||= []
    hash[:conditions] ||= ""

    sql = ["SELECT * FROM books"]
    hash[:joins].each do |join_table|
      sql << "LEFT OUTER JOIN #{join_table} ON"
      sql << "books.#{join_table.to_s.chop}_id"
      sql << "= #{join_table}.id"
    end

    sql << "WHERE #{hash[:conditions]}" unless hash[:conditions].empty?
    sql << "LIMIT 1" if selector == :first

    connection.find(sql.join(" "))
  end
```

Introduce Named Parameter

Our calling code is more fluent, but if we are looking at the class definition, we have to look through the entire method to know the parameters that we need to pass in. We can improve this by using Introduce Assertion. We'll add the assertion to the Hash object itself.

```
module AssertValidKeys
  def assert_valid_keys(*valid_keys)
    unknown_keys = keys - [valid_keys].flatten
    if unknown_keys.any?
      raise(ArgumentError, "Unknown key(s): #{unknown_keys.join(", ")}")
    end
  end
```

```
Hash.send(:include, AssertValidKeys)

class Books...
  def self.find(selector, hash={})
    hash.assert_valid_keys :conditions, :joins

    hash[:joins] ||= []
    hash[:conditions] ||= ""

    sql = ["SELECT * FROM books"]
    hash[:joins].each do |join_table|
      sql << "LEFT OUTER JOIN #{join_table}"
      sql << "ON books.#{join_table.to_s.chop}_id = #{join_table}.id"
    end

    sql << "WHERE #{hash[:conditions]}" unless hash[:conditions].empty?
    sql << "LIMIT 1" if selector == :first

    connection.find(sql.join(" "))
  end
```

This has two advantages: We get quick feedback on misspelled keys that we pass to the method, and the assertion serves as a declarative statement to communicate to any reader the expected parameters.

Remove Named Parameter

The fluency that the named parameter brings is no longer worth the complexity on the receiver.

Convert the named parameter Hash to a standard parameter list.

```
IsbnSearch.new(:isbn => "0201485672")
```

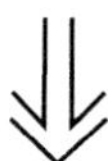

```
IsbnSearch.new("0201485672")
```

Motivation

Introduce Named Parameter brings a fluency to the calling code that can be beneficial. But named parameters do come at a price—they add complexity to the receiving method. The parameters are clumped together into one `Hash`, which can rarely have a better name than "`params`" or "`options`", because the parameters contained within the `Hash` are not cohesive enough to have a domain-related name. Even if they are named well, it is impossible to tell exactly the contents of the `Hash`, without examining the method body or the calling code. Most of the time, this added complexity is worth the increased readability on the calling side, but sometimes the receiver changes in such a way that the added complexity is no longer justified. Perhaps the number of parameters has reduced, or one of the optional parameters becomes required, so we remove the required parameter from the named parameter `Hash`. Or perhaps we perform Extract Method or Extract Class and take only one of the parameters with us. The newly created method or class might now be able to be named in such a way that the parameter is obvious. In these cases, you want to remove the named parameter.

Mechanics

Remove Named Parameter

1. Choose the parameter that you want to remove from the named parameter `Hash`. In the receiving method, replace the named parameter with a standard parameter in the parameter list.

   ⇒ *If you have other named parameters that you don't want to remove, place the unnamed parameter earlier in the parameter list than the named parameters, so that you can still call the method without curly braces for your named parameter* `Hash`.

2. Replace the named parameter in the calling code with a standard parameter.

3. Test.

Example

Let's go back to our books example, but this time suppose that all of the parameters have been implemented as named parameters. They are all optional. This means that the calling code can call the method in many different ways:

```
Books.find
Books.find(:selector => :all,
           :conditions => "authors.name = 'Jenny James'",
           :joins => [:authors])
Books.find(:selector => :first,
           :conditions => "authors.name = 'JennyJames'",
           :joins => [:authors])
```

This code has a couple of problems. For starters, without looking at the implementation of the `find` method, it is difficult to predict the result of calling `Books.find` without any parameters. Does it return one result? Does it return all results? For this, I need to go to the implementation:

```
class Books...

  def self.find(hash={})
    hash[:joins] ||= []
    hash[:conditions] ||= ""

    sql = ["SELECT * FROM books"]
    hash[:joins].each do |join_table|
      sql << "LEFT OUTER JOIN #{join_table}"
      sql << "ON books.#{join_table.to_s.chop}_id = #{join_table}.id"
    end

    sql << "WHERE #{hash[:conditions]}" unless hash[:conditions].empty?
    sql << "LIMIT 1" if hash[:selector] == :first

    connection.find(sql.join(" "))
  end
```


After sifting through the entire method, I see that if I don't provide any parameters, all books will be returned. So we've introduced named parameters, but haven't removed the need to switch to the implementation to understand the calling code.

The second problem is the name of the `:selector` parameter. "`:selector`" doesn't mean anything in the domain of SQL. "`:limit`" would perhaps be a better name, but `:limit => :all` is a little strange. Changing the selector parameter to be required will solve both problems. The name "`selector`" will be removed, and if we want to return all books we will use the syntax `Books.find(:all)`.

The first step is to introduce the `selector` parameter into the `find` method:

```
def self.find(selector, hash={})
  hash[:joins] ||= []
  hash[:conditions] ||= ""
```

```
  sql = ["SELECT * FROM books"]
  hash[:joins].each do |join_table|
    sql << "LEFT OUTER JOIN #{join_table} ON"
    sql << "books.#{join_table.to_s.chop}_id = #{join_table}.id"
  end

  sql << "WHERE #{hash[:conditions]}" unless hash[:conditions].empty?
  sql << "LIMIT 1" if selector == :first

  connection.find(sql.join(" "))
end
```

The next step is to modify the calling code:

```
Books.find
```

becomes

```
Books.find(:all)
```

```
Books.find(:selector => :all,
           :conditions => "authors.name = 'Jenny James'",
           :joins => [:authors])
```

becomes

```
Books.find(:all, :conditions => "authors.name = 'Jenny James'",
                 :joins =>[:authors])
```

and

```
Books.find(:selector => :first,
           :conditions => "authors.name = 'JennyJames'",
           :joins => [:authors])
```

becomes

```
Books.find(:first, :conditions => "authors.name = 'Jenny James'",
                   :joins =>[:authors])
```


Remove Unused Default Parameter

A parameter has a default value, but the method is never called without the parameter.

Remove the default value.

```
def product_count_items(search_criteria=nil)
```

```
  criteria = search_criteria | @search_criteria
  ProductCountItem.find_all_by_criteria(criteria)
end
```

```
def product_count_items(search_criteria)
  ProductCountItem.find_all_by_criteria(search_criteria)
end
```

Motivation

Adding a default value to a parameter can improve the fluency of calling code. Without the default, callers that don't require the parameter will have to explicitly pass `nil` or an empty collection to the method when they don't require it, and the fluency of the calling code is reduced. When required, default values are a good thing. But sometimes, as code evolves over time, fewer and fewer callers require the default value, until finally the default value is unused. Unused flexibility in software is a bad thing. Maintenance of this flexibility takes time, allows opportunities for bugs, and makes refactoring more difficult. Unused default parameters should be removed.

Mechanics

1. Remove the default from the parameter in the method signature.
2. Test.
3. Remove any code within the method that checks for the default value.
4. Test.

Example

In this example, `search_criteria` defaults to `nil` in the parameter list, but then performs some conditional logic to use the `@search_criteria` instance variable if `search_criteria` isn't explicitly passed in:

```
def product_count_items(search_criteria=nil)
  criteria = search_criteria | @search_criteria
  ProductCountItem.find_all_by_criteria(criteria)
end
```

If we never call `product_count_items` without a parameter, then the use of `@search_criteria` is misleading. If this is the only use of the instance variable within the class, then our default value is preventing us from removing the instance variable entirely.

First, we remove the default value:

```
def product_count_items(search_criteria = nil)
  criteria = search_criteria | @search_criteria
  ProductCountItem.find_all_by_criteria(criteria)
end
```

Our tests should still pass since no one calls the method without a parameter.

All going well, we should now be able to remove the conditional logic:

```
def product_count_items(search_criteria)
  ProductCountItem.find_all_by_criteria(search_criteria)
end
```

We now have the option to perform Inline Method, which could remove a layer of indirection and simplify our code.

Dynamic Method Definition

You have methods that can be defined more concisely if defined dynamically.

Define the methods dynamically.

```
def failure
  self.state = :failure
end

def error
  self.state = :error
end
```

```
def_each :failure, :error do |method_name|
  self.state = method_name
end
```

Motivation

I use Dynamic Method Definition frequently. Of course, I default to defining methods explicitly, but at the point when duplication begins to appear I quickly move to the dynamic definitions.

Dynamically defined methods can help guard against method definition mistakes, since adding another method usually means adding one more argument; however, this is not the primary reason for Dynamic Method Definition.

The primary goal for Dynamic Method Definition is to more concisely express the method definition in a readable and maintainable format.

Mechanics

1. Dynamically define one of the similar methods.

2. Test.

3. Convert the additional similar methods to use the dynamic definition.

4. Test.

Example: Using def_each to Define Similar Methods

Defining several similar methods is verbose and often unnecessary. For example, each of the following methods is simply calling the state method.

```
def failure
  self.state = :failure
end

def error
  self.state = :error
end

def success
  self.state = :success
end
```

The preceding code executes perfectly well, but it's too similar to justify 11 lines in our source file. The following example could be a first step to removing the duplication.

```
[:failure, :error, :success].each do |method|
  define_method method do
    self.state = method
  end
end
```

Dynamically defining methods in a loop creates a more concise definition, but it's not a particularly readable one. To address this issue I define the def_each method. The motivation for defining a def_each method is that it is easy to notice and understand while scanning a source file.

```
class Class
  def def_each(*method_names, &block)
    method_names.each do |method_name|
      define_method method_name do
        instance_exec method_name, &block
      end
    end
  end
end
```

The instance_exec Method

Ruby 1.9 includes instance_exec by default; however, Ruby 1.8 has no such feature. To address this limitation I generally include the following code created by Mauricio Fernandez.


```
class Object
  module InstanceExecHelper; end
  include InstanceExecHelper
  def instance_exec(*args, &block)
    begin
      old_critical, Thread.critical = Thread.critical, true
      n = 0
      n += 1 while respond_to?(mname="__instance_exec#{n}")
      InstanceExecHelper.module_eval{ define_method(mname, &block) }
    ensure
      Thread.critical = old_critical
    end
    begin
      ret = send(mname, *args)
    ensure
      InstanceExecHelper.module_eval{ remove_method(mname) } rescue nil
    end
```

```
    ret
  end
end
```

With def_each now available I can define the methods like so:

```
def_each :failure, :error, :success do |method_name|
  self.state = method_name
end
```

Example: Defining Instance Methods with a Class Annotation

The def_each method is a great tool for defining several similar methods, but often the similar methods represent a concept that can be used within code to make the code itself more descriptive.

For example, the previous method definitions were all about setting the state of the class. Instead of using def_each you could use Introduce Class Annotation to generate the state setting methods. Defining a states class annotation helps create more expressive code.

```
def error
  self.state = :error
end

def failure
  self.state = :failure
end

def success
  self.state = :success
end
```

```
class Post
  def self.states(*args)
    args.each do |arg|
      define_method arg do
        self.state = arg
      end
    end
```

```
  end

  states :failure, :error, :success
end
```

Example: Defining Methods By Extending a Dynamically Defined Module

Sometimes you have an object and you simply want to delegate method calls to another object. For example, you might want your object to decorate a Hash so that you can get values by calling methods that match keys of that Hash.

As long as you know what keys to expect, you could define the decorator explicitly.

```
class PostData
  def initialize(post_data)
    @post_data = post_data
  end

  def params
    @post_data[:params]
  end

  def session
    @post_data[:session]
  end
end
```


While this works, it's truly unnecessary in Ruby. Additionally, it's a headache if you want to add new delegation methods. You could define method_missing to delegate directly to the Hash, but I find debugging method_missing problematic and avoid it whenever possible. I'm going to skip straight to defining the methods dynamically from the keys of the Hash. Let's also assume that the PostData instances can be passed different Hashes, thus we'll need to define the methods on individual instances of PostData instead of defining the methods on the class itself.

```
class PostData
  def initialize(post_data)
    (class << self; self; end).class_eval do
      post_data.each_pair do |key, value|
        define_method key.to_sym do
          value
        end
```

```
      end
    end
  end
end
```

The preceding code works perfectly well, but it suffers from readability pain. In cases like these I like to take a step back and look at what I'm trying to accomplish.

What I'm looking for is the keys of the Hash to become methods and the values of the Hash to be returned by those respective methods. The two ways to add methods to an instance are to define methods on the metaclass and to extend a module.

Fortunately, Ruby allows me to define anonymous modules. I have a Hash and a decorator, but what I want is a way to define methods of the decorator by extending a Hash, so I simply need to convert the Hash to a module.

The following code converts a Hash to a module with a method for each key that returns the associated value.

```
class Hash
  def to_module
    hash = self
    Module.new do
      hash.each_pair do |key, value|
        define_method key do
          value
        end
      end
    end
  end
end
```


With the preceding code in place, it's possible to define the PostData class like the following example.

```
class PostData
  def initialize(post_data)
    self.extend post_data.to_module
  end
end
```

Replace Dynamic Receptor with Dynamic Method Definition

You have methods you want to handle dynamically without the pain of debugging method_missing.

Use dynamic method definition to define the necessary methods.

Motivation

Debugging classes that use `method_missing` can often be painful. At best you often get a `NoMethodError` on an object that you didn't expect, and at worst you get stack level too deep (`SystemStackError`).

There are times that `method_missing` is required. If the object must support unexpected method calls you may not be able to avoid the use of `method_missing`. However, often you know how an object will be used and using Dynamic Method Definition you can achieve the same behavior without relying on `method_missing`.

Mechanics

1. Dynamically define the necessary methods.
2. Test.
3. Remove `method_missing`.
4. Test.

Example: Dynamic Delegation Without method_missing

Delegation is a common task while developing software. Delegation can be handled explicitly by defining methods yourself or by utilizing something from the Ruby Standard Library such as `Forwardable`. (See the Hide Delegate section in Chapter 7 for an explanation of `Forwardable`.) Using these techniques gives you control over what methods you want to delegate to the subject object; however, sometimes you want to delegate all methods without specifying them. Ruby's Standard Library also provides this capability with the delegate library, but we'll assume we need to implement our own for this example.

The simple way to handle delegation (ignoring the fact that you would want to undefine all the standard methods a class gets by default) is to use `method_missing` to pass any method calls straight to the subject.

```
class Decorator
  def initialize(subject)
    @subject = subject
  end

  def method_missing(sym, *args, &block)
    @subject.send sym, *args, &block
  end
end
```

This solution does work, but it can be problematic when mistakes are made. For example, calling a method that does not exist on the subject results in the subject raising a `NoMethodError`. Since the method call is being called on the decorator but the subject is raising the error, it may be painful to track down where the problem resides.

The wrong object raising a `NoMethodError` is significantly better than the dreaded stack level too deep (`SystemStackError`). This can be caused by something as simple as forgetting to use the subject instance variable and trying to use a nonexistent subject method or any misspelled method. When this happens the only feedback you have is that something went wrong, but Ruby isn't sure exactly what it was.

These problems can be avoided entirely by using the available data to dynamically define methods at runtime. The following example defines an instance method on the decorator for each public method of the subject.


```
class Decorator
  def initialize(subject)
    subject.public_methods(false).each do |meth|
      (class << self; self; end).class_eval do
        define_method meth do |*args|
          subject.send meth, *args
        end
      end
    end
  end
end
```

Using this technique any invalid method calls will be correctly reported as NoMethodErrors on the decorator. Additionally, there's no `method_missing` definition, which should help avoid the stack level too deep problem entirely.

Example: Using User-Defined Data to Define Methods

Often you can use the information from a class definition to define methods instead of relying on `method_missing`. For example, the following code relies on `method_missing` to determine whether any of the attributes are `nil`.

```
class Person
  attr_accessor :name, :age

  def method_missing(sym, *args, &block)
    empty?(sym.to_s.sub(/^empty_/,"").chomp("?"))
  end

  def empty?(sym)
    self.send(sym).nil?
  end
end
```

The code works, but it suffers from the same debugging issues that the previous example does. Utilizing Dynamic Method Definition and Introduce Class Annotation the issue can be avoided by defining the attributes and creating the `empty_attribute?` methods at the same time.

```
class Person
  def self.attrs_with_empty_predicate(*args)
    attr_accessor *args

    args.each do |attribute|
      define_method "empty_#{attribute}?" do
        self.send(attribute).nil?
      end
    end
  end

  attrs_with_empty_predicate :name, :age
end
```


Isolate Dynamic Receptor

A class utilizing method_missing has become painful to alter.

Introduce a new class and move the method_missing logic to that class.

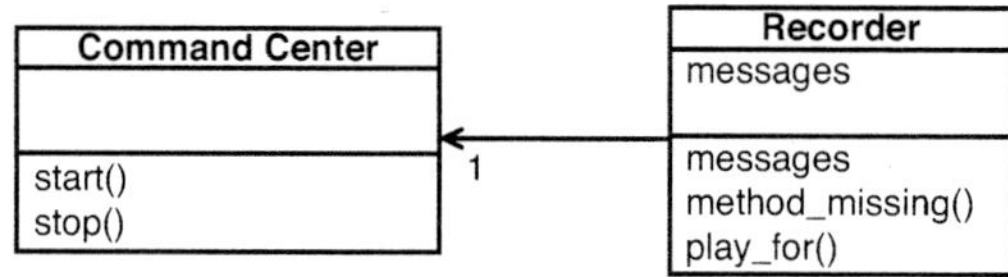

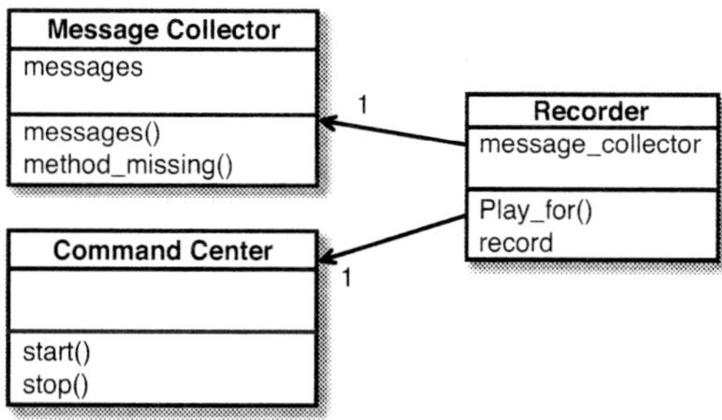

Motivation

As I mentioned in the section "Replace Dynamic Receptor with Dynamic Method Definition" earlier in the chapter, objects that use `method_missing` often raise `NoMethodError` errors unexpectedly. Even worse is when you get no more information than stack level too deep (`SystemStackError`).

Despite the added complexity, `method_missing` is a powerful tool that needs to be used when the interface of a class cannot be predetermined. On those occasions I like to use Isolate Dynamic Receptor to move the `method_missing` behavior to a new class: a class whose sole responsibility is to handle the `method_missing` cases.

The `ActiveRecord::Base` (AR::B) class defines `method_missing` to handle dynamic find messages. The implementation of `method_missing` allows you to send find messages that use attributes of a class as limiting conditions for the results that will be returned by the dynamic find messages. For example, given a `Person` subclass of `AR::B` that has both a first name and a ssn attribute, it's possible to send the messages `Person.find_by_first_name`, `Person.find_by_ssn`, and `Person.find_by_first_name_and_ssn`.

It's possible, though not realistic, to dynamically define methods for all possible combinations of the attributes of an `AR::B` subclass. Utilizing `method_missing` is a good alternative. However, by defining `method_missing` on the `AR::B` class itself the complexity of the class is increased significantly. `AR::B` would benefit from a maintainability perspective if instead the dynamic finder logic were defined on a class whose single responsibility was to handle dynamic find messages. For example, the previous `Person` class could support find with the following syntax: `Person.find.by_first_name`, `Person.find.by_ssn`, or `Person.find.by_first_name_and_ssn`.

Tip Very often it's possible to know all valid method calls ahead of time, in which case I prefer Replace Dynamic Receptor with Dynamic Method Definition.

Mechanics

1. Create a new class whose sole responsibility is to handle the dynamic method calls.

2. Copy the logic from `method_missing` on the original class to the `method_missing` of the focused class.

3. Create a method on the original class to return an instance of the focused class.

4. Change all client code that previously called the dynamic methods on the original object to call the new method first.

5. Remove the `method_missing` from the original object.

6. Test.

Example

The following example is a `Recorder` class that records all calls to `method_missing`.

```
class Recorder
  instance_methods.each do |meth|
    undef_method meth unless meth =~ /^(__|inspect)/
  end
```

```
  def messages
    @messages ||= []
  end

  def method_missing(sym, *args)
    messages << [sym, args]
    self
  end
end
```

The `Recorder` class may need additional behavior such as the ability to play back all the messages on an object and the ability to represent all the calls as `Strings`.

```
class Recorder...
  def play_for(obj)
    messages.inject(obj) do |result, message|
      result.send message.first, *message.last
    end
  end

  def to_s
    messages.inject([]) do |result, message|
      result << "#{message.first}(args: #{message.last.inspect})"
    end.join(".")
  end
end
```

It might be used like this:

```
class CommandCenter

  def start(command_string)
    ...
    self
  end

  def stop(command_string)
    ...
    self
  end

end

recorder = Recorder.new
recorder.start("LRMMMMRL")
```

```
recorder.stop("LRMMMMRL")
recorder.play_for(CommandCenter.new)
```

As the behavior of Recorder grows it becomes harder to identify the messages that are dynamically handled from those that are actually explicitly defined. By design the functionality of method_missing should handle any unknown message, but how do you know if you've broken something by adding an explicitly defined method?

The solution to this problem is to introduce an additional class that has the single responsibility of handling the dynamic method calls. In this case we have a class Recorder that handles recording unknown messages as well as playing back the messages or printing them. To reduce complexity we will introduce the MesageCollector class that handles the method_missing calls.

```
class MessageCollector
  instance_methods.each do |meth|
    undef_method meth unless meth =~ /^(__|inspect)/
  end

  def messages
    @messages ||= []
  end

  def method_missing(sym, *args)
    messages << [sym, args]
    self
  end
end
```

Isolate Dynamic Receptor

The record method of Recorder will create a new instance of the MessageCollector class and each additional chained call will be recorded. The play back and printing capabilities will remain on the Recorder object.

```
class Recorder
  def play_for(obj)
    @message_collector.messages.inject(obj) do |result, message|
      result.send message.first, *message.last
    end
  end

  def record
    @message_collector ||= MessageCollector.new
  end
```

```
  def to_s
    @message_collector.messages.inject([]) do |result, message|
      result << "#{message.first}(args: #{message.last.inspect})"
    end.join(".")
  end
end
```

And now our usage will change to call the `record` method:

```
recorder = Recorder.new
recorder.record.start("LRMMMMRL")
recorder.record.stop("LRMMMMRL")
recorder.play_for(CommandCenter.new)
```

Move Eval from Runtime to Parse Time

You need to use `eval` but want to limit the number of times `eval` is necessary.

Move the use of eval from within the method definition to defining the method itself.

```
class Person
  def self.attr_with_default(options)
    options.each_pair do |attribute, default_value|
      define_method attribute do
        eval "@#{attribute} ||= #{default_value}"
      end
    end
  end

  attr_with_default :emails => "[]",
                    :employee_number =>"EmployeeNumberGenerator.next"
end
```

```
class Person
  def self.attr_with_default(options)
    options.each_pair do |attribute, default_value|
      eval "define_method #{attribute} do
```

```
        @#{attribute} ||= #{default_value}
        end"
    end
  end

  attr_with_default :emails => "[]",
                    :employee_number =>"EmployeeNumberGenerator.next"
end
```

Motivation

As Donald Knuth once said, "Premature optimization is the root of all evil". I'll never advocate for premature optimization, but this refactoring can be helpful when you determine that `eval` is a source of performance pain. The `Kernel#eval` method can be the right solution in some cases, but it is almost always more expensive (in terms of performance) than its alternatives. In the cases where `eval` is necessary, it's often better to move an `eval` call from runtime to parse time.

Mechanics

1. Expand the scope of the string being `eval`'d.

2. Test.

It's also worth noting that evaluating the entire method definition allows you to change the `define_method` to `def` in this example. All current versions of Ruby execute methods defined with `def` significantly faster than methods defined using `define_method`; therefore, this refactoring could yield benefits for multiple reasons. Of course, you should always measure to ensure that you've actually refactored in the right direction.

Chapter 7

Moving Features Between Objects

One of the most fundamental, if not *the* fundamental, decision in object design is deciding where to put responsibilities. I've been working with objects for more than a decade, but I still never get it right the first time. That used to bother me, but now I realize that I can use refactoring to change my mind in these cases.

Often I can resolve these problems simply by using Move Method and Move Field to move the behavior around. If I need to use both, I prefer to use Move Field first and then Move Method.

Often classes become bloated with too many responsibilities. In this case I use Extract Class or Extract Module to separate some of these responsibilities. If a class becomes too irresponsible, I use Inline Class to merge it into another class. The same applies to modules. If another class is being used, it often is helpful to hide this fact with Hide Delegate. Sometimes hiding the delegate class results in constantly changing the owner's interface, in which case you need to use Remove Middle Man.

Move Method

A method is, or will be, using or used by more features of another class than the class on which it is defined.

Create a new method with a similar body in the class it uses most. Either turn the old method into a simple delegation, or remove it altogether.

Class 1
a_method()

Class 1

Class 2

Class 2
a_method()

Motivation

Moving methods is the bread and butter of refactoring. I move methods when classes have too much behavior or when classes are collaborating too much and are too highly coupled. By moving methods around, I can make the classes simpler, and they end up being a more crisp implementation of a set of responsibilities.

I usually look through the methods on a class to find a method that seems to reference another object more than the object it lives on. A good time to do this is after I have moved some attributes. Once I see a likely method to move, I take a look at the methods that call it, the methods it calls, and any redefining methods in the hierarchy. I assess whether to go ahead on the basis of the object with which the method seems to have more interaction.

It's not always an easy decision to make. If I am not sure whether to move a method, I go on to look at other methods. Moving other methods often makes the decision easier. Sometimes the decision still is hard to make. Actually it is then no big deal. If it is difficult to make the decision, it probably does not matter that much. Then I choose according to instinct; after all, I can always change it again later.

Mechanics

1. Examine all features used by the source method that are defined on the source class. Consider whether they also should be moved.

   ⟹ *If a feature is used only by the method you are about to move, you might as well move it, too. If the feature is used by other methods, consider moving them as well. Sometimes it is easier to move a clutch of methods than to move them one at a time.*

2. Check the sub- and superclasses of the source class for other definitions of the method.

   ⟹ *If there are any other definitions, you may not be able to make the move, unless the polymorphism can also be expressed on the target.*

3. Define the method in the target class.

   ⟹ *You may choose to use a different name, one that makes more sense in the target class.*

4. Copy the code from the source method to the target. Adjust the method to make it work in its new home.

   ⟹ *If the method uses its source, you need to determine how to reference the source object from the target method. If there is no mechanism in the target class, pass the source object reference to the new method as a parameter.*

   ⟹ *If the method includes exception handlers, decide which class should logically handle the exception. If the source class should be responsible, leave the handlers behind.*

5. Determine how to reference the correct target object from the source.

   ⟹ *There may be an existing attribute or method that will give you the target. If not, see whether you can easily create a method that will do so. Failing that, you need to create a new attribute in the source that can store the target. This may be a permanent change, but you can also make it temporarily until you have refactored enough to remove it.*

6. Turn the source method into a delegating method.

7. Test.

8. Decide whether to remove the source method or retain it as a delegating method.

   ⟹ *Leaving the source as a delegating method is easier if you have many references.*

9. If you remove the source method, replace all the references with references to the target method.

   ⟹ *You can test after changing each reference, although it is usually easier to change all references with one search and replace.*

10. Test.

Example

An account class illustrates this refactoring:

```
class Account...
  def overdraft_charge
    if @account_type.premium?
      result = 10
      result += (@days_overdrawn - 7) * 0.85 if @days_overdrawn > 7
      result
    else
      @days_overdrawn * 1.75
    end
  end

  def bank_charge
      result = 4.5
      result += overdraft_charge if @days_overdrawn > 0
      result
  end
```


Let's imagine that there are going to be several new account types, each of which has its own rule for calculating the overdraft charge. So I want to move the overdraft_charge method over to the account type.

The first step is to look at the features that the overdraft_charge method uses and consider whether it is worth moving a batch of methods together. In this case I need the @days_overdrawn instance variable to remain on the account class, because that will vary with individual accounts.

Next I copy the method body over to the account type and get it to fit.

```
class AccountType...
  def overdraft_charge(days_overdrawn)
    if premium?
      result = 10
      result += (days_overdrawn - 7) * 0.85 if days_overdrawn > 7
```

```
    result
  else
    days_overdrawn * 1.75
  end
end
```

In this case fitting means removing the @account_type from uses of features of the account type, and doing something about the features of account that I still need. When I need to use a feature of the source class I can do one of four things: (1) move this feature to the target class as well, (2) create or use a reference from the target class to the source, (3) pass the source object as a parameter to the method, or (4) if the feature is a variable, pass it in as a parameter.

In this case I pass the variable as a parameter.

Once the method fits in the target class, I can replace the source method body with a simple delegation:

```
class Account...
  def overdraft_charge
    @account_type.overdraft_charge(@days_overdrawn)
  end
```

At this point I can test.

I can leave things like this, or I can remove the method in the source class. To remove the method I need to find all callers of the method and redirect them to call the method in account type:

```
class Account...
  def bank_charge
    result = 4.5
    if @days_overdrawn > 0
      result += @account_type.overdraft_charge(@days_overdrawn)
    end
    result
  end
```


Once I've replaced all the callers, I can remove the method definition in account. I can test after each removal, or do them in a batch. If the method isn't private, I need to look for other classes that use this method. In a statically typed language like Java or C#, the compilation after removal of the source definition finds anything I missed. In an interpreted language such as Ruby, there's no compilation to catch these mistakes. A comprehensive test suite is vitally important, even more-so in dynamic languages!

In this case the method referred only to a single instance variable, so I could just pass this instance variable in as a variable. If the method called for another method on the account, I wouldn't have been able to do that. In those cases I need to pass in the source object:

```
class AccountType...
  def overdraft_charge(account)
    if premium?
      result = 10
      if  (account.days_overdrawn > 7)
        result += (account.days_overdrawn - 7) * 0.85
      end
      result
    else
      account.days_overdrawn * 1.75
    end
  end
```

I also pass in the source object if I need several features of the class, although if there are too many, further refactoring is needed. Typically I need to decompose and move some pieces back.

Move Field

A field is, or will be, used by another class more than the class on which it is defined.

Create a new attribute reader (and if necessary, a writer) in the target class, and change all its users.

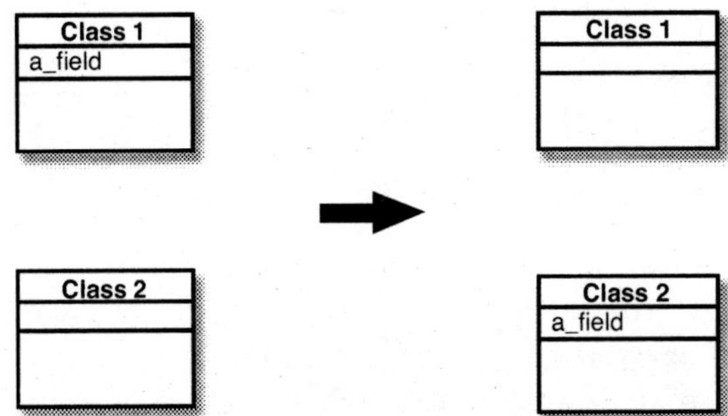

Motivation

Moving state and behavior between classes is the essence of refactoring. As the system develops, you find the need for new classes and the need to shuffle responsibilities around. A design decision that is reasonable and correct one week can become incorrect in another. That is not a problem; the only problem is not to do something about it.

I consider moving a field if I see more methods on another class using the information in the field than the class itself. I may choose to move the methods; this decision is based on interface. But if the methods seem sensible where they are, I move the field.

Another reason for field moving is when doing Extract Class. In that case the fields go first and then the methods.

Mechanics

1. If you are likely to be moving the methods that access the field frequently or if a lot of methods access the field, you may find it useful to use Self Encapsulate Field.

2. Test.

3. Create in the target class an attribute reader and, if necessary, a writer.

4. Determine how to reference the target object from the source.

   ⟹ *An existing field or method may give you the target. If not, see whether you can easily create a method that will do so. Failing that, you need to create a new field in the source that can store the target. This may be a permanent change, but you can also do it temporarily until you have refactored enough to remove it.*

5. Replace all references to the source field with references to the appropriate method on the target.

   ⟹ *For accesses to the variable, replace the reference with a call to the target object's reader; for assignments, replace the reference with a call to the writer.*

   ⟹ *Look in all the subclasses of the source for references to the field.*

6. Test.

Example

Here is part of an account class:

```
class Account...

  def interest_for_amount_days(amount, days)
    @interest_rate * amount * days / 365;
  end
```

I want to move the `@interest_rate` field to the account type. There are several methods with that reference, of which `interest_for_amount_days` is one example. I next create the attribute in the account type:

```
class AccountType...
  attr_accessor :interest_rate
```

Now I redirect the methods from the account class to use the account type and remove the interest rate instance variable in the account.

```
def interest_for_amount_days(amount, days)
  @account_type.interest_rate * amount * days / 365
end
```

Example: Using Self-Encapsulation

If a lot of methods use the interest rate instance variable, I might start by using Self Encapsulate Field:

```
class Account...
  attr_accessor :interest_rate

  def interest_for_amount_days(amount, days)
    interest_rate * amount * days / 365
  end
```


That way I only need to do the redirection for the appropriate accessors:

```
class Account...

  attr_accessor :interest_rate

  def interest_for_amount_and_days(amount, days)

    interest_rate * amount * days / 365
  end
```

```
  def interest_rate
    @account_type.interest_rate
  end
```

Or, I can extend Forwardable and declare delegating accessors like this:

```
extend Forwardable

def_delegator :@account_type, :interest_rate, :interest_rate=

def interest_for_amount_and_days(amount, days)
  interest_rate * amount * days / 365
end
```

I can redirect the clients of the accessors to use the new object later if I want. Using self-encapsulation allows me to take a smaller step. This is useful if I'm doing a lot of things with the class. In particular, it simplifies use of Move Method to move methods to the target class. If they refer to the accessor, such references don't need to change Self Encapsulate Field.

Extract Class

You have one class doing work that should be done by two.

Create a new class and move the relevant fields and methods from the old class into the new class.

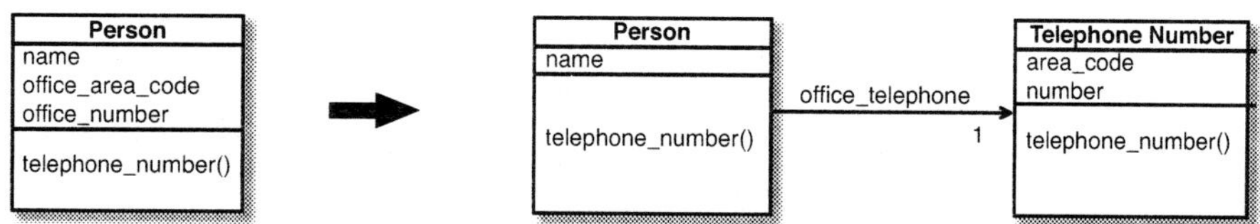

Motivation

You've probably heard that a class should be a crisp abstraction, handle a few clear responsibilities, or some similar guideline. In practice, classes grow. You add some operations here, a bit of data there. You add a responsibility to a class feeling that it's not worth a separate class, but as that responsibility grows and breeds, the class becomes too complicated. Soon your class is as crisp as a microwaved duck.

Such a class is one with many methods and a lot of data—a class that is too big to understand easily. You need to consider where it can be split, and you split it. A good sign is that a subset of the data and a subset of the methods seem to go together. Other good signs are subsets of data that usually change together or are particularly dependent on each other. A useful test is to ask yourself what would happen if you removed a piece of data or a method. What other fields and methods would become nonsense?

One sign that often crops up later in development is the way the class is subtyped. You may find that subtyping affects only a few features or that some features need to be subtyped one way and other features a different way.

Mechanics

1. Decide how to split the responsibilities of the class.

2. Create a new class to express the split-off responsibilities.

   ⟹ *If the responsibilities of the old class no longer match its name, rename the old class.*

3. Make a link from the old to the new class.

   ⟹ *You may need a two-way link. But don't make the back link until you find you need it.*

4. Use Move Field on each field you want to move.

5. Test after each move.

6. Use Move Method to move methods over from old to new. Start with lower-level methods (called rather than calling) and build to the higher level.

7. Test after each move.

8. Review and reduce the interfaces of each class.

   ⟹ *If you did have a two-way link, examine to see whether it can be made one-way.*

9. Decide whether multiple clients will be able to access the class. If you do allow access to multiple clients, decide whether to expose the new class as a reference object or as an immutable value object.

Example

I start with a simple person class:

```
class Person...
  attr_reader :name
  attr_accessor :office_area_code
  attr_accessor :office_number
  def telephone_number
    '(' + @office_area_code + ') ' + @office_number
  end
```

In this case I can separate the telephone number behavior into its own class. I start by defining a telephone number class:

```
class TelephoneNumber
end
```

That was easy! I next make a link from the person to the telephone number:

```
class Person...
  def initialize
    @office_telephone = TelephoneNumber.new
  end
```

Now I use Move Field on one of the fields:

```
class TelephoneNumber
  attr_accessor :area_code
end

class Person...

  def telephone_number
    '(' + office_area_code + ') ' + @office_number
  end

  def office_area_code
    @office_telephone.area_code
  end
```

```
  def office_area_code=(arg)
    @office_telephone.area_code = arg
  end
```

I can then move the other field and use Move Method on the telephone number:

```
class Person...
  attr_reader :name

  def initialize
    @office_telephone = TelephoneNumber.new
  end

  def telephone_number
    @office_telephone.telephone_number
  end

  def office_telephone
    @office_telephone
  end

class TelephoneNumber...
  attr_accessor :area_code, :number

  def telephone_number
    '(' + area_code + ') ' + number
  end
```

The decision then is how much to expose the new class to my clients. I can completely hide it by providing delegating methods for its interface, or I can expose it.

If I choose to expose the class, I need to consider the dangers of aliasing. If I expose the telephone number and a client changes the area code in that object, how do I feel about it? It may not be a direct client that makes this change. It might be the client of a client of a client.

I have the following options:

- I accept that any object may change any part of the telephone number. This makes the telephone number a reference object, and I should consider Change Value to Reference. In this case the person would be the access point for the telephone number.
- I don't want anybody to change the value of the telephone number without going through the person. I should make the telephone number immutable.

- A third option that reduces that confusion is to clone and then freeze the telephone number before passing it out.

Extract Class is a common technique for improving the liveness of a concurrent program because it allows you to have separate locks on the two resulting classes. If you don't need to lock both objects you don't have to. For more on this see Brian Goetz's book *Java Concurrency in Practice* [Goetz].

However, there is a danger there. If you need to ensure that both objects are locked together, you get into the area of transactions and other kinds of shared locks. This is complex territory and requires heavier machinery than it is typically worth. Transactions are useful when you use them, but writing transaction managers is more than most programmers should attempt.

Inline Class

A class isn't doing very much.

Move all its features into another class and delete it.

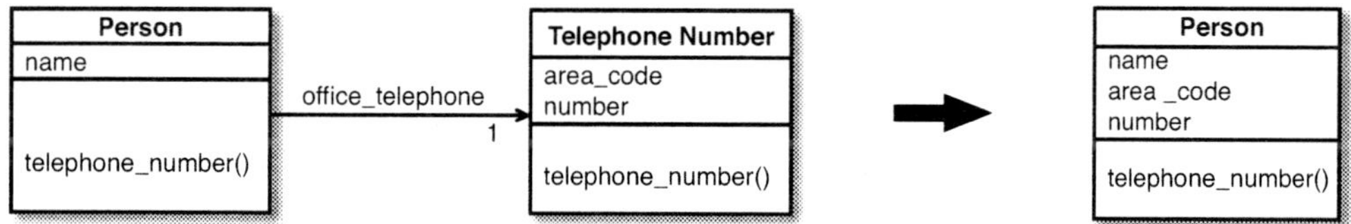

Motivation

Inline Class is the reverse of Extract Class. I use Inline Class if a class is no longer pulling its weight and shouldn't be around any more. Often this is the result of refactoring that moves other responsibilities out of the class so there are little left. Then I want to fold this class into another class, picking one that seems to use the runt class the most.

Mechanics

1. Declare the public protocol of the source class onto the absorbing class. Delegate all these methods to the source class.

2. Change all references from the source class to the absorbing class.

3. Test.

4. Use Move Method and Move Field to move features from the source class to the absorbing class until there is nothing left.

5. Hold a short, simple funeral service.

Example

Let's assume that the `TelephoneNumber` class we extracted in the Extract Class example isn't pulling its weight. I now inline it back into `Person`. I start with separate classes:

```
class Person...
  attr_reader :name

  def initialize
    @office_telephone = TelephoneNumber.new
  end

  def telephone_number
    @office_telephone.telephone_number
  end

  def office_telephone
    @office_telephone
  end

class TelephoneNumber...
  attr_accessor :area_code, :number

  def telephone_number
```

```
    '(' + area_code + ') ' + number
  end
```

I begin by declaring all the visible methods on telephone number on person:

```
class Person...

  def area_code
    @office_telephone.area_code
  end

  def area_code=(arg)
    @office_telephone.area_code = arg
  end

  def number
    @office_telephone.number
  end

  def number=(arg)
    @office_telephone.number = arg
  end
```

Now I find clients of telephone number and switch them to use the person's interface. So:

```
martin = Person.new
martin.office_telephone.area_code = "781"
```

becomes

```
martin = Person.new
martin.area_code = "781"
```

Now I can use Move Method and Move Field until the telephone class is no more.

Hide Delegate

A client is calling a delegate class of an object.

Create methods on the server to hide the delegate.

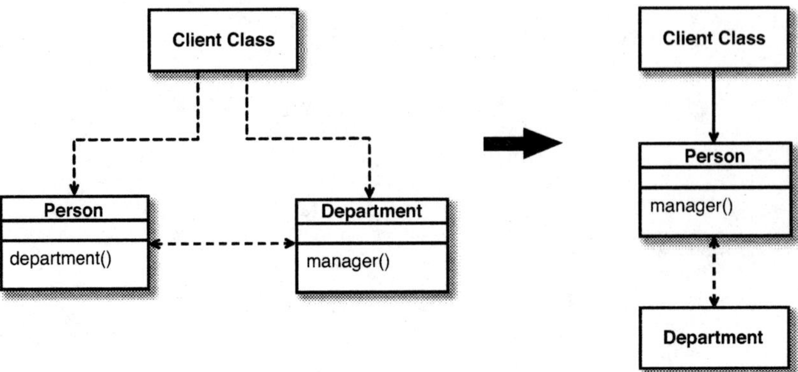

Motivation

One of the keys, if not the key, to objects is encapsulation. Encapsulation means that objects need to know less about other parts of the system. Then when things change, fewer objects need to be told about the change—which makes the change easier to make.

Anyone involved in objects knows that you should hide your fields. As you become more sophisticated, you realize there is more you can encapsulate.

If a client calls a method defined on one of the fields of the server object, the client needs to know about this delegate object. If the delegate changes, the client also may have to change. You can remove this dependency by placing a simple delegating method on the server, which hides the delegate (see Figure 7.1). Changes become limited to the server and don't propagate to the client.

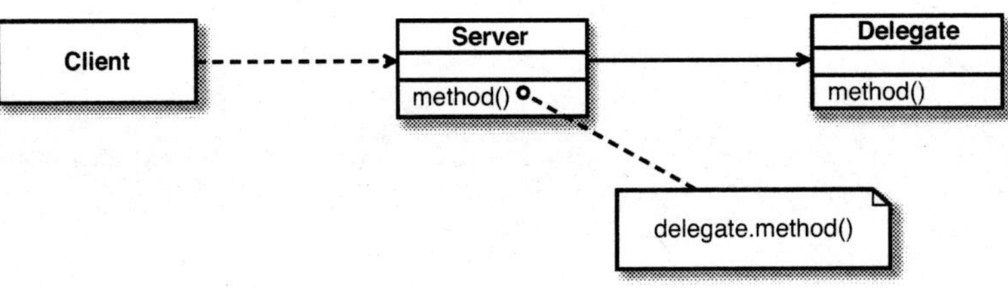

Figure 7.1 Simple delegation.

You may find it is worthwhile to use Hide Delegate for some clients of the server or all clients. If you hide from all clients, you can remove all mention of the delegate from the interface of the server.

Mechanics

1. For each method on the delegate, create a simple delegating method on the server.

2. Adjust the client to call the server.

3. Test after adjusting each method.

4. If no client needs to access the delegate anymore, remove the server's accessor for the delegate.

5. Test.

Example

I start with a person and a department:

```
class Person
  attr_accessor :department
end

class Department
  attr_reader :manager

  def initialize(manager)
    @manager = manager
  end

  ...
```


If a client wants to know a person's manager, it needs to get the department first:

```
manager = john.department.manager
```

This reveals to the client how the department class works and that the department is responsible for tracking the manager. I can reduce this coupling by hiding the department class from the client. I do this by creating a simple delegating method on person:

```
def manager

  @department.manager
end
```

Or, extend Forwardable and declare the delegating method:

```
class Person
  extend Forwardable

  def_delegator :@department, :manager
  ...
```

Forwardable is a module included within the Ruby Standard Library.

From the documentation:

> The Forwardable module provides delegation of specified methods to a designated object, using the methods #def_delegator and #def_delegators. For example, say you have a class RecordCollection which contains an array +@records+. You could provide the lookup method #record_number(), which simply calls #[] on the +@records+ array, like this:

```
class RecordCollection
    extend Forwardable
    def_delegator :@records, :[], :record_number
end
```

> Further, if you wish to provide the methods #size, #<<, and #map, all of which delegate to @records, this is how you can do it:

Hide Delegate

```
class RecordCollection
    # extend Forwardable, but we did that above
    def_delegators :@records, :size, :<<, :map
end
```

I now need to change all clients of person to use this new method:

```
manager = john.manager
```

Once I've made the change for all methods of department and for all the clients of person, I can remove the department reader on person.

Remove Middle Man

A class is doing too much simple delegation.

Get the client to call the delegate directly.

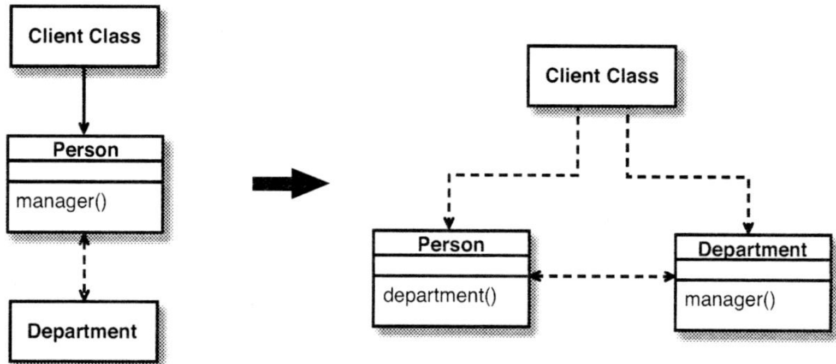

Motivation

In the motivation for Hide Delegate, I talked about the advantages of encapsulating the use of a delegated object. There is a price for this. The price is that every time the client wants to use a new feature of the delegate, you have to add a simple delegating method to the server. After adding features for a while, it becomes painful. The server class is just a middle man, and perhaps it's time for the client to call the delegate directly.

It's hard to figure out what the right amount of hiding is. Fortunately, with Hide Delegate and Remove Middle Man it does not matter so much. You can adjust your system as time goes on. As the system changes, the basis for how much you hide also changes. A good encapsulation six months ago may be awkward now. Refactoring means you never have to say you're sorry: You just fix it.

Mechanics

1. Create an accessor for the delegate.

2. For each client use of a delegate method, remove the method from the server and replace the call in the client to call the method on the delegate.

3. Test after each method.

Example

For an example I use person and department flipped the other way. I start with person hiding the department:

```
class Person...

  def initialize(department)
    @department = department
  end

  def manager
    @department.manager
  end

class Department
  attr_reader :manager

  def initialize(manager)
    @manager = manager
  end
  ...
```

To find a person's manager, clients ask:

```
manager = john.manager
```

This is simple to use and encapsulates the department. However, if a lot of methods are doing this, I end up with too many of these simple delegations on the person. That's when it is good to remove the middle man. First I make an accessor for the delegate:


```
class Person...

  attr_reader :department
```

Then I take each method at a time. I find clients that use the method on person and change it to first get the delegate. Then I use it:

```
manager = john.department.manager
```

I can then remove the delegating manager method from person. A test run shows whether I missed anything.

I may want to keep some of these delegations for convenience. I also may want to hide the delegate from some clients but show it to others. That also will leave some of the simple delegations in place.

Chapter 8

Organizing Data

In this chapter I discuss several refactorings that make working with data easier. For many people Self Encapsulate Field seems unnecessary. It's long been a matter of good-natured debate about whether an object should access its own data directly or through accessors. Sometimes you do need the accessors, and then you can get them with Self Encapsulate Field. I generally use direct access because I find it simple to do this refactoring when I need it.

One of the useful things about object languages is that they allow you to define new types that go beyond what can be done with the simple data types of traditional languages. It takes a while to get used to how to do this, however. Often you start with a simple data value and then realize that an object would be more useful. Replace Data Value with Object allows you to turn dumb data into articulate objects. When you realize that these objects are instances that will be needed in many parts of the program, you can use Change Value to Reference to make them into reference objects.

If you see an `Array` or `Hash` acting as a data structure, you can make the data structure clearer with Replace Array with Object or Replace Hash with Object. In all these cases the object is but the first step. The real advantage comes when you use Move Method to add behavior to the new objects.

Magic numbers—numbers with special meaning—have long been a problem. I remember being told in my earliest programming days not to use them. They do keep appearing, however, and I use Replace Magic Number with Symbolic Constant to get rid of magic numbers whenever I figure out what they are doing.

Links between objects can be one-way or two-way. One-way links are easier, but sometimes you need to Change Unidirectional Association to Bidirectional to support a new function. Change Bidirectional Association to Unidirectional removes unnecessary complexity should you find you no longer need the two-way link.

One of the key tenets of Object-Oriented programming is encapsulation. If a collection is exposed, use Encapsulate Collection to cover it up. If an entire record is naked, use Replace Record with Data Class.

One form of data that requires particular treatment is the type code: a special value that indicates something particular about a type of instance. These are often implemented as integers. If the behavior of a class is affected by a type code, try to use Replace Type Code with Polymorphism. If you can't do that, use one of the more complicated (but more flexible) Replace Type Code with Module Extension or Replace Type Code with State/Strategy.

Self Encapsulate Field

You are accessing a field directly, but the coupling to the field is becoming awkward.

Create getting and setting methods for the field and use only those to access the field.

```
def total
  @base_price * (1 + @tax_rate)
end
```

```
attr_reader :base_price, :tax_rate

def total
  base_price * (1 + tax_rate)
end
```

Motivation

When it comes to accessing fields, there are two schools of thought. One is that within the class where the variable is defined, you should access the variable freely (direct variable access). The other school is that even within the class, you should always use accessors (indirect variable access). Debates between the two can be heated. (See also the discussion in Smalltalk Best Practices [Beck].)

Essentially the advantages of *indirect variable access* are that it allows a subclass to override how to get that information with a method and that it supports more flexibility in managing the data, such as lazy initialization, which initializes the value only when you need to use it.

The advantage of *direct variable access* is that the code is easier to read. You don't need to stop and say, "This is just a getting method."

I'm always of two minds with this choice. I'm usually happy to do what the rest of the team wants to do. Left to myself, though, I like to use direct variable access as a first resort, until it gets in the way. Once things start becoming awkward, I switch to indirect variable access. Refactoring gives you the freedom to change your mind.

The most important time to use Self Encapsulate Field is when you are accessing a field in a superclass but you want to override this variable access with a computed value in the subclass. Self-encapsulating the field is the first step. After that you can override the getting and setting methods as you need to.

Mechanics

1. Create a getting and setting method for the field.

2. Find all references to the field and replace them with a getting or setting method.

   ⟹ *Replace accesses to the field with a call to the getting method; replace assignments with a call to the setting method.*

3. Double check that you have caught all references.

4. Test.

Example

This seems almost too simple for an example, but, hey, at least it is quick to write:

```
class Item

  def initialize(base_price, tax_rate)
    @base_price = base_price
    @tax_rate = tax_rate
  end
```

```
  def raise_base_price_by(percent)
    @base_price = @base_price * (1 + percent/100.0)
  end

  def total
    @base_price * (1 + @tax_rate)
  end
```

To self-encapsulate I define getting and setting methods (if they don't already exist) and use those:

```
class Item...

  attr_accessor :base_price, :tax_rate

  def raise_base_price_by(percent)
    self.base_price = base_price * (1 + percent/100.0)
  end

  def total
    base_price * (1 + tax_rate)
  end
```

When you are using self-encapsulation you have to be careful about using the setting method in the constructor. Often it is assumed that you use the setting method for changes after the object is created, so you may have different behavior in the setter than you have when initializing. In cases like this I prefer using either direct access from the constructor or a separate initialization method:

```
def initialize(base_price, tax_rate)
  setup(base_price, tax_rate)
end

def setup(base_price, tax_rate)
  @base_price = base_price
  @tax_rate = tax_rate
end
```


The value in doing all this comes when you have a subclass, as follows:

```
class ImportedItem < Item

  attr_reader :import_duty

  def initialize(base_price, tax_rate, import_duty)
```

```
    super(base_price, tax_rate)
    @import_duty = import_duty
  end

  def tax_rate
    super + import_duty
  end
```

I can override all of the behavior of Item to take into account the `import_duty` without changing any of that behavior.

Replace Data Value with Object

You have a data item that needs additional data or behavior.

Turn the data item into an object.

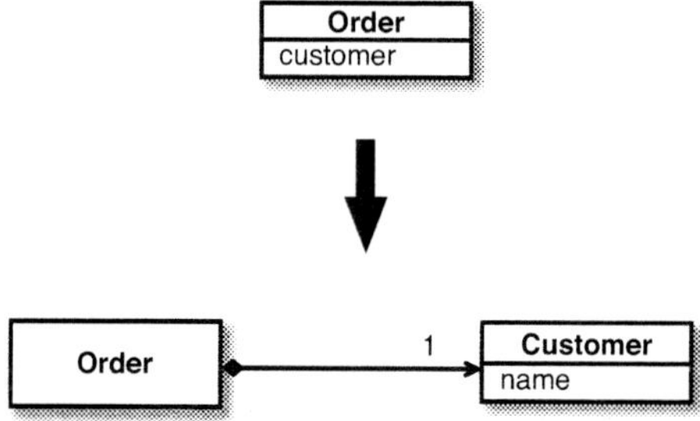

Motivation

Often in early stages of development you make decisions about representing simple facts as simple data items. As development proceeds you realize that those simple items aren't so simple anymore. A telephone number may be represented as a string for a while, but later you realize that the telephone needs special behavior for formatting, extracting the area code, and the like. For one or two items you may put the methods in the owning object, but quickly the code smells of duplication and feature envy. When the smell begins, turn the data value into an object.

Mechanics

1. Create the class for the value. Give it an equivalent field to the field in the source class. Add an attribute reader and a constructor that takes the field as an argument.

2. Change the attribute reader in the source class to call the reader in the new class.

3. If the field is mentioned in the source class constructor, assign the field using the constructor of the new class.

4. Change the attribute reader to create a new instance of the new class.

5. Test.

6. You may now need to use Change Value to Reference on the new object.

Example

I start with an `Order` class that has stored the customer of the order as a string and wants to turn the customer into an object. This way I have somewhere to store data, such as an address or credit rating, and useful behavior that uses this information.

```
class Order...
  attr_accessor :customer

  def initialize(customer)
    @customer = customer
  end
```

Some client code that uses this looks like:


```
private

def self.number_of_orders_for(orders, customer)
  orders.select { |order| order.customer == customer }.size
end
```

First I create the new `Customer` class. I give it a field for a string attribute, because that is what the order currently uses. I call it name, because that seems to be what the string is used for. I also add an attribute reader and provide a constructor that uses the attribute:

```
class Customer
  attr_reader :name

  def initialize(name)
    @name = name
  end
end
```

Now I change methods that reference the customer field to use the appropriate references on the `Customer` class. The attribute reader and constructor are obvious. For the attribute writer I create a new customer:

```
class Order...
  attr_accessor :customer

  def initialize(customer)
    @customer = Customer.new(customer)
  end

  def customer
    @customer.name
  end

  def customer=(value)
    @customer = Customer.new(value)
  end
```

The setter creates a new customer because the old string attribute was a value object, and thus the customer currently also is a value object. This means that each order has its own customer object. As a rule, value objects should be immutable; this avoids some nasty aliasing bugs. Later I will want customer to be a reference object, but that's another refactoring. At this point I can test.

Now I look at the methods on `Order` that manipulate `Customer` and make some changes to make the new state of affairs clearer. With the getter I use Rename Method to make it clear that it is the name not the object that is returned:


```
class Order...

  def customer_name
    @customer.name
  end
```

On the constructor and attribute writer, I don't need to change the signature, but the name of the arguments should change:

```
class Order...

  def initialize(customer_name)
    @customer = Customer.new(customer_name)
  end

  def customer=(customer_name)
    @customer = Customer.new(customer_name)
  end
```

Further refactoring may well cause me to add a new constructor and attribute writer that take an existing customer.

This finishes this refactoring, but in this case, as in many others, there is another step. If I want to add such things as credit ratings and addresses to our customer, I cannot do so now. This is because the customer is treated as a value object. Each order has its own customer object. To give a customer these attributes I need to apply Change Value to Reference to the customer so that all orders for the same customer share the same customer object. You'll find this example continued there.

Change Value to Reference

You have a class with many equal instances that you want to replace with a single object.

Turn the object into a reference object.

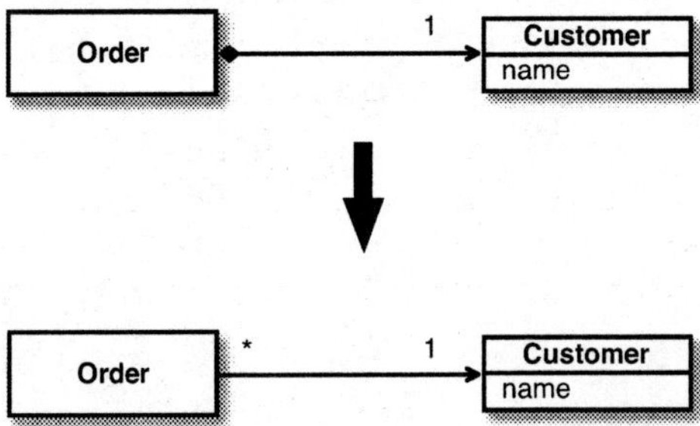

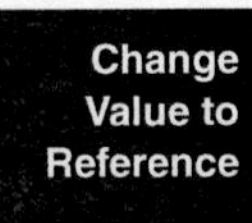

Motivation

You can make a useful classification of objects in many systems: reference objects and value objects. *Reference objects* are things like customer or account. Each object stands for one object in the real world, and you use the object identity to test whether they are equal. *Value objects* are things like date or money. They are defined entirely through their data values. You don't mind that copies exist; you may have hundreds of "1/1/2010" objects around your system. You do need to tell whether two of the objects are equal, so you need to override the `eql?` method (and the `hash` method too).

The decision between reference and value is not always clear. Sometimes you start with a simple value with a small amount of immutable data. Then you want to give it some changeable data and ensure that the changes ripple to everyone referring to the object. At this point you need to turn it into a reference object.

Mechanics

1. Use Replace Constructor with Factory Method.

2. Test.

3. Decide what object is responsible for providing access to the objects.

   ⟹ *This may be a hash or a registry object.*

   ⟹ *You may have more than one object that acts as an access point for the new object.*

4. Decide whether the objects are precreated or created on the fly.

   ⟹ *If the objects are precreated and you are retrieving them from memory, you need to ensure they are loaded before they are needed.*

5. Alter the factory method to return the reference object.

   ⟹ *If the objects are precomputed, you need to decide how to handle errors if someone asks for an object that does not exist.*

   ⟹ *You may want to use Rename Method on the factory to convey that it returns an existing object.*

6. Test.

Example

I start where I left off in the example for Replace Data Value with Object. I have the following `Customer` class:

```
class Customer
  attr_reader :name

  def initialize(name)
    @name = name
  end
end
```

It is used by an `Order` class:

```
class Order...

  def initialize(customer_name)
    @customer = Customer.new(customer_name)
  end

  def customer=(customer_name)
    @customer = Customer.new(customer_name)
  end

  def customer_name
    @customer.name
  end
```

and some client code:

```
private

def self.number_of_orders_for(orders, customer)
  orders.select { |order| order.customer_name == customer.name }.size
end
```


At the moment `Customer` is a value object. Each order has its own `customer` object even if they are for the same conceptual customer. I want to change this so that if we have several orders for the same conceptual customer, they share a single customer object. For this case this means that there should be only one customer object for each `customer` name.

I begin by using Replace Constructor with Factory Method. This allows me to take control of the creation process, which will become important later. I define the factory method on `Customer`:

```
class Customer

  def self.create(name)
    Customer.new(name)
  end
```

Then I replace the calls to the constructor with calls to the factory:

```
class Order

  def initialize(customer_name)
    @customer = Customer.create(customer_name)
  end
```

Now I have to decide how to access the customers. My preference is to use another object. Such a situation works well with something like the line items on an order. The order is responsible for providing access to the line items. However, in this situation there isn't such an obvious object. In this situation I usually create a registry object to be the access point. For simplicity in this example, however, I store them using a field on `Customer`, making the `Customer` class the access point:

```
class Customer...

  Instances = {}
```

Then I decide whether to create customers on the fly when asked or to create them in advance. I'll use the latter. In my application startup code I load the customers that are in use. These could come from a database or from a file. For simplicity I use explicit code. I can always use Substitute Algorithm to change it later.

```
class Customer...

  def self.load_customers
    new("Lemon Car Hire").store
    new("Associated Coffee Machines").store
    new("Bilston Gasworks").store
  end

  def store
    Instances[name] = self
  end
```


Now I alter the factory method to return the precreated customer:

```
class Customer

  def self.create(name)
    Instances[name]
  end
```

Because the create method always returns an existing customer, I should make this clear by using Rename Method.

```
class Customer

  def self.with_name(name)
    Instances[name]
  end
```

Change Reference to Value

You have a reference object that is small, immutable, and awkward to manage.

Turn it into a value object.

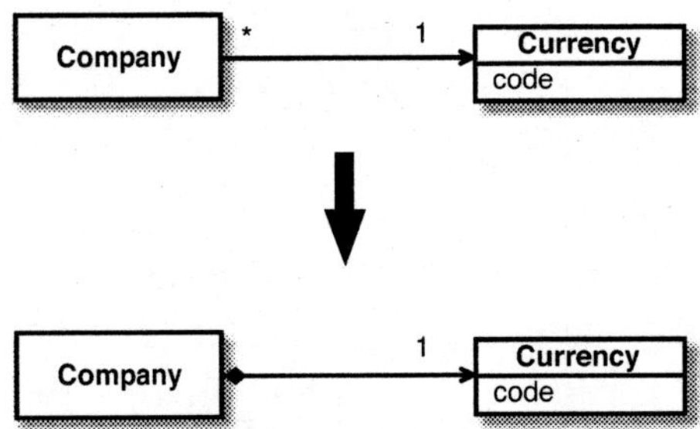

Motivation

As with Change Value to Reference, the decision between a reference and a value object is not always clear. It is a decision that often needs reversing.

The trigger for going from a reference to a value is that working with the reference object becomes awkward. Reference objects have to be controlled in some way. You always need to ask the controller for the appropriate object. The memory links also can be awkward. Value objects are particularly useful for distributed and concurrent systems.

An important property of value objects is that they should be immutable. Any time you invoke a query on one, you should get the same result. If this is true, there is no problem having many objects represent the same thing. If the value is mutable, you have to ensure that changing any object also updates all the other objects that represent the same thing. That's so much of a pain that the easiest thing to do is to make it a reference object.

It's important to be clear on what *immutable* means. If you have a money class with a currency and a value, that's usually an immutable value object. That does not mean your salary cannot change. It means that to change your salary, you need to replace the existing money object with a new money object rather than changing the amount on an existing money object. Your relationship can change, but the money object itself does not.

Mechanics

1. Check that the candidate object is immutable or can become immutable.

   ⟹ *If the object isn't currently immutable, use Remove Setting Method until it is.*

   ⟹ *If the candidate cannot become immutable, you should abandon this refactoring.*

2. Create an == method and an eql? method (the eql? method can delegate to the == method).

3. Create a hash method.

4. Test.

5. Consider removing any factory method and making a constructor public.

Example

I begin with a currency class:

```
class Currency

  attr_reader :code
```

```
  def initialize(code)
  @code = code
  end
```

All this class does is hold and return a code. It is a reference object, so to get an instance I need to use use a method that will return the same instance of currency for a given currency code:

```
class Currency...

  def self.get(code)
    ... return currency from a registry
  end

usd = Currency.get("USD")
```

The currency class maintains a list of instances. I can't just use a constructor.

```
Currency.new("USD") == Currency.new("USD") # returns false

Currency.new("USD").eql?(Currency.new("USD")) # returns false
```

To convert this to a value object, the key thing to do is verify that the object is immutable. If it isn't, I don't try to make this change, as a mutable value causes no end of painful aliasing.

In this case the object is immutable, so the next step is to define an `eql?` method:

```
def eql?(other)
  self == (other)
end

def ==(other)
  other.equal?(self) ||
    (other.instance_of?(self.class) &&
     other.code == code)
end
```


I've delegated the `eql?` method to the == method, since I don't desire different behavior for these two methods. If I define `eql?`, I also need to define `hash`. The simple way to do this is to take the hash codes of all the fields used in the `eql?` method and do a bitwise xor (^) on them. Here it's easy because there's only one:

```
def hash
  code.hash
end
```

With both methods replaced, I can test. I need to do both; otherwise Hash and any collection that relies on hashing, such as Array's uniq method, may act strangely.

Now I can create as many equal currencies as I like. I can get rid of all the controller behavior on the class and the factory method and just use the constructor.

```
Currency.send(:new, "USD") == Currency.new("USD") # returns true
Currency.send(:new, "USD").eql?(Currency.new("USD")) # returns true
```

Replace Array with Object

You have an Array in which certain elements mean different things.

Replace the Array with an object that has a field for each element.

```
row = []
row[0] = "Liverpool"
row[1] = "15"
```

```
row = Performance.new
row.name = "Liverpool"
row.wins = "15"
```

Motivation

Arrays are a common structure for organizing data. However, they should be used only to contain a collection of similar objects in some order. Sometimes, however, you see them used to contain a number of different things. Conventions such as "the first element on the Array is the person's name" are hard to remember. With an object you can use names of fields and methods to convey this information so you don't have to remember it or hope the comments are up to date. You can also encapsulate the information and use Move Method to add behavior to it.

Mechanics

1. Create a new class to represent the information in the Array. Give it a method called [] so that callers that read the Array can be changed one by one. Give it a method called []= so that callers that write to the Array can be changed one by one.

2. Construct the new object wherever the Array was instantiated.

3. Test.

4. One by one, add attribute readers for each element in the Array that is read by a client. Name the attr_reader after the purpose of the Array element. Change the clients to use the attr_reader. Test after each change.

5. Add attribute writers for any attribute in the Array that is written to by a client. Name the attr_writer after the purpose of the Array element. Change the clients to use the attr_writer. Test after each change.

6. When all Array accesses are replaced by custom accessors, remove the [] and []= methods.

7. Test.

Example

I start with an Array that's used to hold the name, wins, and losses of a sports team. It would be declared as follows:

```
row = []
```

It would be used with code such as the following:


```
row[0] = "Liverpool"
row[1] = "15"

name = row[0]
wins = row[1].to_i
```

To turn this into a custom object, I begin by creating a class:

```
class Performance

end
```

I then need to implement the Array accessor methods so that I can change the calling code one-by-one. I also need to initialize my Array to be empty.

```
class Performance

  def initialize
    @data = []
  end

  def []=(index, value)
    @data.insert(index, value)
  end

  def [](index)
    @data[index]
  end
end
```

Now I find the spots that create the Array, and modify them to construct the Performance object.

```
row = Performance.new
```

I should be able to run my tests now, because all callers should be able to interact with the Performance object in the same way they did the Array.

One by one, I add attr_readers for any attributes that are read from the Array by clients. I start with the name:

```
class Performance

  attr_reader :name


...

name = row.name
wins = row[1].to_i
```

I can do the same with the second element. To make matters easier, I can encapsulate the data type conversion:

```
class Performance
  attr_reader :name
```

```
  def wins
    @wins.to_i
  end

...

name = row.name
wins = row.wins
```

One by one, I add attr_writers (or convert attr_readers to attr_accessors) for any attributes that are written to the Array. I start with the name:

```
class Performance
  attr_accessor :name

  def wins
    @wins.to_i
  end

...

row = Performance.new
row.name = "Liverpool"
row[1] = "15"
```

And then wins:

```
class Performance
  attr_accessor :name
  attr_writer :wins

  def wins
    @wins.to_i
  end

...

row = Performance.new
row.name = "Liverpool"
row.wins = "15"
```


Once I've done this for each element, I can remove the Array element readers and writers:

```
class Performance...

  def []=(index, value)
```

```
  @data, insert(index, value)
end

def [](index)
  @data[index]
end
```

I now have an object with an interface that reveals the intention of its attributes. I also have the opportunity now to use Move Method to move any behavior that relates to the performance onto the `Performance` object.

Refactor with Deprecation

If you're developing a library that is being consumed by others, you may not want to remove old methods (like the `Array` element readers and writers in the previous example) straight away. You could deprecate the methods and leave them on the object, warning consumers that the method will be removed in future releases. By Adding a method to class Module, this can be done pretty easily:

```
class Module
  def deprecate(methodName, &block)
    module_eval <<-END
      alias_method :deprecated_#{methodName}, :#{methodName}
      def #{methodName}(*args, &block)
        $stderr.puts "Warning: calling deprecated method\
#{self}.#{methodName}. This method will be removed in a future release."
        deprecated_#{methodName}(*args, &block)
      end
    END
  end
end
```

Then you can deprecate a method on any class:

```
class Foo
  def foo
    puts "in the foo method"
  end

  deprecate :foo
end

Foo.new.foo
```

produces:

```
in the foo method
Warning: calling deprecated method Foo.foo. This method will be removed in a
future release.
```

Replace Hash with Object

You have a Hash that stores several different types of objects, and is passed around and used for more than one purpose.

Replace the Hash with an object that has a field for each key.

```
new_network = { :nodes => [], :old_networks => [] }

new_network[:old_networks] << node.network
new_network[:nodes] << node

new_network[:name] = new_network[:old_networks].collect do |network|
  network.name
end.join(" - ")
```

```
new_network = NetworkResult.new

new_network.old_networks << node.network
new_network.nodes << node

new_network.name = new_network.old_networks.collect do |network|
  network.name
end.join(" - ")
```


Motivation

Like Arrays, Hashes are a common structure for organizing data. Outside the context of named parameters, they should only be used to store a collection of similar objects. Sometimes, however, you see them used to contain a number of different things. If they are then passed around from method to method, it becomes difficult to remember the keys that the Hash contains. With an object, you can define a class with a public interface to represent the way the object can be interacted with, and one does not have to traverse the entire algorithm to see how the object might behave. As with Replace Array With Object, you can also encapsulate the information and use Move Method to add behavior to it.

Mechanics

1. Create a new class to represent the information in the `Hash`. Give it a method called [] so that callers that read the `Hash` can be changed one by one. Give it a method called []= so that callers that write to the `Hash` can be changed one by one.

2. Construct the new object wherever the `Hash` was instantiated.

3. Test.

4. One by one, add attribute readers for any attribute in the `Hash` that is read by a client. Name the `attr_reader` after the key. Change the clients to use the `attr_reader`. Test after each change.

5. Add attribute writers for any attribute in the Hash that is written to by a client. Name the `attr_writer` after the key. Change the clients to use the `attr_writer`. Test after each change.

6. When all `Hash` accesses are replaced by custom accessors, remove the [] and []= methods.

7. Test.

Example

I start with a `Hash` that's used to store the nodes for a network, and the old networks from which the nodes just came:

```
new_network = { :nodes => [], :old_networks => [] }

new_network[:old_networks] << node.network
new_network[:nodes] << node

new_network[:name] = new_network[:old_networks].collect do |network|
  network.name
end.join(" - ")
```

To turn the Hash into an object, I begin by creating a class:

```
class NetworkResult

end
```

I then need to implement the Hash accessor methods so that I can change the calling code one-by-one.

```
class NetworkResult

  def [](attribute)
    instance_variable_get "@#{attribute}"
  end

  def []=(attribute, value)
    instance_variable_set "@#{attribute}", value
  end

end
```

I need to initialize each of @old_networks and @nodes to an empty Array.

```
class NetworkResult...

  def initialize
    @old_networks, @nodes = [], []
  end
```

I can then instantiate my new object wherever I was instantiating the Hash.

```
new_network = { :nodes => [], :old_networks => [] }
```

becomes

```
new_network = NetworkResult.new
```

My tests should pass if I haven't made any mistakes.

One-by-one, I can replace each of the calls to the Hash reader with calls to an attr_reader. First I add an attr_reader for :old_networks.

Replace Hash with Object

```
class NetworkResult...
  attr_reader :old_networks
```

and replace calls to the Hash reader using the :old_networks key with calls to our new attr_reader.

```
new_network[:old_networks] << node.network
```

becomes:

```
new_network.old_networks << node.network
```

Then I can do the same with `:nodes`:

```
new_network[:nodes] << node
```

becomes

```
class NetworkResult...

  attr_reader :old_networks, :nodes

...

new_network.nodes << node
```

I can then replace calls to the Hash writer with an `attr_accessor`.

```
new_network[:name] = new_network.old_networks.collect do |network|
  network.name
end.join(" - ")
```

becomes:

```
class NetworkResult...
  attr_reader :old_networks, :nodes
  attr_accessor :name

...

new_network.name = new_network.old_networks.collect do |network|
  network.name
end.join(" - ")
```

And finally, I can remove my `Hash accessor` methods from `NetworkResult`:

```
class NetworkResult...

  def [](attribute)
    instance_variable_get "@#{attribute}"
  end

  def []=(attribute, value)
    instance_variable_set "@#{attribute}", value
  end
```


As with many of these refactorings, the true benefit comes when you can move behavior onto the newly created object. Take for example, the name attribute, which is set using data from the old networks. We can make `name` a method on `NetworkResult` and remove the `attr_accessor` for name.

```
class NetworkResult...
  attr_reader :old_networks, :nodes
  attr_accessor :name

  def name
    @old_networks.collect { | network | network.name }.join(" - ")
  end
```

Change Unidirectional Association to Bidirectional

You have two classes that need to use each other's features, but there is only a one-way link.

Add back pointers, and change modifiers to update both sets.

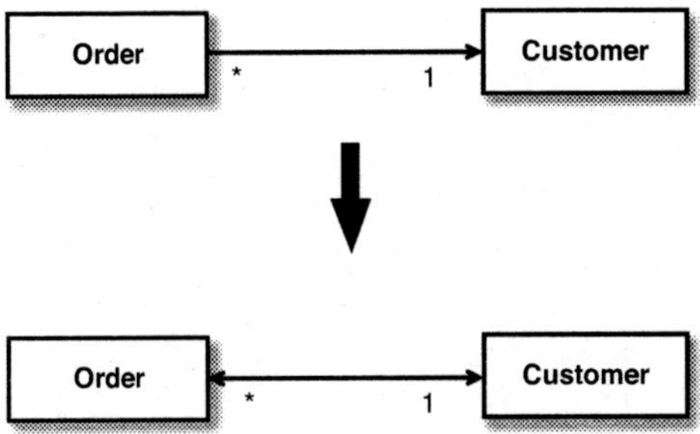

Motivation

You may find that you have initially set up two classes so that one class refers to the other. Over time you may find that a client of the referred class needs to get to the objects that refer to it. This effectively means navigating backward along the pointer. Pointers are one-way links, so you can't do this. Often you can get around this problem by finding another route. This may cost in computation but is reasonable, and you can have a method on the referred class that uses this behavior. Sometimes, however, this is not easy, and you need to set up a two-way reference, sometimes called a *back pointer*. If you aren't used to back pointers, it's easy to become tangled up using them. Once you get used to the idiom, however, it is not too complicated.

The idiom is awkward enough that you should have tests, at least until you are comfortable with the idiom. Because I usually don't bother testing accessors (the risk is not high enough), this is the rare case of a refactoring that adds a test.

This refactoring uses back pointers to implement bidirectionality. Other techniques, such as link objects, require other refactorings.

Mechanics

1. Add a field for the back pointer.
2. Decide which class will control the association.
3. Create a helper method on the noncontrolling side of the association. Name this method to clearly indicate its restricted use.
4. If the existing modifier is on the controlling side, modify it to update the back pointers.
5. If the existing modifier is on the controlled side, create a controlling method on the controlling side and call it from the existing modifier.

Example

A simple program has an order that refers to a customer:

```
class Order...
  attr_accessor :customer

end
```

The `Customer` class has no reference to the `Order`.

I start the refactoring by adding a field to the `Customer`. As a customer can have several orders, so this field is a collection. Because I don't want a customer to have the same order more than once in its collection, the correct collection is a set:

```
require 'set'

class Customer

  def initialize
```

```
    @orders = Set.new
  end
```

Now I need to decide which class will take charge of the association. I prefer to let one class take charge because it keeps all the logic for manipulating the association in one place. My decision process runs as follows:

- If both objects are reference objects and the association is one to many, then the object that has the one reference is the controller. (That is, if one customer has many orders, the order controls the association.)
- If one object is a component of the other, the composite should control the association.
- If both objects are reference objects and the association is many to many, it doesn't matter whether the order or the customer controls the association.

Because the order will take charge, I need to add a helper method to the customer that allows direct access to the orders collection. The order's modifier will use this to synchronize both sets of pointers. I use the name `friend_orders` to signal that this method is to be used only in this special case:

```
class Customer...
  def friend_orders
    #should only be used by Order when modifying the association
    @orders
  end
```

Now I replace the `attr_accessor` with an `attr_reader` and a custom attribute writer to update the back pointers:

```
class Order...
  attr_accessor :customer
  attr_reader :customer


  def customer=(value)
    customer.friend_orders.subtract(self) unless customer.nil?
    @customer = value
    customer.friend_orders.add(self) unless customer.nil?
  end
```


The exact code in the controlling modifier varies with the multiplicity of the association. If the customer is not allowed to be nil, I can forgo the nil checks, but I need to check for a nil argument. The basic pattern is always the same, however: First tell the other object to remove its pointer to you, set your pointer to the new object, and then tell the new object to add a pointer to you.

If you want to modify the link through the customer, let it call the controlling method:

```
class Customer...

  def add_order(order)
    order.customer = self
  end
```

If an order can have many customers, you have a many-to-many case, and the methods look like this:

```
class Order...
  #controlling methods
  def add_customer(customer)
    customer.friend_orders.add(self)
    @customers.add(customer)
  end

  def remove_customer(customer)
    customer.friend_orders.subtract(self)
    @customers.subtract(customer)
  end

class Customer...
  def add_order(order)
    order.add_customer(self)
  end

  def remove_order(order)
    order.remove_customer(self)
  end
```


Change Bidirectional Association to Unidirectional

You have a two-way association but one class no longer needs features from the other.

Drop the unneeded end of the association.

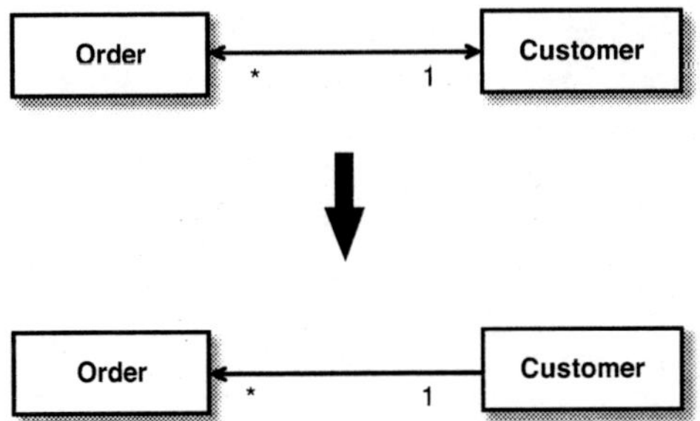

Motivation

Bidirectional associations are useful, but they carry a price. The price is the added complexity of maintaining the two-way links and ensuring that objects are properly created and removed. Bidirectional associations are not natural for many programmers, so they often are a source of errors.

Having many two-way links also makes it easy for mistakes to lead to zombies: objects that should be dead but still hang around because of a reference that was not cleared.

Bidirectional associations force an interdependency between the two classes. Any change to one class may cause a change to another. Many interdependencies lead to a highly coupled system, in which any little change leads to a lot of unpredictable ramifications.

You should use bidirectional associations when you need to but avoid them when you don't. As soon as you see a bidirectional association is no longer pulling its weight, drop the unnecessary end.

Mechanics

1. Examine all the readers of the field that holds the pointer that you want to remove to see whether the removal is feasible.

   ⟹ *Look at direct readers and further methods that call those methods.*

   ⟹ *Consider whether it is possible to determine the other object without using the pointer. If so you will be able to use Substitute Algorithm on the attribute reader to allow clients to use the reader even if there is no pointer.*

⟹ *Consider adding the object as an argument to all methods that use the field.*

2. If clients need to use the attribute reader, use Self Encapsulate Field, carry out Substitute Algorithm on the attribute reader, and test.

3. If clients don't need the attribute reader, change each user of the field so that it gets the object in the field another way. Test after each change.

4. When no reader is left in the field, remove all updates to the field, and remove the field.

   ⟹ *If there are many places that assign the field, use Self Encapsulate Field so that they all use a single attribute writer. Test. Change the attribute writer to have an empty body. Test. If that works, remove the field, the attribute reader, and all calls to the attribute writer.*

5. Test.

Example

This example starts from where I ended up in the example in the section "Change Unidirectional Association to Bidirectional." I have a customer and order with a bidirectional link:

```
class Order...
  attr_reader :customer

  def customer=(value)
    customer.friend_orders.subtract(self) unless customer.nil?
    @customer = value
    customer.friend_orders.add(self) unless customer.nil?
  end

class Customer..

  def initialize
    @orders = Set.new
  end

  def add_order(order)
```

```
    order.set_customer(self)
  end

  def friend_orders
    #should only be used by Order when modifying the association
    @orders
  end
```

I've found that in my application I don't have orders unless I already have a customer, so I want to break the link from order to customer.

The most difficult part of this refactoring is checking that I can do it. Once I know it's safe to do, it's easy. The issue is whether code relies on the customer fields being there. To remove the field, I need to provide an alternative.

My first move is to study all the readers of the field and the methods that use those readers. Can I find another way to provide the customer object? Often this means passing in the customer as an argument for an operation. Here's a simplistic example of this:

```
class Order...
  def discounted_price
    gross_price * (1 - @customer.discount)
  end
```

changes to

```
class Order...
  def discounted_price(customer)
    gross_price * (1 - customer.discount)
  end
```

This works particularly well when the behavior is being called by the customer, because then it's easy to pass itself in as an argument. So:

```
class Customer...

  def price_for(order)
    assert { @orders.include?(order) } # see Introduce Assertion
    order.discounted_price
  end
```


becomes:

```
class Customer...

  def price_for(order)
```

```
    assert { @orders.include?(order) } # see Introduce Assertion
    order.discounted_price(self)
  end
```

Another alternative I consider is changing the attribute reader so that it gets the customer without using the field. If it does, I can use Substitute Algorithm on the body of `Order.customer`. I might do something like this:

```
def customer
  Customer::Instances.each do |customer|
    return customer if customer.has_order?(self)
  end
end
```

Slow, but it works. In a database context it may not even be that slow if I use a database query. If the `Order` class contains methods that use the `customer` field, I can change them to use the `customer` reader by using Self Encapsulate Field.

If I retain the accessor, the association is still bidirectional in interface but is unidirectional in implementation. I remove the back-pointer but retain the interdependencies between the two classes.

If I substitute the attribute reader, I substitute that and leave the rest till later. Otherwise, I change the callers one at a time to use the customer from another source. I test after each change. In practice, this process usually is pretty rapid. If it were complicated, I would give up on this refactoring.

Once I've eliminated the readers of the field, I can work on the writers of the field. This is as simple as removing any assignments to the field and then removing the field. Because nobody is reading it any more, that shouldn't matter.

Replace Magic Number with Symbolic Constant

You have a literal number with a particular meaning.

Create a constant, name it after the meaning, and replace the number with it.

```
def potential_energy(mass, height)
  mass * 9.81 * height
end
```

```
GRAVITATIONAL_CONSTANT = 9.81

def potential_energy(mass, height)
  mass * GRAVITATIONAL_CONSTANT * height
end
```

Motivation

Magic numbers are one of oldest ills in computing. They are numbers with special values that usually are not obvious. Magic numbers are really nasty when you need to reference the same logical number in more than one place. If the numbers might ever change, making the change is a nightmare. Even if you don't make a change, you have the difficulty of figuring out what is going on.

Many languages allow you to declare a constant. There is no cost in performance and there is a great improvement in readability.

Before you do this refactoring, always look for an alternative. Look at how the magic number is used. Often you can find a better way to use it. If the magic number is a type code, consider Replace Type Code with Polymorphism. If the magic number is the length of an `Array`, use `an_array.size` instead.

Mechanics

1. Declare a constant and set it to the value of the magic number.

2. Find all occurrences of the magic number.

3. See whether the magic number matches the usage of the constant; if it does, change the magic number to use the constant.

4. When all magic numbers are changed, test. At this point all should work as if nothing has been changed.

   ⟹ *A good test is to see whether you can change the constant easily. This may mean altering some expected results to match the new value. This isn't always possible, but it is a good trick when it works.*

Encapsulate Collection

A method returns a collection.

Make it return a copy of the collection and provide add/remove methods.

Motivation

Often a class contains a collection of instances. This collection might be an Array or a Hash. Such cases often have the usual attribute reader and writer for the collection.

However, collections should use a protocol slightly different from that for other kinds of data. The attribute reader should not return the collection object itself, because that allows clients to manipulate the contents of the collection without the owning class knowing what is going on. It also reveals too much to clients about the object's internal data structures. An attribute reader for a multivalued attribute should return something that prevents manipulation of the collection and hides unnecessary details about its structure.

In addition there should not be an attribute writer for the collection: rather, there should be operations to add and remove elements. This gives the owning object control over adding and removing elements from the collection.

With this protocol the collection is properly encapsulated, which reduces the coupling of the owning class to its clients.

Mechanics

1. Add add and remove methods for the collection.

2. Initialize the field to an empty collection.

3. Find callers of the attribute writer. Either modify the writer to use the `add` and `remove` operations or have the clients call those operations instead.

   ⟹ *Attribute writers are used in two cases: when the collection is empty and when the attribute writer is replacing a nonempty collection.*

   ⟹ *You may want to use Rename Method to rename the attribute writer. Change it to* `initialize_x` *or* `replace_x`, *where "*`x`*" is the name of your collection.*

4. Test.

5. Find all users of the attribute reader that modify the collection. Change them to use the add and `remove` methods. Test after each change.

6. When all uses of the attribute reader that modify have been changed, modify the reader to return a copy of the collection.

7. Test.

8. Find the users of the attribute reader. Look for code that should be on the host object. Use Extract Method and Move Method to move the code to the host object.

9. Test.

Example

A person is taking courses. Our `Course` is pretty simple:

```
class Course...
  def initialize(name, advanced)
    @name = name
    @advanced = advanced
  end
```


I'm not going to bother with anything else on the `Course`. The interesting class is the `Person`:

```
class Person...
  attr_accessor :courses
```

With this interface, clients add courses with code such as:

```
kent = Person.new
courses = []
courses << Course.new("Smalltalk Programming", false)
courses << Course.new("Appreciating Single Malts", true)
kent.courses = courses
assert_equal 2, kent.courses.size
refactoring = Course.new("Refactoring", true)
kent.courses << refactoring
kent.courses << Course.new("Brutal Sarcasm", false)
assert_equal 4, kent.courses.size
kent.courses.delete(refactoring)
assert_equal 3, kent.courses.size
```

A client that wants to know about advanced courses might do it this way:

```
person.courses.select { |course| course.advanced? }.size
```

The first thing I want to do is to create the proper modifiers for the collection as follows:

```
class Person...


  def add_course(course)
    @courses << course
  end

  def remove_course(course)
    @courses.delete(course)
  end
```

Life will be easier if I initialize the field as well:

```
def initialize
  @courses = []
end
```

I then look at the users of the attribute writer. If there are many clients and the writer is used heavily, I need to replace the body of the writer to use the add and remove operations. The complexity of this process depends on how the writer is used. There are two cases. In the simplest case the client uses the writer to initialize the values, that is, there are no courses before the writer is applied. In this case I replace the attribute accessor with an explicit writer that uses the add method:


```
class Person...
  def courses=(courses)
```

```
    raise "Courses should be empty" unless @courses.empty?
    courses.each { |course| add_course(course) }
  end
```

After changing the body this way, it is wise to use Rename Method to make the intention clearer.

```
class Person...
  def initialize_courses(courses)
    raise "Courses should be empty" unless @courses.empty?
    courses.each { |course| add_course(course) }
  end
```

In the more general case I have to use the remove method to remove every element first and then add the elements. But I find that occurs rarely (as general cases often do).

If I know that I don't have any additional behavior when adding elements as I initialize, I can remove the loop and use +=.

```
def initialize_courses(courses)
  raise "Courses should be empty" unless @courses.empty?
  @courses += courses
end
```

I can't just assign the Array, even though the previous Array was empty. If the client were to modify the Array after passing it in, that would violate encapsulation. I have to make a copy.

If the clients simply create an Array and use the attribute writer, I can get them to use the add and remove methods directly and remove the writer completely. Code such as:

```
kent = Person.new
courses = []
courses << Course.new("Smalltalk Programming", false)
courses << Course.new("Appreciating Single Malts", true)
kent.initialize_courses(courses)
```

becomes:

```
kent = Person.new
kent.add_course(Course.new("Smalltalk Programming", false))
kent.add_course(Course.new("Appreciating Single Malts", true))
```

Now I start looking at users of the attribute reader. My first concern is cases in which someone uses the reader to modify the underlying collection, for example:

```
kent.courses << Course.new("Brutal Sarcasm", false)
```

I need to replace this with a call to the new modifier:

```
kent.add_course(Course.new("Brutal Sarcasm", false))
```

Once I've done this for everyone, I can ensure that nobody is modifying through the attribute reader by changing the reader body to return a copy of the collection:

```
def courses
  @courses.dup
end
```

At this point I've encapsulated the collection. No one can change the elements of the collection except through methods on the `Person`.

Moving Behavior into the Class

I have the right interface. Now I like to look at the users of the attribute reader to find code that ought to be on person. Code such as:

```
number_of_advanced_courses = person.courses.select do |course|
  course.advanced?
end.size
```

is better moved to `Person` because it uses only `Person's` data. First I use Extract Method on the code:

```
def number_of_advanced_courses
  person.courses.select { |course| course.advanced? }.size

end
```

And then I use Move Method to move it to person:

```
class Person...

  def number_of_advanced_courses
    @courses.select { |course| course.advanced? }.size
  end
```

A common case is:

```
kent.courses.size
```

which can be changed to the more readable:

```
kent.number_of_courses
```

```
class Person...

  def number_of_courses
    @courses.size
  end
```

A few years ago I was concerned that moving this kind of behavior over to `Person` would lead to a bloated `Person` class. In practice, I've found that this usually isn't a problem.

Replace Record with Data Class

You need to interface with a record structure in a traditional programming environment.

Make a dumb data object for the record.

Motivation

Record structures are a common feature of programming environments. There are various reasons for bringing them into an Object-Oriented program. You could be copying a legacy program, or you could be communicating a structured record with a traditional programming API, or a database record. In these cases it is useful to create an interfacing class to deal with this external element. It is simplest to make the class look like the external record. You move other fields and methods into the class later. A less obvious but very compelling case is an Array in which the element in each index has a special meaning. In this case you use Replace Array with Object.

Mechanics

1. Create a class to represent the record.

2. Give the class a field with an `attribute_accessor` for each data item.

3. You now have a dumb data object. It has no behavior yet but further refactoring will explore that issue.

Replace Type Code with Polymorphism

You have a type code that affects the behavior of a class.

Replace the type code with classes: one for each type code variant.

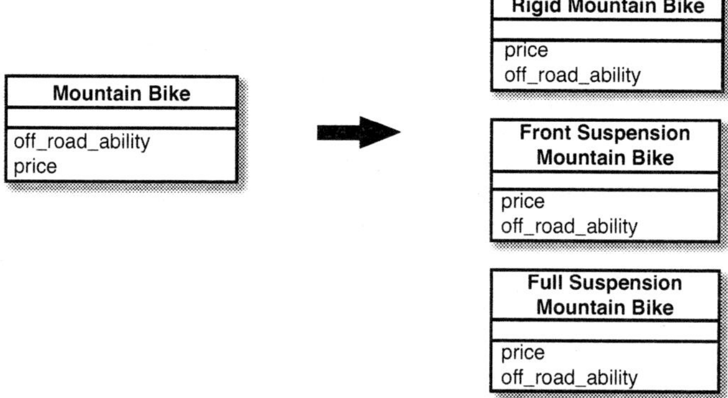

Motivation

This situation is usually indicated by the presence of case-like conditional statements. These may be case statements or if-then-else constructs. In both forms they test the value of the type code and then execute different code depending on the value of the type code.

Removing Conditional Logic

There are three different refactorings to consider when you're trying to remove conditional logic: Replace Type Code with Polymorphism, Replace Type Code with Module Extension, or Replace Type Code with State/Strategy. The choice depends on relatively subtle design differences.

If the methods that use the type code make up a large portion of the class, I use Replace Type Code with Polymorphism. It's the simplest, and just takes advantage of Ruby's duck-typing to remove the conditional statements. It involves blowing away the original class and replacing it with a new class for each type code. Since the original class was heavily reliant on the type code, it generally makes sense for the clients of the original class to construct an instance of one of the new type classes (because they were probably injecting the type into the original class anyway).

If the class has a large chunk of behavior that doesn't use the type code, I choose either Replace Type Code with Module Extension or Replace Type Code with State/Strategy. These have the advantage of enabling me to change the type at runtime. In the former we extend a module, mixing in the module's behavior onto the object. Instance variables are shared automatically between the object and the module, which can simplify things. Replace Type Code with State/Strategy uses delegation: The parent object delegates to the state object for state-specific behavior. The state object can be swapped out at runtime when a change in behavior is required. Because of the delegation, sharing of instance variables between the parent object and the state object can be awkward. So the question becomes, why would you choose State/Strategy over Module Extension? It turns out that you can't unmix a module in Ruby, so removing undesired behavior can be difficult. When the state changes become complex enough that unwanted behavior cannot be removed or overridden, I choose Replace Type Code with State/Strategy.

The great thing about Ruby is that you can do Replace Type Code with Polymorphism without inheritance or implementing an interface, something that is impossible in a language such as Java or C#.

Mechanics

1. Create a class to represent each type code variant.

2. Change the class that uses the type code into a module. Include the module into each of the new type classes.

3. Change the callers of the original class to create an instance of the desired type instead.

4. Test.

5. Choose one of the methods that use the type code. Override the method on one of the type classes,

6. Test.

7. Do the same for the other type classes, removing the method on the module when you're done.

8. Test.

9. Repeat for the other methods that use the type code.

10. Test.

11. Remove the module if it no longer houses useful behavior.

Example

For this case I'm modeling mountain bikes. An instance of the `MountainBike` can either be `:rigid` (having no suspension), `:front_suspension`, or `:full_suspension` (having both front and rear suspension). The `@type_code` determines how things like `off_road_ability` and `price` are calculated:

```
class MountainBike...

def initialize(params)
    params.each { |key, value| instance_variable_set "@#{key}", value }
  end

  def off_road_ability
    result = @tire_width * TIRE_WIDTH_FACTOR
    if @type_code == :front_suspension || @type_code == :full_suspension
      result += @front_fork_travel * FRONT_SUSPENSION_FACTOR
    end
    if @type_code == :full_suspension
      result += @rear_fork_travel * REAR_SUSPENSION_FACTOR
    end
    result
  end

  def price
    case @type_code
      when :rigid
        (1 + @commission) * @base_price
      when :front_suspension
        (1 + @commission) * @base_price + @front_suspension_price
      when :full_suspension
        (1 + @commission) * @base_price + @front_suspension_price +
        @rear_suspension_price
  end
end
```

It can be used like this:

```
bike = MountainBike.new(:type_code => :rigid, :tire_width => 2.5)
bike2 = MountainBike.new(:type_code => :front_suspension, :tire_width => 2,
          :front_fork_travel => 3)
```

We'll start by creating a class for each type. We'll change `MountainBike` to a module, and include it in each of our new classes.

```
class RigidMountainBike
  include MountainBike
end

class FrontSuspensionMountainBike
  include MountainBike
end

class FullSuspensionMountainBike
  include MountainBike
end
```

```
~~class~~ module MountainBike...

  def wheel_circumference
    Math::PI * (@wheel_diameter + @tire_diameter)
  end

  def off_road_ability
    result = @tire_width * TIRE_WIDTH_FACTOR
    if @type_code == :front_suspension || @type_code == :full_suspension
      result += @front_fork_travel * FRONT_SUSPENSION_FACTOR
    end
    if @type_code == :full_suspension
      result += @rear_fork_travel * REAR_SUSPENSION_FACTOR
    end
    result
  end

  def price
    case @type_code
      when :rigid
        (1 + @commission) * @base_price
      when :front_suspension
        (1 + @commission) * @base_price + @front_suspension_price
      when :full_suspension
```

```
        (1 + @commission) * @base_price + @front_suspension_price +
        @rear_suspension_price
    end
  end
end
```

The callers will need to change to create our new type.

```
bike = MountainBike.new(:type_code => :front_suspension, :tire_width => 2,
  :front_fork_travel => 3)
```

becomes

```
bike = FrontSuspensionMountainBike.new(:type_code => :front_suspension,
  :tire_width => 2,
  :front_fork_travel => 3)
```

Although we haven't gotten far, we should be able to run the tests and they should still pass.

Next we use Replace Conditional with Polymorphism on one of the methods that we want to call polymorphically, overriding it for one of our new classes. I choose `price` and start with `RigidMountainBike`.

```
class RigidMountainBike
  include MountainBike

  def price
    (1 + @commission) * @base_price
  end
end
```

This new method overrides the whole `case` statement for rigid mountain bikes. Because I'm paranoid, I sometimes put a trap in the `case` statement:

```
module MountainBike...

  def price
    case @type_code
      when :rigid
        raise "shouldn't get here"
      when :front_suspension
        (1 + @commission) * @base_price + @front_suspension_price
      when :full_suspension
        (1 + @commission) * @base_price + @front_suspension_price +
        @rear_suspension_price
    end
  end
end
```

All going well, the tests should pass.

I then do the same for the other type classes, removing the `price` method in the `MountainBike` module when I'm done.

```
class RigidMountainBike
  include MountainBike

  def price
    (1 + @commission) * @base_price
  end
end

class FrontSuspensionMountainBike
  include MountainBike

  def price
    (1 + @commission) * @base_price + @front_suspension_price
  end
end

class FullSuspensionMountainBike
  include MountainBike

  def price
    (1 + @commission) * @base_price + @front_suspension_price +
    @rear_suspension_price
  end
end

module MountainBike...
  def price
    case @type_code
    ...
    end
  end
end
```

I can then do the same for `off_road_ability`.

```
class RigidMountainBike
  include MountainBike

  def price
    (1 + @commission) * @base_price
  end

  def off_road_ability
    @tire_width * TIRE_WIDTH_FACTOR
  end
end

class FrontSuspensionMountainBike
  include MountainBike

  def price
    (1 + @commission) * @base_price + @front_suspension_price
  end

  def off_road_ability
    @tire_width * TIRE_WIDTH_FACTOR + @front_fork_travel *
    FRONT_SUSPENSION_FACTOR
  end
end

class FullSuspensionMountainBike
  include MountainBike

  def price
    (1 + @commission) * @base_price + @front_suspension_price +
    @rear_suspension_price
  end

  def off_road_ability
    @tire_width * TIRE_WIDTH_FACTOR + @front_fork_travel *
    FRONT_SUSPENSION_FACTOR + @rear_fork_travel * REAR_SUSPENSION_FACTOR
  end
end
```

```
module MountainBike
  def off_road_ability
    result = @tire_width * TIRE_WIDTH_FACTOR
    if @type_code == :front_suspension || @type_code == :full_suspension
      result += @front_fork_travel * FRONT_SUSPENSION_FACTOR
    end
    if @type_code == :full_suspension
      result += @rear_fork_travel * REAR_SUSPENSION_FACTOR
    end
    result
  end
end
```

Since we're no longer using the type code, I can remove it from the callers.

```
bike = FrontSuspensionMountainBike.new(:type_code => :front_suspension,
  :tire_width => 2,
  :front_fork_travel => 3)
```

becomes

```
bike = FrontSuspensionMountainBike.new(:tire_width => 2, :front_fork_travel => 3)
```

We'll keep the `MountainBike` module in this case since it still houses some useful code that would otherwise need to be duplicated.

Replace Type Code with Module Extension

You have a type code that affects the behavior of a class.

Replace the type code with dynamic module extension.

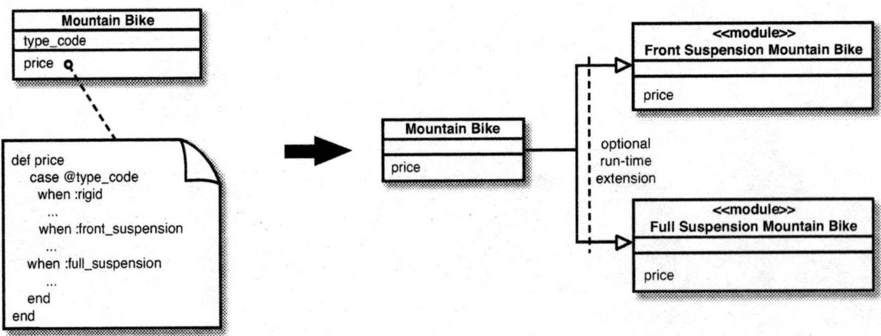

Motivation

Like Replace Type Code with Polymorphism, Replace Type Code with Module Extension aims to remove conditional logic. By extending a module, we can change the behavior of an object at runtime. Both the original class and the module that is being extended can access the same instance variables. This removes some of the headache that comes along with a more traditional state/strategy pattern that uses delegation.

The one catch with module extension is that modules cannot be unmixed easily. Once they are mixed into an object, their behavior is hard to remove. So use Replace Type Code with Module Extension when you don't care about removing behavior. If you do care, use Replace Type Code with State/Strategy instead.

Mechanics

1. Perform Self-encapsulate Field on the type code.
2. Create a module for each type code variant.
3. Make the type code writer extend the type module appropriately.
4. Choose one of the methods that use the type code. Override the method on one of the type modules.
5. Test.
6. Do the same for the other type modules. Modify the implementation on the class to return the default behavior.
7. Test.
8. Repeat for the other methods that use the type code.
9. Test.
10. Pass the module into the type code setter instead of the old type code.
11. Test.

Example

We'll use a similar example to Replace Type Code with Polymorphism. Let's say we have a mountain bike object in the system that at some stage in its life cycle we decide to add front suspension to.

```
bike = MountainBike.new(:type_code => :rigid)
...
bike.type_code = :front_suspension
```

MountainBike might look something like this:

```
class MountainBike...

  attr_writer :type_code

  def initialize(params)
    @type_code = params[:type_code]
    @commission = params[:commission]
    ...
  end

  def off_road_ability
    result = @tire_width * TIRE_WIDTH_FACTOR
    if @type_code == :front_suspension || @type_code == :full_suspension
      result += @front_fork_travel * FRONT_SUSPENSION_FACTOR
    end
    if @type_code == :full_suspension
      result += @rear_fork_travel * REAR_SUSPENSION_FACTOR
    end
    result
  end

  def price
    case @type_code
      when :rigid
        (1 + @commission) * @base_price
      when :front_suspension
        (1 + @commission) * @base_price + @front_suspension_price
      when :full_suspension
        (1 + @commission) * @base_price + @front_suspension_price +
        @rear_suspension_price
    end
  end
end
```

The first step is to use Self Encapsulate Field on the type code. I'll create a custom attribute writer because it will do something more interesting soon, and call it from the constructor.

```
class MountainBike...

  attr_reader :type_code

  def initialize(params)
    self.type_code = params[:type_code]
    @commission = params[:commission]
    ...
  end

  def type_code=(value)
    @type_code = value
  end

  def off_road_ability
    result = @tire_width * TIRE_WIDTH_FACTOR
    if type_code == :front_suspension || type_code == :full_suspension
      result += @front_fork_travel * FRONT_SUSPENSION_FACTOR
    end
    if type_code == :full_suspension
      result += @rear_fork_travel * REAR_SUSPENSION_FACTOR
    end
    result
  end

  def price
    case type_code
      when :rigid
        (1 + @commission) * @base_price
      when :front_suspension
        (1 + @commission) * @base_price + @front_suspension_price
      when :full_suspension
        (1 + @commission) * @base_price + @front_suspension_price +
        @rear_suspension_price
    end
  end
```


The next step is to create a module for each of the types. We'll make rigid the default, and add modules for `FrontSuspensionMountainBike` and `FullSuspensionMountainBike`.

I need to change the type code setter to extend the appropriate module. The case statement I'm introducing will be removed by the time we've finished this refactoring; it's just there to make the next step a bit smaller.

```
class MountainBike...

  def type_code=(value)
    @type_code = value
    case type_code
      when :front_suspension: extend(FrontSuspensionMountainBike)
      when :full_suspension: extend(FullSuspensionMountainBike)
    end
  end
```

I then begin Replace Conditional with Polymorphism. I'll start with price, and override it on FrontSuspensionMountainBike.

```
module FrontSuspensionMountainBike
  def price
    (1 + @commission) * @base_price + @front_suspension_price
  end
end

module FullSuspensionMountainBike

end
```

I can put a trap in the case statement to make sure it's being overridden:

```
class MountainBike...

  def price
    case type_code
      when :rigid
        (1 + @commission) * @base_price
      when :front_suspension
        raise "shouldn't get here"
      when :full_suspension
        (1 + @commission) * @base_price + @front_suspension_price +
        @rear_suspension_price
    end
  end
end
```

At this point we haven't gotten far, but our tests should pass.

I then repeat the process for FullSuspensionMountainBike. I can remove the case statement in price, and just return the default implementation for rigid mountain bikes.

```
module FrontSuspensionMountainBike
  def price
    (1 + @commission) * @base_price + @front_suspension_price
  end
end

module FullSuspensionMountainBike
  def price
    (1 + @commission) * @base_price + @front_suspension_price +
    @rear_suspension_price
  end
end

class MountainBike...

  def price
    (1 + @commission) * @base_price
  end
end
```

I then do the same for off_road_ability. The constants will have to be scoped to access them on MountainBike.

```
module FrontSuspensionMountainBike
  def price
    (1 + @commission) * @base_price + @front_suspension_price
  end

  def off_road_ability
    @tire_width * MountainBike::TIRE_WIDTH_FACTOR + @front_fork_travel *
    MountainBike::FRONT_SUSPENSION_FACTOR
  end
end

module FullSuspensionMountainBike
  def price
    (1 + @commission) * @base_price + @front_suspension_price +
    @rear_suspension_price
  end

  def off_road_ability
    @tire_width * MountainBike::TIRE_WIDTH_FACTOR +
    @front_fork_travel * MountainBike::FRONT_SUSPENSION_FACTOR +
```

```
    @rear_fork_travel * MountainBike::REAR_SUSPENSION_FACTOR
  end
end

class MountainBike...

  def off_road_ability
    @tire_width * TIRE_WIDTH_FACTOR
  end

  def price
    (1 + @commission) * @base_price
  end
end
```

I can remove the case statement I created by getting the callers to pass in the appropriate module.

```
bike = MountainBike.new(:type_code => :rigid)
...
bike.type_code = :front_suspension
```

becomes

```
bike = MountainBike.new
...
bike.type_code = FrontSuspensionMountainBike

class MountainBike...

  def type_code=(mod)
    extend(mod)
  end
```

I should now have removed all traces of @type_code.

Replace Type Code with State/Strategy

You have a type code that affects the behavior of a class and the type code changes at runtime.

Replace the type code with a state object.

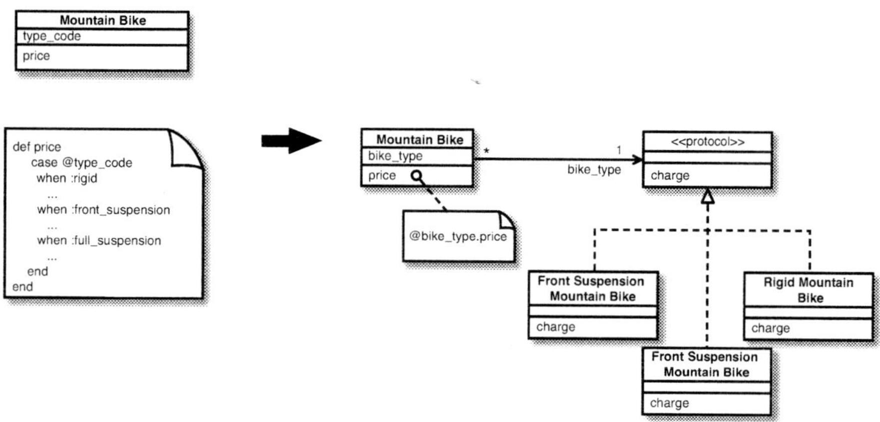

Motivation

This refactoring has the same goal as Replace Type Code with Polymorphism and Replace Type Code with Module Extension: removing conditional logic. I use Replace Type Code with State/Strategy when the type code is changed at runtime and the type changes are complex enough that I can't get away with Module Extension.

State and strategy are similar, and the refactoring is the same whichever you use. Choose the pattern that better fits the specific circumstances. If you are trying to simplify a single algorithm, strategy is the better term. If you are going to move state-specific data and you think of the object as changing state, use the state pattern.

Mechanics

1. Perform Self-encapsulate Field on the type code.

2. Create empty classes for each of the polymorphic objects. Create a new instance variable to represent the type. This will be the object that we'll delegate to.

3. Use the old type code to determine which of the new type classes should be assigned to the type instance variable.

4. Choose one of the methods that you want to behave polymorphically. Add a method with the same name on one of the new type classes, and delegate to it from the parent object

   ⟹ *You'll need to pass in any state that needs to be shared with the object being delegated to, or pass a reference to the original object.*

5. Test.

6. Repeat step 4 for the other type classes.

7. Test.

8. Repeat steps 4 through 7 for each of the other methods that use the type code.

Example

To easily demonstrate the differences between Replace Type Code with State/Strategy and the other Replace Type Code refactorings, we'll use a similar example. This time we'll add methods for upgrading the mountain bike to add front suspension and rear suspension.

```
class MountainBike...

  def initialize(params)
    set_state_from_hash(params)
  end

  def add_front_suspension(params)
    @type_code = :front_suspension
    set_state_from_hash(params)
  end

  def add_rear_suspension(params)
    unless @type_code == :front_suspension
```

```
      raise "You can't add rear suspension unless you have front suspension"
    end
    @type_code = :full_suspension
    set_state_from_hash(params)
  end

  def off_road_ability
    result = @tire_width * TIRE_WIDTH_FACTOR
    if @type_code == :front_suspension || @type_code == :full_suspension
      result += @front_fork_travel * FRONT_SUSPENSION_FACTOR
    end
    if @type_code == :full_suspension
      result += @rear_fork_travel * REAR_SUSPENSION_FACTOR
    end
    result
  end

  def price
    case @type_code
      when :rigid
        (1 + @commission) * @base_price
      when :front_suspension
        (1 + @commission) * @base_price + @front_suspension_price
      when :full_suspension
        (1 + @commission) * @base_price + @front_suspension_price +
        @rear_suspension_price
    end
  end

  private

  def set_state_from_hash(hash)
    @base_price = hash[:base_price] if hash.has_key?(:base_price)
    if hash.has_key?(:front_suspension_price)
      @front_suspension_price = hash[:front_suspension_price]
    end
    if hash.has_key?(:rear_suspension_price)
      @rear_suspension_price = hash[:rear_suspension_price]
    end
    if hash.has_key?(:commission)
      @commission = hash[:commission]
    end
    if hash.has_key?(:tire_width)
      @tire_width = hash[:tire_width]
    end
    if hash.has_key?(:front_fork_travel)
```

```
      @front_fork_travel = hash[:front_fork_travel]
    end
    if hash.has_key?(:rear_fork_travel)
      @rear_fork_travel = hash[:rear_fork_travel]
    end
    @type_code = hash[:type_code] if hash.has_key?(:type_code)
  end
end
```

The first step is to perform Self-encapsulate Field on the type code. By confining all access to the type code to just the getter and setter, we can more easily perform parallel tasks when the type is being accessed. This enables us to take smaller steps during the refactoring.

We add an `attr_reader`, and a custom attribute writer, which will do something more interesting soon.

```
class MountainBike...
  attr_reader :type_code

  def initialize(params)
    set_state_from_hash(params)
  end

  def type_code=(value)
    @type_code = value
  end

  def add_front_suspension(params)
    self.type_code = :front_suspension
    set_state_from_hash(params)
  end

  def add_rear_suspension(params)
    unless type_code == :front_suspension
      raise "You can't add rear suspension unless you have front suspension"
    end
    self.type_code = :full_suspension
    set_state_from_hash(params)
  end

  def off_road_ability
    result = @tire_width * TIRE_WIDTH_FACTOR
    if type_code == :front_suspension || type_code == :full_suspension
      result += @front_fork_travel * FRONT_SUSPENSION_FACTOR
    end
```

```
    if type_code == :full_suspension
      result += @rear_fork_travel * REAR_SUSPENSION_FACTOR
    end
    result
  end

  def price
    case type_code
      when :rigid
        (1 + @commission) * @base_price
      when :front_suspension
        (1 + @commission) * @base_price + @front_suspension_price
      when :full_suspension
        (1 + @commission) * @base_price + @front_suspension_price +
        @rear_suspension_price
    end
  end

  private

  def set_state_from_hash(hash)
    @base_price = hash[:base_price] if hash.has_key?(:base_price)
    if hash.has_key?(:front_suspension_price)
      @front_suspension_price = hash[:front_suspension_price]
    end
    if hash.has_key?(:rear_suspension_price)
      @rear_suspension_price = hash[:rear_suspension_price]
    end
    if hash.has_key?(:commission)
      @commission = hash[:commission]
    end
    if hash.has_key?(:tire_width)
      @tire_width = hash[:tire_width]
    end
    if hash.has_key?(:front_fork_travel)
      @front_fork_travel = hash[:front_fork_travel]
    end
    if hash.has_key?(:rear_fork_travel)
      @rear_fork_travel = hash[:rear_fork_travel]
    end
    self.type_code = hash[:type_code] if hash.has_key?(:type_code)
  end
```

Next we create empty classes for each variant of type code.

```
class RigidMountainBike

end

class FrontSuspensionMountainBike

end

class FullSuspensionMountainBike

end
```

We need a new instance variable to represent the type. We'll assign to it an instance of one of our new classes. This will be the object that we'll delegate to.

```
class MountainBike...

  def type_code=(value)
    @type_code = value
    @bike_type = case type_code
      when :rigid: RigidMountainBike.new
      when :front_suspension: FrontSuspensionMountainBike.new
      when :full_suspension: FullSuspensionMountainBike.new
    end
  end

end
```

It may seem strange that we're introducing a `case` statement when the purpose of this refactoring is, in fact, to *remove* conditional logic. The `case` statement just enables a smaller step to the refactoring, by giving us the ability to modify the internals of the class without modifying the callers. Rest assured that it won't last long: By the time we finish the refactoring all conditional logic will be removed.

Now the fun begins. We want to use Replace Conditional with Polymorphism on the conditional logic. I'll start with `off_road_ability`, and add it to `RigidMountainBike`. We have to pass in the instance variables that are needed by the state object.


```
class RigidMountainBike...

  def initialize(params)
    @tire_width = params[:tire_width]
  end

  def off_road_ability
    @tire_width * MountainBike::TIRE_WIDTH_FACTOR
  end
```

```
end

class FrontSuspensionMountainBike

end

class FullSuspensionMountainBike

end

class MountainBike...

  def type_code=(value)
    @type_code = value
    @bike_type = case type_code
      when :rigid: RigidMountainBike.new(:tire_width => @tire_width)
      when :front_suspension: FrontSuspensionMountainBike.new
      when :full_suspension: FullSuspensionMountainBike.new
    end
  end

  def off_road_ability
    return @bike_type.off_road_ability if type_code == :rigid
    result = @tire_width * TIRE_WIDTH_FACTOR
    if type_code == :front_suspension || type_code == :full_suspension
      result += @front_fork_travel * FRONT_SUSPENSION_FACTOR
    end
    if type_code == :full_suspension
      result += @rear_fork_travel * REAR_SUSPENSION_FACTOR
    end
    result
  end

end
```

At this stage we shouldn't have broken anything.

We do the same with the other new classes.

```
class FrontSuspensionMountainBike

  def initialize(params)
    @tire_width = params[:tire_width]
    @front_fork_travel = params[:front_fork_travel]
  end
```

```
  def off_road_ability
    @tire_width * MountainBike::TIRE_WIDTH_FACTOR + @front_fork_travel *
    MountainBike::FRONT_SUSPENSION_FACTOR
  end

end

class FullSuspensionMountainBike

  def initialize(params)
    @tire_width = params[:tire_width]
    @front_fork_travel = params[:front_fork_travel]
    @rear_fork_travel = params[:rear_fork_travel]
  end

  def off_road_ability
    @tire_width * MountainBike::TIRE_WIDTH_FACTOR +
    @front_fork_travel * MountainBike::FRONT_SUSPENSION_FACTOR +
    @rear_fork_travel * MountainBike::REAR_SUSPENSION_FACTOR
  end

end
```

We can then make `off_road_ability` in mountain bike delegate to the type using `Forwardable`. (See the Hide Delegate section in Chapter 7 for an explanation of `Forwardable`.)

```
class MountainBike...

  extend Forwardable
  def_delegators :@bike_type, :off_road_ability

  attr_reader :type_code

  def type_code=(value)
    @type_code = value
    @bike_type = case type_code
      when :rigid: RigidMountainBike.new(:tire_width => @tire_width)
      when :front_suspension: FrontSuspensionMountainBike.new(
        :tire_width => @tire_width,
        :front_fork_travel => @front_fork_travel
      )
      when :full_suspension: FullSuspensionMountainBike.new(
        :tire_width => @tire_width,
        :front_fork_travel => @front_fork_travel,
        :rear_fork_travel => @rear_fork_travel
      )
```

```
    end
  end

end
```

Our add_front_suspension and add_rear_suspension methods need to change to set the type object to an instance of one of our new classes.

```
class MountainBike...

  def add_front_suspension(params)
    self.type_code = :front_suspension
    @bike_type = FrontSuspensionMountainBike.new(
      { :tire_width => @tire_width}.merge(params)
    )
    set_state_from_hash(params)
  end

  def add_rear_suspension(params)
    unless type_code == :front_suspension
      raise "You can't add rear suspension unless you have front suspension"
    end
    self.type_code = :full_suspension
    @bike_type = FullSuspensionMountainBike.new({
      :tire_width => @tire_width,
      :front_fork_travel => @front_fork_travel
    }.merge(params))
    set_state_from_hash(params)
  end
end
```

We can then do the same with the price method.

```
class RigidMountainBike...

  def price
    (1 + @commission) * @base_price
  end

end

class FrontSuspensionMountainBike...

  def price
    (1 + @commission) * @base_price + @front_suspension_price
  end

end
```

```
class FullSuspensionMountainBike...

  def price
    (1 + @commission) * @base_price + @front_suspension_price +
    @rear_suspension_price
  end

end
```

Since `price` is the last method that we need to move, we can start to remove `type_code`.

```
class MountainBike...

  def_delegators :@bike_type, :off_road_ability, :price

  def type_code=(value)
    @type_code = value
    @bike_type = case type_code
      when :rigid: RigidMountainBike.new(
          :tire_width => @tire_width,
          :base_price => @base_price,
          :commission => @commission
        )
      when :front_suspension: FrontSuspensionMountainBike.new(
          :tire_width => @tire_width,
          :front_fork_travel => @front_fork_travel,
          :front_suspension_price => @front_suspension_price,
          :base_price => @base_price,
          :commission => @commission
        )
      when :full_suspension: FullSuspensionMountainBike.new(
          :tire_width => @tire_width,
          :front_fork_travel => @front_fork_travel,
          :rear_fork_travel => @rear_fork_travel,
          :front_suspension_price => @front_suspension_price,
          :rear_suspension_price => @rear_suspension_price,
          :base_price => @base_price,
          :commission => @commission
        )
    end

  end
```

```
  def add_front_suspension(params)
    self.type_code = :front_suspension
    @bike_type = FrontSuspensionMountainBike.new({
      :tire_width => @bike_type.tire_width,
      :base_price => @bike_type.base_price,
      :commission => @bike_type.commission
     }.merge(params))
  end

  def add_rear_suspension(params)
    unless @bike_type.is_a?(FrontSuspensionMountainBike)
      raise "You can't add rear suspension unless you have front suspension"
    end
    self.type_code = :full_suspension
    @bike_type = FullSuspensionMountainBike.new({
      :tire_width => @bike_type.tire_width,
      :front_fork_travel => @bike_type.front_fork_travel,
      :front_suspension_price => @bike_type.front_suspension_price,
      :base_price => @bike_type.base_price,
      :commission => @bike_type.commission
    }.merge(params))
  end
```

Then we can change the callers of `MountainBike` and remove the `case` statement from our `initialize` method.

```
bike = MountainBike.new(
  :type => :front_suspension,
  :tire_width => @tire_width,
  :front_fork_travel => @front_fork_travel,
  :front_suspension_price => @front_suspension_price,
  :base_price => @base_price,
  :commission => @commission
```

becomes

```
bike = MountainBike.new(FrontSuspensionMountainBike.new(
  :type => :front_suspension,
  :tire_width => @tire_width,
  :front_fork_travel => @front_fork_travel,
  :front_suspension_price => @front_suspension_price,
  :base_price => @base_price,
  :commission => @commission
```

And with most of the instance data being set directly on the type object, we can remove all that instance variable setting in MountainBike.

```
class MountainBike...
  def initialize(bike_type)
    set_state_from_hash(params)
    @bike_type = bike_type
  end

  def set_state_from_hash(hash)
    @base_price = hash[:base_price] if hash.has_key?(:base_price)
    if hash.has_key?(:front_suspension_price)
      @front_suspension_price = hash[:front_suspension_price]
    end
    if hash.has_key?(:rear_suspension_price)
      @rear_suspension_price = hash[:rear_suspension_price]
    end
    if hash.has_key?(:commission)
      @commission = hash[:commission]
    end
    @tire_width = hash[:tire_width] if hash.has_key?(:tire_width)
    if hash.has_key?(:front_fork_travel)
      @front_fork_travel = hash[:front_fork_travel]
    end
    if hash.has_key?(:rear_fork_travel)
      @rear_fork_travel = hash[:rear_fork_travel]
    end
    self.type_code = hash[:type_code] if hash.has_key?(:type_code)
  end
end
```

Rather than reach into the type object when we're upgrading, we can use Extract Method to encapsulate the upgradable parameters.

```
class RigidMountainBike...
  attr_reader :tire_width, :front_fork_travel, :front_suspension_price,
              :base_price, :commission

  def upgradable_parameters
    {
      :tire_width => @tire_width,
      :base_price => @base_price,
      :commission => @commission
    }
  end
end
```

```
class FrontSuspensionMountainBike...
  attr_reader :tire_width, :front_fork_travel, :front_suspension_price,
              :base_price, :commission
  def upgradable_parameters
    {
      :tire_width => @tire_width,
      :front_fork_travel => @front_fork_travel,
      :front_suspension_price => @front_suspension_price,
      :base_price => @base_price,
      :commission => @commission
    }
  end
end

class MountainBike...
  def add_front_suspension(params)
    @bike_type = FrontSuspensionMountainBike.new(
      @bike_type.upgradable_parameters.merge(params)
    )
  end

  def add_rear_suspension(params)
    unless @bike_type.is_a?(FrontSuspensionMountainBike)
      raise "You can't add rear suspension unless you have front suspension"
    end
    @bike_type = FullSuspensionMountainBike.new(
      @bike_type.upgradable_parameters.merge(params)
    )
  end
end
```

We could then use Extract Module to remove any duplication in our new classes.

Replace Subclass with Fields

You have subclasses that vary only in methods that return constant data.

Change the methods to superclass fields and eliminate the subclasses.

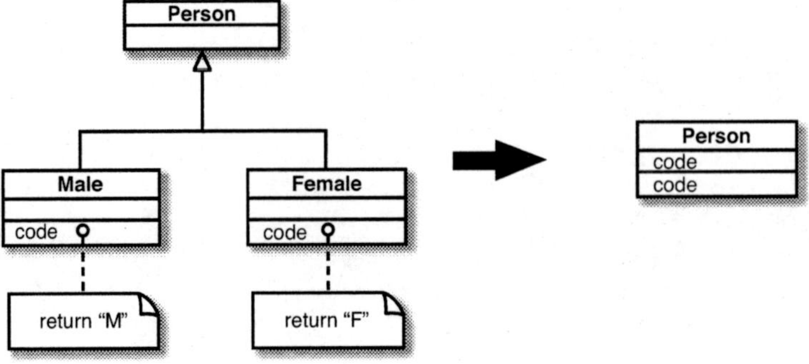

Motivation

You create subclasses to add features or allow behavior to vary. One form of variant behavior is the constant method [Beck]. A constant method is one that returns a hard-coded value. This can be useful on subclasses that return different values for an accessor. You define the accessor in the superclass and override it with different values on the subclass.

Although constant methods are useful, a subclass that consists only of constant methods is not doing enough to justify its existence. You can remove such subclasses completely by putting fields in the superclass. By doing that you remove the extra complexity of the subclasses.

Mechanics

1. Use Replace Constructor with Factory Method on the subclasses.

2. Modify the superclass constructor to initialize a field for each constant method.

3. Add or modify subclass constructors to call the new superclass constructor.

4. Test.

5. Implement each constant method in the superclass to return the field and remove the method from the subclasses.

6. Test after each removal.

7. When all the subclass methods have been removed, use Inline Method to inline the constructor into the factory method of the superclass.

8. Test.

9. Remove the subclass.

10. Test.

11. Repeat inlining the constructor and eliminating each subclass until they are all gone.

Example

I begin with a `Person` and sex-oriented subclasses:

```
class Person...

class Female < Person

  def female?
    true
  end

  def code
    'F'
  end

end

class Male < Person

  def female?
    false
  end

  def code
    'M'
  end

end
```

Here the only difference between the subclasses is that they have implementations of methods that return a hard-coded constant method [Beck]. I remove these lazy subclasses.

First I need to use Replace Constructor with Factory Method. In this case I want a factory method for each subclass:

```
class Person...

  def self.create_female
    Female.new
  end

  def self.create_male
    Male.new
  end
```

I then replace calls of the form:

```
bree = Female.new
```

with

```
bree = Person.create_female
```

Once I've replaced all of these calls I shouldn't have any references to the subclasses. I can check this with a text search or by enclosing the class in a module namespace and running the tests.

I add an `initialize` method on the superclass, assigning an instance variable for each:

```
class Person...

  def initialize(female, code)
    @female = female
    @code = code
  end
```

I add constructors that call this new constructor:


```
class Female...
  def initialize
    super(true, 'F')
  end

class Male...
  def initialize
    super(false, 'M')
  end
```

With that done I can run my tests. The fields are created and initialized, but so far they aren't being used. I can now start bringing the fields into play by putting accessors on the superclass and eliminating the subclass methods:

```
class Person...

  def female?
    @female
  end

class Female
  def female?
    true
  end
```

I can do this one field and one subclass at a time or all in one go if I'm feeling lucky.

After all the subclasses are empty, I use Inline Method to inline the subclass constructor into the superclass:

```
class Person...

  def self.create_female
    Person.new(true, 'M')
  end
```

After testing I delete the `Female` class and repeat the process for the `Male` class.

Lazily Initialized Attribute

Initialize an attribute on access instead of at construction time.

```
class Employee
  def initialize
    @emails = []
  end
end
```

```
class Employee
  def emails
```

```
    @emails ||= []
  end
end
```

Motivation

The motivation for converting attributes to be lazily initialized is for code readability purposes. While the preceding example is trivial, when the `Employee` class has multiple attributes that need to be initialized the constructor needs to contain all the initialization logic. Classes that initialize instance variables in the constructor need to worry about both attributes and instance variables. The procedural behavior of initializing each attribute in a constructor is sometimes unnecessary and less maintainable than a class that deals exclusively with attributes. Lazily Initialized Attributes can encapsulate all their initialization logic within the methods themselves.

Mechanics

1. Move the initialization logic to the attribute reader.

2. Test.

Example using ||=

The following code is an `Employee` class with the `email` attribute initialized in the constructor.

```
class Employee
  attr_reader :emails, :voice_mails

  def initialize
    @emails = []
    @voice_mails = []
  end
end
```


Moving to a Lazily Initialized Attribute generally means moving the initialization logic to the getter method and initializing on the first access.

```
class Employee
  def emails
```

```
    @emails ||= []
  end

  def voice_mails
    @voice_mails ||= []
  end
end
```

Example Using instance_variable_defined?

Using ||= for Lazily Initialized Attributes is a common idiom; however, this idiom falls down when nil or false are valid values for the attribute.

```
class Employee...
  def initialize
    @assistant = Employee.find_by_boss_id(self.id)
  end
```

In the preceding example it's not practical to use an ||= operator for a Lazily Initialized Attribute because the `find_by_boss_id` might return `nil`. In the case where nil is returned, each time the `assistant` attribute is accessed another database trip will occur. A superior solution is to use code similar to the following example that utilizes the `instance_variable_defined?` method that was introduced in Ruby 1.8.6.

```
class Employee...
  def assistant
    unless instance_variable_defined? :@assistant
      @assistant = Employee.find_by_boss_id(self.id)
    end
    @assistant
  end
```

Eagerly Initialized Attribute

Initialize an attribute at construction time instead of on the first access.

```
class Employee
  def emails
    @emails ||= []
  end
end
```

```
class Employee
  def initialize
    @emails = []
  end
end
```

Motivation

The motivation for converting attributes to be eagerly initialized is for code readability purposes. Lazily initialized attributes change their value upon access. Lazily initialized attributes can be problematic to debug because their values change upon access. Eagerly Initialized Attributes initialize their attributes in the constructor of the class. This leads to encapsulating all initialization logic in the constructor and consistent results when querying the value of the instance variable.

Discussion

I prefer Lazily Initialized Attributes, but Martin prefers Eagerly Initialized Attributes. I opened up the discussion to the reviewers of *Refactoring: Ruby Edition* and my current ThoughtWorks team, but in the end it was split 50/50 on preference. Based on that fact, I told Martin I didn't think it was a good candidate for *Refactoring: Ruby Edition*. Not surprisingly, he had a better solution: Provide examples of both refactoring to Eagerly Initialized Attribute and refactoring to Lazily Initialized Attribute.

Martin and I agree that this isn't something worth being religious about. Additionally, we both think it's valuable for a team to standardize on Lazily or Eagerly Initialized Attributes.

Mechanics

1. Move the initialization logic to the constructor.

2. Test.

Example

The following code is an `Employee` class with both the `email` and `voice_mail` attributes lazily initialized.

```
class Employee
  def emails
    @emails ||= []
  end

  def voice_mails
    @voice_mails ||= []
  end
end
```

Moving to an Eagerly Initialized Attribute generally means moving the initialization logic from the getter methods into the constructor.

```
class Employee
  attr_reader :emails, :voice_mails

  def initialize
    @emails = []
    @voice_mails = []
  end
end
```

Chapter 9

Simplifying Conditional Expressions

Conditional logic has a way of getting tricky, so here are a number of refactorings you can use to simplify it. The core refactoring here is Decompose Conditional, which entails breaking a conditional into pieces. It is important because it separates the switching logic from the details of what happens.

The other refactorings in this chapter involve other important cases. Use Recompose Conditional to use more readable, idiomatic Ruby. Use Consolidate Conditional Expression when you have several tests and all have the same effect. Use Consolidate Duplicate Conditional Fragments to remove any duplication within the conditional code.

If you are working with code developed in a one exit point mentality, you often find control flags that allow the conditions to work with this rule. I don't follow the rule about one exit point from a method. Hence I use Replace Nested Conditional with Guard Clauses to clarify special case conditionals and Remove Control Flag to get rid of the awkward control flags.

Object-Oriented programs often have less conditional behavior than procedural programs because much of the conditional behavior is handled by polymorphism. Polymorphism is better because the caller does not need to know about the conditional behavior, and it is thus easier to extend the conditions. As a result, Object-Oriented programs rarely have `case` statements. Any that show up are prime candidates for Replace Conditional with Polymorphism.

One of the most useful, but less obvious, uses of polymorphism is to use Introduce Null Object to remove checks for a null value.

Decompose Conditional

You have a complicated conditional (if-then-else) statement.

Extract methods from the condition, "then" part, and "else" parts.

```
if date < SUMMER_START || date > SUMMER_END
  charge = quantity * @winter_rate + @winter_service_charge
else
  charge = quantity * @summer_rate
end
```

```
if not_summer(date)
  charge = winter_charge(quantity)
else
  charge = summer_charge(quantity)
end
```

Motivation

One of the most common areas of complexity in a program lies in complex conditional logic. As you write code to test conditions and to do various things depending on various conditions, you quickly end up with a pretty long method. Length of a method is in itself a factor that makes it harder to read, but conditions increase the difficulty. The problem usually lies in the fact that the code, both in the condition checks and in the actions, tells you what happens but can easily obscure why it happens.

As with any large block of code, you can make your intention clearer by decomposing it and replacing chunks of code with a method call named after the intention of that block of code. With conditions you can receive further benefit by doing this for the conditional part and each of the alternatives. This way you highlight the condition and make it clear the logic on which you are branching. You also highlight the reason for the branching.

Mechanics

1. Extract the condition into its own method.

2. Extract the "then" part and the "else" part into their own methods.

If I find a nested conditional, I usually first look to see whether I should use Replace Nested Conditional with Guard Clauses. If that does not make sense, I decompose each of the conditionals.

Example

Suppose I'm calculating the charge for something that has separate rates for winter and summer:

```
if date < SUMMER_START || date > SUMMER_END
  charge = quantity * @winter_rate + @winter_service_charge
else
  charge = quantity * @summer_rate
end
```

I extract the conditional and each leg as follows:

```
if not_summer(date)
  charge = winter_charge(quantity)
else
  charge = summer_charge(quantity)
end

def not_summer(date)
  date < SUMMER_START || date > SUMMER_END
end

def winter_charge(quantity)
  quantity * @winter_rate + @winter_service_charge
end

def summer_charge(quantity)
  quantity * @summer_rate
end
```

Here I show the result of the complete refactoring for clarity. In practice, however, I do each extraction separately and test after each one.

Many programmers don't extract the condition parts in situations such as this. The conditions often are short, so it hardly seems worth it. Although the condition is often short, there often is a big gap between the intention of the code and its body. Even in this little case, reading "`not_summer date`" conveys a clearer message to me than does the original code. With the original I have to look at the code and figure out what it is doing. It's not difficult to do that here, but even so the extracted method reads more like a comment.

Recompose Conditional

You have conditional code that is unnecessarily verbose and does not use the most readable Ruby construct.

Replace the conditional code with the more idiomatic Ruby construct.

```
parameters = params ? params : []
```

```
parameters = params || []
```

Motivation

Ruby has some expressive constructs for forming conditional logic with which newcomers to the language aren't necessarily familiar. Throughout this book we have been on a constant quest to improve the expressiveness of our code, and choosing the best construct from the Ruby language is a great place to start.

Example: Replace Ternary Assignment with "Or" Assignment

In this example, we want to default our parameters variable to an empty array, if the params method returns nil.

```
parameters = params ? params : []
```

We can use the "Or" operator to make the assignment more expressive:

```
parameters = params || []
```

Example: Replace Conditional with Explicit Return

In this method we check the result of `days_rented` to determine how many reward points to return:

```
def reward_points
  if days_rented > 2
```

```
    2
  else
    1
  end
end
```

We can make our code more English-like if we use the "return if" syntax:

```
def reward_points
  return 2 if days_rented > 2
  1
end
```

Consolidate Conditional Expression

You have a sequence of conditional tests with the same result.

Combine them into a single conditional expression and extract it.

```
def disability_amount
  return 0 if @seniority < 2
  return 0 if @months_disabled > 12
  return 0 if @is_part_time
  # compute the disability amount
```

```
def disability_amount
  return 0 if ineligable_for_disability?
  # compute the disability amount
```

Motivation

Sometimes you see a series of conditional checks in which each check is different yet the resulting action is the same. When you see this, you should use ands and ors to consolidate them into a single conditional check with a single result.

Consolidating the conditional code is important for two reasons. First, it makes the check clearer by showing that you are really making a single check that's or-ing the other checks together. The sequence has the same effect, but it communicates carrying out a sequence of separate checks that just happen to be done together. The second reason for this refactoring is that it often sets you up for Extract Method. Extracting a condition is one of the most useful things you can do to clarify your code. It replaces a statement of what you are doing with why you are doing it.

The reasons in favor of consolidating conditionals also point to reasons for not doing it. If you think the checks are really independent and shouldn't be thought of as a single check, don't do the refactoring. Your code already communicates your intention.

Mechanics

1. Check that none of the conditionals has side effects.

   ⟹ *If there are side effects, you won't be able to do this refactoring.*

2. Replace the string of conditionals with a single conditional statement using logical operators.

3. Test.

4. Consider using Extract Method on the condition.

Example: Ors

The state of the code is along the lines of the following:

```
def disability_amount
  return 0 if @seniority < 2
  return 0 if @months_disabled > 12
  return 0 if @is_part_time
  # compute the disability amount
```

Here we see a sequence of conditional checks that all result in the same thing. With sequential code like this, the checks are the equivalent of an or statement:

```
def disability_amount
  return 0 if @seniority < 2 || @months_disabled > 12 || @is_part_time
  # compute the disability amount
  ...
```


Now I can look at the condition and use Extract Method to communicate what the condition is looking for:

```
def disability_amount
  return 0 if ineligable_for_disability?
  # compute the disability amount
  ...
end

def ineligible_for_disability?
  @seniority < 2 || @months_disabled > 12 || @is_part_time
end
```

Example: Ands

That example showed ors, but I can do the same with ands. Here the setup is something like the following:

```
if on_vacation?
  if length_of_service > 10
    return 1
  end
end
0.5
```

This would be changed to

```
if on_vacation? && length_of_service > 10
  return 1
end
0.5
```

You may well find you get a combination of these that yields an expression with ands, ors, and nots. In these cases the conditions may be messy, so I try to use Extract Method on parts of the expression to make it simpler.

If the routine I'm looking at tests only the condition and returns a value, I can increase fluency by moving the conditional onto the same line as the return statement:

```
if on_vacation? && length_of_service > 10
  return 1
end
0.5
```

becomes

```
return 1 if on_vacation? && length_of_service > 10
0.5
```

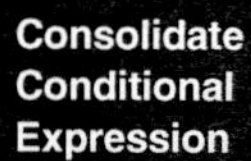

Consolidate Duplicate Conditional Fragments

The same fragment of code is in all branches of a conditional expression.

Move it outside the expression.

```
if special_deal?
  total = price * 0.95
  send_order
else
  total = price * 0.98
  send_order
end
```

```
if special_deal?
  total = price * 0.95
else
  total = price * 0.98
end
send_order
```

Motivation

Sometimes you find the same code executed in all legs of a conditional. In that case you should move the code to outside the conditional. This makes clearer what varies and what stays the same.

Mechanics

1. Identify code that is executed the same way regardless of the condition.

2. If the common code is at the beginning, move it to before the conditional.

3. If the common code is at the end, move it to after the conditional.

4. If the common code is in the middle, look to see whether the code before or after it changes anything. If it does, you can move the common code

forward or backward to the ends. You can then move it as described for code at the end or the beginning.

5. If there is more than a single statement, you should extract that code into a method.

Example

You find this situation with code such as the following:

```
if special_deal?
  total = price * 0.95
  send_order
else
  total = price * 0.98
  send_order
end
```

Because the `send_order` method is executed in either case, I should move it out of the conditional:

```
if special_deal?
  total = price * 0.95
else
  total = price * 0.98
end
send_order
```

The same situation can apply to exceptions. If code is repeated after an exception-causing statement in the `begin` block and all the `rescue` blocks, I can move it to the `ensure` block.

Remove Control Flag

You have a variable that is acting as a control flag for a series of boolean expressions.

Use a break or return instead.

Motivation

When you have a series of conditional expressions, you often see a control flag used to determine when to stop looking, as in the following code:

```
done = false

until done do
  if (condition)
    # do something
    done = true
  end
  value -= 1
end
```

Such control flags are more trouble than they are worth. They come from rules of structured programming that call for routines with one entry and one exit point. I agree with (and modern languages enforce) one entry point, but the one exit point rule leads you to convoluted conditionals with these awkward flags in the code. This is why languages have `break` and `next` (or `continue`) statements to get out of a complex conditional. It is often surprising what you can do when you get rid of a control flag. The real purpose of the conditional becomes so much clearer.

Mechanics

The obvious way to deal with control flags is to use the break or next statements present in Ruby.

1. Find the value of the control flag that gets you out of the logic statement.

2. Replace assignments of the break-out value with a `break` or `next` statement.

3. Test after each replacement.

Another approach, also usable in languages without break and next, is as follows:

1. Extract the logic into a method.

2. Find the value of the control flag that gets you out of the logic statement.

3. Replace assignments of the break-out value with a return.

4. Test after each replacement.

Even in languages with a `break` or `next`, I usually prefer to use an extraction and return. The return clearly signals that no more code in the method is executed. If you have that kind of code, you often need to extract that piece anyway.

Keep an eye on whether the control flag also indicates result information. If it does, you still need the control flag if you use the break, or you can return the value if you have extracted a method.

Example: Simple Control Flag Replaced with Break

The following function checks to see whether a list of people contains a couple of hard-coded suspicious characters:

```
def check_security(people)
  found = false
  people.each do |person|
    unless found
      if person == "Don"
        send_alert
        found = true
      end
      if person == "John"
        send_alert
        found = true
      end
    end
  end
end
```

In a case like this, it is easy to see the control flag. It's the piece that sets the found variable to true. I can introduce the breaks one at a time:

```
def check_security(people)
  found = false
  people.each do |person|
    unless found
      if person == "Don"
        send_alert
        break
      end
      if person == "John"
        send_alert
```

```
        found = true
      end
    end
  end
end
```

until I have them all:

```
def check_security(people)
  found = false
  people.each do |person|
    unless found
      if person == "Don"
        send_alert
        break
      end
      if person == "John"
        send_alert
        break
      end
    end
  end
end
```

Then I can remove all references to the control flag:

```
def check_security(people)
  people.each do |person|
    if person == "Don"
      send_alert
      break
    end
    if person == "John"
      send_alert
      break
    end
  end
end
```

Example: Using Return with a Control Flag Result

The other style of this refactoring uses a return. I illustrate this with a variant that uses the control flag as a result value:

```
def check_security(people)
```

```
  found = ""
  people.each do |person|
    if found == ""
      if person == "Don"
        send_alert
        found = "Don"
      end
      if person == "John"
        send_alert
        found = "John"
      end
    end
  end
  some_later_code(found)
end
```

Here found does two things. It indicates a result and acts as a control flag. When I see this, I like to extract the code that is determining found into its own method:

```
def check_security(people)
  found = found_miscreant(people)
  some_later_code(found)
end

def found_miscreant(people)
  found = ""
  people.each do |person|
    if found == ""
      if person == "Don"
        send_alert
        found = "Don"
      end
      if person == "John"
        send_alert
        found = "John"
      end
    end
  end
  found
end
```

Then I can replace the control flag with a return:

```
def found_miscreant(people)
```

```
  found = ""
  people.each do |person|
    if found == ""
      if person == "Don"
        send_alert
        return "Don"
      end
      if person == "John"
        send_alert
        found = "John"
      end
    end
  end
  found
end
```

until I have removed the control flag:

```
def found_miscreant(people)
  people.each do |person|
    if person == "Don"
      send_alert
      return "Don"
    end
    if person == "John"
      send_alert
      return "John"
    end
  end
  ""
end
```

You can also use the return style when you're not returning a value. Just use return without the argument.

Our refactoring is not yet finished—the found_miscreant method is a function with side effects. To fix it, we need to use Separate Query from Modifier. You'll find this example continued there.

Replace Nested Conditional with Guard Clauses

A method has conditional behavior that does not make clear the normal path of execution.

Use guard clauses for all the special cases.

```
def pay_amount
  if @dead
    result = dead_amount
  else
    if @separated
      result = separated_amount
    else
      if @retired
        result = retired_amount
      else
        result = normal_pay_amount
      end
    end
  end
  result
end
```

```
def pay_amount
  return dead_amount if @dead
  return separated_amount if @separated
  return retired_amount if @retired
  normal_pay_amount
end
```

Motivation

I often find that conditional expressions come in two forms. The first form is a check where either course is part of the normal behavior. The second form is a situation in which one answer from the conditional indicates normal behavior and the other indicates an unusual condition.

These kinds of conditionals have different intentions, and these intentions should come through in the code. If both are part of normal behavior, use a condition with an `if` and an `else` leg. If the condition is an unusual condition, check the condition and return if the condition is true. This kind of check is often called a guard clause [Beck].

The key point about Replace Nested Conditional with Guard Clauses is one of emphasis. If you are using an if-then-else construct you are giving equal weight to the `if` leg and the `else` leg. This communicates to the reader that the legs are equally likely and important. Instead the guard clause says, "This is rare, and if it happens, do something and get out."

I often find I use Replace Nested Conditional with Guard Clauses when I'm working with a programmer who has been taught to have only one entry point and one exit point from a method. One entry point is enforced by modern languages, and one exit point is really not a useful rule. Clarity is the key principle: If the method is clearer with one exit point, use one exit point; otherwise don't.

Mechanics

1. For each check put in the guard clause.

   ⟹ *The guard clause either returns, or throws an exception.*

2. Test after each check is replaced with a guard clause.

   ⟹ *If all guard clauses yield the same result, use Consolidate Conditional Expressions.*

Example

Imagine a run of a payroll system in which you have special rules for dead, separated, and retired employees. Such cases are unusual, but they do happen from time to time.

If I see the code like this:

```
def pay_amount
  if @dead
    result = dead_amount
  else
    if @separated
      result = separated_amount
    else
      if @retired
        result = retired_amount
      else
        result = normal_pay_amount
      end
    end
  end
  result
```

```
end
```

Then the checking is masking the normal course of action behind the checking. So instead it is clearer to use guard clauses. I can introduce these one at a time. I like to start at the top:

```
def pay_amount
  return dead_amount if @dead
  if @separated
    result = separated_amount
  else
    if @retired
      result = retired_amount
    else
      result = normal_pay_amount
    end
  end
  result
end
```

I continue one at a time:

```
def pay_amount
  return dead_amount if @dead
  return separated_amount if @separated
  if @retired
    result = retired_amount
  else
    result = normal_pay_amount
  end
  result
end
```

and then:

```
def pay_amount
  return dead_amount if @dead
  return separated_amount if @separated
  return retired_amount if @retired
  result = normal_pay_amount
  result
end
```


By this point the `result` temp isn't pulling its weight so I nuke it:

```
def pay_amount
  return dead_amount if @dead
```

```
  return separated_amount if @separated
  return retired_amount if @retired
  normal_pay_amount
end
```

Nested conditional code often is written by programmers who are taught to have one exit point from a method. I've found that is a too simplistic rule. When I have no further interest in a method, I signal my lack of interest by getting out. Directing the reader to look at an empty else block only gets in the way of comprehension.

Example: Reversing the Conditions

In reviewing the manuscript of this book, Joshua Kerievsky pointed out that you often do Replace Nested Conditional with Guard Clauses by reversing the conditional expressions. He kindly came up with an example to save further taxing of my imagination:

```
def adjusted_capital
  result = 0.0
  if @capital > 0.0
    if @interest_rate > 0.0 && @duration > 0.0
      result = (@income / @duration) * ADJ_FACTOR
    end
  end
  result
end
```

Again I make the replacements one at a time, but this time I reverse the conditional as I put in the guard clause:

```
def adjusted_capital
  result = 0.0
  return result if @capital <= 0.0
  if @interest_rate > 0.0 && @duration > 0.0
    result = (@income / @duration) * ADJ_FACTOR
  end
  result
end
```


Because the next conditional is a bit more complicated, I can reverse it in two steps. First I add a not:

```
def adjusted_capital
  result = 0.0
```

```
  return result if @capital <= 0.0
  return result if !(@interest_rate > 0.0 && @duration > 0.0)
  result = (@income / @duration) * ADJ_FACTOR
  result
end
```

Leaving nots in a conditional like that twists my mind around at a painful angle, so I simplify it as follows:

```
def adjusted_capital
  result = 0.0
  return result if @capital <= 0.0
  return result if @interest_rate <= 0.0 || @duration <= 0.0
  result = (@income / @duration) * ADJ_FACTOR
  result
end
```

In these situations I prefer to put an explicit value on the returns from the guards. That way you can easily see the result of the guard's failing. (I would also consider Replace Magic Number with Symbolic Constant here.)

```
def adjusted_capital
  result = 0.0
  return 0.0 if @capital <= 0.0
  return 0.0 if @interest_rate <= 0.0 || @duration <= 0.0
  result = (@income / @duration) * ADJ_FACTOR
  result
end
```

With that done I can also remove the temp:

```
def adjusted_capital
  return 0.0 if @capital <= 0.0
  return 0.0 if @interest_rate <= 0.0 || @duration <= 0.0
  (@income / @duration) * ADJ_FACTOR
end
```

Replace Conditional with Polymorphism

You have a conditional that chooses different behavior depending on the type of an object.

Move each leg of the conditional to a method in an object that can be called polymorphically.

```
class MountainBike...
  def price
    case @type_code
      when :rigid
        (1 + @commission) * @base_price
      when :front_suspension
        (1 + @commission) * @base_price + @front_suspension_price
      when :full_suspension
        (1 + @commission) * @base_price + @front_suspension_price +
        @rear_suspension_price
    end
  end
end
```

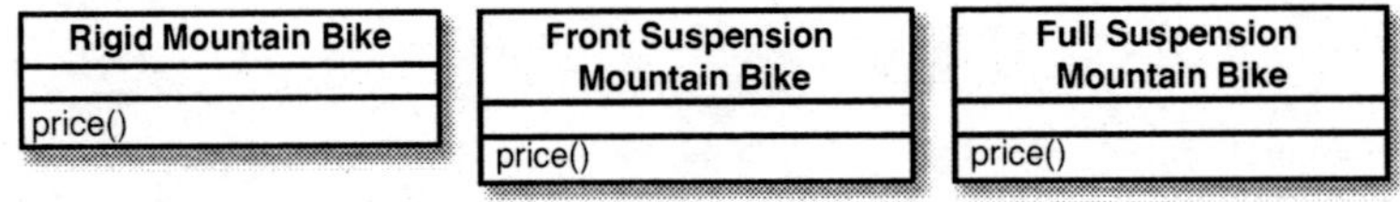

Motivation

One of the grandest sounding words in object jargon is polymorphism. The essence of polymorphsim is that it allows you to avoid writing an explicit conditional when you have objects whose behavior varies depending on their types.

As a result you find that case statements or if-then-else statements that switch on type codes are much less common in an Object-Oriented program.

Polymorphism gives you many advantages. The biggest gain occurs when this same set of conditions appears in many places in the program. If you want to add a new type, you have to find and update all the conditionals. But with polymorphism you just create a new class and provide the appropriate methods. Clients of the class don't need to know about the polymorphism, which reduces the dependencies in your system and makes it easier to update.

Ruby's duck typing makes it easy to introduce polymorphism. In a statically typed language like Java, you need inheritance or implementation of an interface to be able to call a method polymorphically. But in Ruby, an object's current set of methods—not its inheritance from a particular class—determines its valid semantics. So long as objects A and B have the same method, you can call them in the same way.

Mechanics

Polymorphism in Ruby can be achieved in a couple of ways. In its simplest form, you can implement the same method signature on multiple objects and call these methods polymorphically. You can introduce a module hierarchy and have the method that is to be called polymorphically on the module. Or you can introduce an inheritance hierarchy and have the method that is to be called polymorphically on the subclasses. In each case, the mechanics are the same.

The code you target may be a `case` statement or an `if` statement.

1. If the conditional statement is one part of a larger method, take apart the conditional statement and use Extract Method.

2. If necessary use Move Method to place the conditional at the appropriate place in the object structure.

3. Pick one of the polymorphic objects. Create a method on the polymorphic object that will override the conditional statement method. Copy the body of that leg of the conditional statement into the polymorphic method and adjust it to fit.

4. Test.

5. Remove the copied leg of the conditional statement.

6. Test.

7. Repeat with each leg of the conditional statement until all legs are turned into polymorphic methods.

Example

This is the same example we used in Replace Type Code with Polymorphism. The important thing to note is that to do this refactoring you need to have the polymorphic objects in place—either objects that you are calling polymorphically (as in this case), or a module or inheritance hierarchy. For an example using a module hierarchy see Replace Type Code with Module Extension. For an example using inheritance, see Extract Subclass.

We already have our clients creating specific mountain bike objects, and calling them polymorphically:

```
rigid_bike = RigidMountainBike.new(
  :type_code => :rigid
  :base_price => 300,
  :commission => 0.1
)
total += rigid_bike.price
...

front_suspension_bike = FrontSuspensionMountainBike.new(
  :type_code => :front_suspension,
  :base_price => 500,
  :commission => 0.15
)
total += front_suspension_bike.price
```

Each mountain bike class includes a common module that has the conditional logic:

```
module MountainBike...
  def price
    case @type_code
      when :rigid
        (1 + @commission) * @base_price
      when :front_suspension
        (1 + @commission) * @base_price + @front_suspension_price
      when :full_suspension
        (1 + @commission) * @base_price + @front_suspension_price +
        @rear_suspension_price
    end
  end
end

class RigidMountainBike
  include MountainBike
end
```

```
class FrontSuspensionMountainBike
  include MountainBike
end

class FullSuspensionMountainBike
  include MountainBike
end
```

The case statement is already nicely extracted and placed on our polymorphic objects via the module, so there is nothing to do there. For an example that isn't so nicely factored, see "Replacing the Conditional Logic on Price Code with Polymorphism" in Chapter 1, "Refactoring, a First Example."

I can go to work immediately on the case statement. It's rather like the way small boys kill insects: I remove one leg at a time. First I copy the RigidMountainBike leg of the case statement onto the RigidMountainBike class.

```
class RigidMountainBike
  include MountainBike

  def price
    (1 + @commission) * @base_price
  end
end
```

This new method overrides the whole case statement for rigid mountain bikes. Because I'm paranoid, I sometimes put a trap in the case statement:

```
module MountainBike...
  def price
    case @type_code
      when :rigid
        raise "should never get here"
      when :front_suspension
        (1 + @commission) * @base_price + @front_suspension_price
      when :full_suspension
        (1 + @commission) * @base_price + @front_suspension_price +
        @rear_suspension_price
    end
  end
end
```

I carry on until all the legs are removed. I can delete the price method on the MountainBike module when I'm done. If this is the only method left, I can remove the module too.


```
class RigidMountainBike
  include MountainBike
```

```
  def price
    (1 + @commission) * @base_price
  end
end

class FrontSuspensionMountainBike
  include MountainBike

  def price
    (1 + @commission) * @base_price + @front_suspension_price
  end
end

class FullSuspensionMountainBike
  include MountainBike
  def price
    (1 + @commission) * @base_price + @front_suspension_price +
    @rear_suspension_price
  end
end

module MountainBike...
  def price
    case @type_code
    ...
    end
  end
end
```

Introduce Null Object

You have repeated checks for a nil value.

Replace the nil value with a null object.

```
plan = customer ? customer.plan : BillingPlan.basic
```

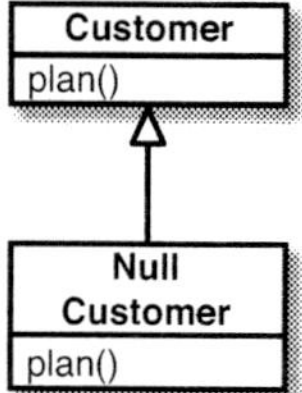

Motivation

The essence of polymorphism is that instead of asking an object what type it is and then invoking some behavior based on the answer, you just invoke the behavior. The object, depending on its type, does the right thing. One of the less intuitive places to do this is where you have a null value in a field. I'll let Ron Jeffries, one of the original implementers of eXtreme Programming, tell the story:

Ron Jeffries

We first started using the null object pattern when Rich Garzaniti found that a lot of code in the system would check objects for presence before sending a message to the object. We might ask an object for its person, then ask the result whether it was null. If the object was present, we would ask it for its rate. We were doing this in several places, and the resulting duplicate code was getting annoying.

So we implemented a missing-person object that answered a zero rate (we call our null objects missing objects). Soon missing person knew a lot of methods, such as rate. Now we have more than 80 null-object classes.

Our most common use of null objects is in the display of information. When we display, for example, a person, the object may or may not have any of perhaps 20 instance variables. If these were allowed to be null, the printing of a person would be complex. Instead we plug in various null objects, all of which know how to display themselves in an orderly way. This got rid of huge amounts of procedural code.

Our most clever use of null objects is the missing Gemstone session. We use the Gemstone database for production, but we prefer to develop without it and push the new code to Gemstone every week or so. There are various points in the code where we have to log in to a Gemstone session. When we are running without Gemstone, we simply plug in a missing Gemstone session. It looks the same as the real thing but allows us to develop and test without realizing the database isn't there.

Another helpful use of null objects is the missing bin. A bin is a collection of payroll values that often have to be summed or looped over. If a particular bin doesn't exist, we answer a missing bin, which acts just like an empty bin. The missing bin knows it has zero balance and no values. By using this approach, we eliminate the creation of tens of empty bins for each of our thousands of employees.

An interesting characteristic of using null objects is that things almost never blow up. Because the null object responds to all the same messages as a real one, the system generally behaves normally. This can sometimes make it difficult to detect or find a problem, because nothing ever breaks. Of course, as soon as you begin inspecting the objects, you'll find the null object somewhere where it shouldn't be.

Remember, null objects are always constant; nothing about them ever changes. Accordingly, we implement them using the Singleton pattern [Gang of Four]. Whenever you ask, for example, for a missing person, you always get the single instance of that class.

You can find more details about the null object pattern in Woolf [Woolf]. It is an example of a Special Case, outlined in Fowler [Fowler].

Ruby allows us two main options for implementing the null object. The traditional route (and the only one available in statically typed languages without extracting an interface on the original class) is to create a subclass of the source class. This way the null object will respond to all the messages that the source class responds to. This is convenient but may lead to bugs if the null object lands in a spot where the default behavior of the source class is undesirable. The other option is to create a new class that does not inherit from the source class, only defining the methods that you want to be able to handle from the null object. This may be more work but is less likely to introduce subtle misbehavior.

When not subclassing the source class, there's another option to consider: whether to implement a message-eating null object. A message-eating null will accept any message sent to it and return another message-eating null object. Ruby's `nil`, the single instance of `NilClass`, is not a message-eating null, but in some languages, including Objective-C, `nil` will accept any message. This provides an interesting halfway point between the levels of effort and risk undertaken with either of the options discussed previously. By making your null object eat all messages, you avoid any strange default behavior in the source class, but you also avoid having to implement every method that might be called on the null object.

There's a third option for Introduce Null Object in Ruby: You could add methods to `NilClass` itself. While this option might be valid in certain specific cases, muddying the interface of NilClass or changing the behavior of such a low-level object should not be undertaken lightly.

When deciding on a name for your Null Object, it is better to use a more meaningful and specific name (a la "`UnknownCustomer`" or even "`MissingPerson`") and avoid the confusion or overloading of "null" or "nil," respectively.

Mechanics

1. Create your null object class, optionally as a subclass of the source class. Create a `missing?` method on the source class and the null class to test for nullity. For the source class it should return `false`, for the null class it should return `true`.

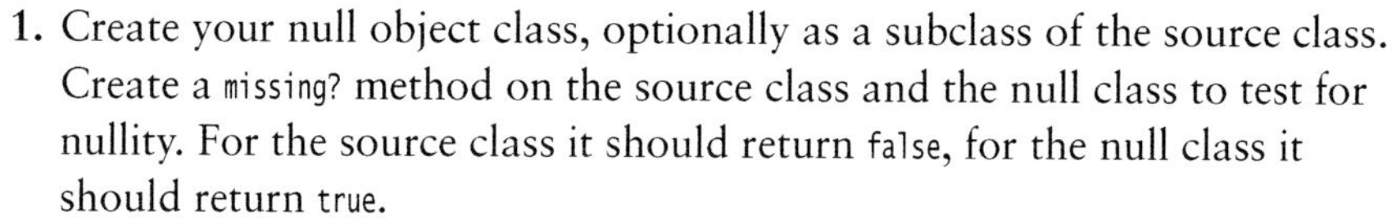

   ⟹ *You may find it useful to create a mixin module for the test method so that "nullability" is declared clearly.*

   ⟹ *As an alternative you can use a testing interface to test for nullness.*

2. Find all places that can give out `nil` when asked for a source object. Replace them to give out the null object instead.

3. Find all places that compare a variable of the source type with null and replace them with a call to `missing?`.

   ⟹ *You may be able to do this by replacing one source and its clients at a time and testing between working on sources.*

   ⟹ *A few assertions that check for null in places where you should no longer see it can be useful.*

4. Test.

5. Look for cases in which clients invoke an operation if not null and do some alternative behavior if null.

6. For each of these cases define the method in the null class with the alternative behavior.

7. Remove the condition check for those that use the overridden behavior and test.

Example

A utility company knows about sites: the houses and apartments that use the utility's services. At any time a site has a customer.

```
class Site...

  attr_reader :customer
```

There are various features of a customer. I look at three of them.

```
class Customer...
  attr_reader :name, :plan, :history
```

The payment history has its own features:

```
class PaymentHistory...
  def weeks_delinquent_in_last_year
    ...
  end
```

The attribute readers I show allow clients to get at this data. However, sometimes I don't have a customer for a site. Someone may have moved out and I don't yet know who has moved in. Because this can happen we have to ensure that any code that uses the customer can handle `nils`. Here are a few example fragments:

```
customer = site.customer
plan = customer ? customer.plan : BillingPlan.basic
...
customer_name = customer ? customer.name : 'occupant'
...
weeks_delinquent = customer.nil? ? 0 :
customer.history.weeks_delinquent_in_last_year
```

In these situations I may have many clients of `Site` and `Customer`, all of which have to check for `nils` and all of which do the same thing when they find one. Sounds like it's time for a null object.

The first step is to create the null customer class and modify the `Customer` class to support a query for a null test:

```
class MissingCustomer
  def missing?; true; end
end

class Customer...
  def missing?; false; end
```

If you like, you can signal the use of a null object by means of a module:

```
module Nullable
  def missing?; false; end
end

class Customer
  include Nullable
```

I like to add a factory method to create null customers. That way clients don't have to know about the null class:

```
class Customer...
  def self.new_missing
    MissingCustomer.new
  end
```

Now comes the difficult bit. Now I have to return this new null object whenever I expect a `nil` and replace the tests for `nil` with tests of the form `foo.missing?`. I find it useful to look for all the places where I ask for a customer and modify them so that they return a null customer rather than `nil`.

```
class Site...
  def customer
    @customer || Customer.new_missing
  end
```

I also have to alter all uses of this value so that they test with `missing?` rather than `nil?` or evaluation as a boolean.

```
customer = site.customer
plan = customer.missing? ? BillingPlan.basic : customer.plan
...
```

```
customer_name = customer.missing? ? 'occupant' : customer.name
...
weeks_delinquent = customer.missing? ? 0 :
customer.history.weeks_delinquent_in_last_year
```

There's no doubt that this is the trickiest part of this refactoring. For each source of a null I replace, I have to find all the times it is tested for nullness and replace them. If the object is widely passed around, these can be hard to track. I have to find every variable of type `Customer` and find everywhere it is used. It is hard to break this process into small steps. Sometimes I find one source that is used in only a few places, and I can replace that source only. But most of the time, however, I have to make many widespread changes. The changes aren't too difficult to back out of, because I can find calls of `missing?` without too much difficulty, but this is still a messy step.

Once this step is done and tested, I can smile. Now the fun begins. As it stands I gain nothing from using `missing?` rather than `nil?`. The gain comes as I move behavior to the null customer and remove conditionals. I can make these moves one at a time. I begin with the name. Currently I have client code that says:

```
customer_name = customer.missing? ? 'occupant' : customer.name
```

I add a suitable name method to the null customer:

```
class NullCustomer...

  def name
    'occupant'
  end
```

Now I can make the conditional code go away:

```
customer_name = customer.name
```

I can do the same for any other method in which there is a sensible general response to a query. I can also do appropriate actions for modifiers. So client code such as:

```
if !customer.missing?

  customer.plan = BillingPlan.special
```

can be replaced with

```
customer.plan = BillingPlan.special

class NullCustomer...
  def plan=; end
```

Remember that this movement of behavior makes sense only when most clients want the same response. Notice that I said most, not all. Any clients who want a different response to the standard one can still test using missing?. You benefit when many clients want to do the same thing; they can simply rely on the default null object behavior.

The example contains a slightly different case—client code that uses the result of a call to customer:

```
weeks_delinquent = customer.missing? ? 0 :
customer.history.weeks_delinquent_in_last_year
```

I can handle this by creating a null payment history:

```
class NullPaymentHistory...
  def weeks_delinquent_in_last_year; 0; end
```

I modify the null customer to return it when asked:

```
class NullCustomer...
  def history
    PaymentHistory.new_null
  end
```

Again I can remove the conditional code:

```
weeks_delinquent = customer.history.weeks_delinquent_in_last_year
```

You often find that null objects return other null objects.

Example: Testing Interface

The testing interface is an alternative to defining a method to test whether you have a null object. In this approach I create a null mixin module with no methods defined:

```
module Null; end
```

I then include this module in my null objects:

```
class NullCustomer ...
  include Null
```

I then test for nullness with the is_a? method:

```
aCustomer.is_a? Null
```

I normally run away screaming from queries on the type of an object, but in this case it is okay to use it. It has the particular advantage that I don't need to change the customer class to introduce the null object.

Other Special Cases

When carrying out this refactoring, you can have several kinds of null. Often there is a difference between having no customer (new building and not yet moved in) and having an unknown customer (we think there is someone there, but we don't know who it is). If that is the case, you can build separate classes for the different null cases. Sometimes null objects actually can carry data, such as usage records for the unknown customer, so that we can bill the customers when we find out who they are.

In essence there is a bigger pattern here, called special case. A special case class is a particular instance of a class with special behavior. So `UnknownCustomer` and `NoCustomer` would both be special cases of `Customer`. You often see special cases with numbers. Floating points in Java have special cases for positive and negative infinity and for not a number (`NaN`). The value of special cases is that they help reduce dealing with errors. Floating point operations don't throw exceptions. Doing any operation with `NaN` yields another `NaN` in the same way that accessors on null objects usually result in other null objects.

Introduce Assertion

A section of code assumes something about the state of the program.

Make the assumption explicit with an assertion.

```
def expense_limit
  # should have either expense limit or a primary project
  (@expense_limit != NULL_EXPENSE) ? \
    @expense_limit : \
    @primary_project.member_expense_limit
end
```

⇓

```
def expense_limit
  assert { (@expense_limit != NULL_EXPENSE) || (!@primary_project.nil?) }

  (@expense_limit != NULL_EXPENSE) ? \
    @expense_limit : \
    @primary_project.member_expense_limit
end
```

Motivation

Often sections of code work only if certain conditions are true. This may be as simple as a square root calculation's working only on a positive input value. With an object it may be assumed that at least one of a group of fields has a value in it.

Such assumptions often are not stated but can only be decoded by looking through an algorithm. Sometimes the assumptions are stated with a comment. A better technique is to make the assumption explicit by writing an assertion.

An assertion is a conditional statement that is assumed to be always true. Failure of an assertion indicates programmer error. As such, assertion failures should always result in an exception. Assertions should never be used by other parts of the system. Indeed assertions usually are removed for production code. It is therefore important to signal something is an assertion.

Assertions act as communication and debugging aids. In communication they help the reader understand the assumptions the code is making. In debugging, assertions can help catch bugs closer to their origin. I've noticed the debugging help is less important when I write self-testing code, but I still appreciate the value of assertions in communication.

Mechanics

Because assertions should not affect the running of a system, adding one is always behavior preserving.

1. When you see that a condition is assumed to be true, add an assertion to state it.

   ⟹ *Have an* `Assertions` *module that you can include for assertion behavior.*

Beware of overusing assertions. Don't use assertions to check everything that you think is true for a section of code. Use assertions only to check things that *need* to be true. Overusing assertions can lead to duplicate logic that is awkward to maintain. Logic that covers an assumption is good because it forces you to rethink the section of the code. If the code works without the assertion, the assertion is confusing rather than helpful and may hinder modification in the future.

Always ask whether the code still works if an assertion fails. If the code does work, remove the assertion.

Beware of duplicate code in assertions. Duplicate code smells just as bad in assertion checks as it does anywhere else. Use Extract Method liberally to get rid of the duplication.

Example

Here's a simple tale of expense limits. Employees can be given an individual expense limit. If they are assigned a primary project, they can use the expense limit of that primary project. They don't have to have an expense limit or a primary project, but they must have one or the other. This assumption is taken for granted in the code that uses expense limits:

```
class Employee...
  NULL_EXPENSE = -1.0

  def initialize
    @expense_limit = NULL_EXPENSE
  end

  def expense_limit
    (@expense_limit != NULL_EXPENSE) ? \
      @expense_limit : \
      @primary_project.member_expense_limit
  end

  def within_limit(expense_amount)
    expense_amount <= expense_limit
  end
```

This code contains an implicit assumption that the employee has either a project or a personal expense limit. Such an assertion should be clearly stated in the code:

```
class Employee..
  include Assertions

  def expense_limit
    assert { (@expense_limit != NULL_EXPENSE) || (!@primary_project.nil?) }

    (@expense_limit != NULL_EXPENSE) ? \
      @expense_limit : \
      @primary_project.member_expense_limit
  end
```

This assertion does not change any aspect of the behavior of the program. Either way, if the condition is not true, I get an exception: either an `ArgumentError` in `within_limit` or a custom error inside `Assertions#assert`. In some circumstances the assertion helps find the bug, because it is closer to where things went wrong. Mostly, however, the assertion helps to communicate how the code works and what it assumes.

I often find I use Extract Method on the conditional inside the assertion. I either use it in several places and eliminate duplicate code or use it simply to clarify the intention of the condition.

One of the complications of assertions is that there is often no simple mechanism to putting them in. Assertions should be easily removable, so they don't affect performance in production code. Having a utility module, such as `Assertions`, certainly helps. But with the flexibility of dynamic languages such as Ruby, we can go even further. By using a block as a parameter to our `assert` method, we can easily prevent the expression inside the block from being evaluated in production. If our `Assertions` module is implemented like this:

```
module Assertions
  class AssertionFailedError < StandardError; end

  def assert(&condition)
    raise AssertionFailedError.new("Assertion Failed") unless condition.call
  end

end
```

then we can easily overwrite the method with a no-op method during deployment to production:

```
Assertions.class_eval do
  def assert; end;
end
```

The Assertion module should have various methods that are named helpfully. In addition to assert, you can have `equals`, and `should_never_reach_here`.

Chapter 10

Making Method Calls Simpler

Objects are all about interfaces. Coming up with interfaces that are easy to understand and use is a key skill in developing good Object-Oriented software. This chapter explores refactorings that make interfaces more straightforward.

Often the simplest and most important thing you can do is to change the name of a method. Naming is a key tool in communication. If you understand what a program is doing, you should not be afraid to use Rename Method to pass on that knowledge. You can (and should) also rename variables and classes. On the whole these renamings are fairly simple text replacements, so I haven't added extra refactorings for them.

Parameters themselves have quite a role to play with interfaces. Add Parameter and Remove Parameter are common refactorings. Programmers new to objects often use long parameter lists, which are typical of other development environments. Objects allow you to keep parameter lists short, and several more involved refactorings give you ways to shorten them. If you are passing several values from an object, use Preserve Whole Object to reduce all the values to a single object. If this object does not exist, you can create it with Introduce Parameter Object. If you can get the data from an object to which the method already has access, you can eliminate parameters with Replace Parameter with Method. If you have parameters that are used to determine conditional behavior, you can use Replace Parameter with Explicit Methods. You can combine several similar methods by adding a parameter with Parameterize Method.

Doug Lea, author of *Concurrent Programming in Java*, gave me a warning about refactorings that reduce parameter lists. Concurrent programming often uses long parameter lists. Typically this occurs so that you can pass in parameters that are immutable, as built-ins and value objects often are. Usually you can replace long parameter lists with immutable objects, but otherwise you need to be cautious about this group of refactorings.

One of the most valuable conventions I've used over the years is to clearly separate methods that change state (modifiers) from those that query state (queries). I don't know how many times I've got myself into trouble, or seen others get into trouble, by mixing these up. So whenever I see them combined, I use Separate Query from Modifier to get rid of them.

Good interfaces show only what they have to and no more. You can improve an interface by hiding things. Of course all data should be hidden (I hope I don't need to tell you to do that), but also any methods that can should be hidden. When refactoring you often need to make things visible for a while and then cover them up with Hide Method and Remove Setting Method.

Constructors are a particularly awkward feature of Ruby and Java, because they force you to know the class of an object you need to create. Often you don't need to know this. The need to know can be removed with Replace Constructor with Factory Method.

Ruby, like many modern languages, has an exception-handling mechanism to make error handling easier. Programmers who are not used to this often use error codes to signal trouble. You can use Replace Error Code with Exception to use the new exceptional features. But sometimes exceptions aren't the right answer; you should test first with Replace Exception with Test.

Rename Method

The name of a method does not reveal its purpose.

Change the name of the method.

Motivation

An important part of the code style I am advocating is small methods to factor complex processes. Done badly, this can lead you on a merry dance to find out what all the little methods do. The key to avoiding this merry dance is naming the methods. Methods should be named in a way that communicates their intention. A good way to do this is to think about the comment you would use to describe the method, and turn that comment into the name of the method.

Life being what it is, you won't get your names right the first time. In this situation you may well be tempted to leave it—after all it's only a name. That is the work of the evil demon *Obfuscatis*; don't listen to him. If you see a badly named method, it is imperative that you change it. Remember your code is for a human first and a computer second. Humans need good names. Take note of when you have spent ages trying to do something that would have been easier if a couple of methods had been better named. Good naming is a skill that requires practice; improving this skill is the key to being a truly skillful programmer. The same applies to other aspects of the signature. If reordering parameters clarifies matters, do it (see Add Parameter and Remove Parameter).

Mechanics

1. Check to see whether the method signature is implemented by a superclass or subclass. If it is, perform these steps for each implementation.

2. Declare a new method with the new name. Copy the old body of code over to the new name and make any alterations to fit.

3. Change the body of the old method so that it calls the new one.

   ⟹ *If you only have a few references, you can reasonably skip this step.*

4. Test.

5. Find all references to the old method name and change them to refer to the new one. Test after each change.

6. Remove the old method.

   ⟹ *If the old method is part of the published interface and you cannot get to all of its callers, leave it in place and mark it as deprecated.*

7. Test.

Example

I have a method to get a person's telephone number:

```
def telephone_number
  "(#{@officeAreaCode}) #{@officeNumber}"
end
```

I want to rename the method to `office_telephone_number`. I begin by creating the new method and copying the body over to the new method. The old method now changes to call the new one:

```
class Person...
  def telephone_number
    office_telephone_number
  end

  def office_telephone_number
    "(#{@officeAreaCode}) #{@officeNumber}"
  end
```

Now I find the callers of the old method, and switch them to call the new one. When I have switched them all, I can remove the old method.

The procedure is the same if I need to add or remove a parameter.

If there aren't many callers, I change the callers to call the new method without using the old method as a delegating method. If my tests throw a wobbly, I back out and make the changes the slow way.

Add Parameter

A method needs more information from its caller.

Add a parameter for an object that can pass on this information.

Motivation

Add Parameter is a common refactoring, one that you almost certainly have already done. The motivation is simple. You have to change a method, and the change requires information that wasn't passed in before, so you add a parameter.

Actually most of what I have to say is motivation against doing this refactoring. Often you have other alternatives to adding a parameter. If available, these alternatives are better because they don't lead to increasing the length of parameter lists. Long parameter lists smell bad because they are hard to remember and often involve data clumps.

Look at the existing parameters. Can you ask one of those objects for the information you need? If not, would it make sense to give them a method to provide that information? What are you using the information for? Should that behavior be on another object, the one that has the information? Look at the existing parameters and think about them with the new parameter. Perhaps you should consider Introduce Parameter Object.

I'm not saying that you should never add parameters; I do it frequently, but you need to be aware of the alternatives.

Mechanics

The mechanics of Add Parameter are similar to those of Rename Method.

1. Check to see whether this method signature is implemented by a superclass or subclass. If it is, check to see whether the parameter needs to be added for all implementations. If you decide not too add the parameter for any of the implementations, any calls to the implementation via super will have to be made explicitly with the receiving method's parameter list.

2. Declare a new method with the added parameter. Copy the old body of code over to the new method.

   ⟹ *If you need to add more than one parameter, it is easier to add them at the same time.*

3. Change the body of the old method so that it calls the new one.

   ⟹ *If you only have a few references, you can reasonably skip this step.*

   ⟹ *Add a default value for the new parameter. You can use any value for the default, but usually you use* `nil` *or an empty* `Array` *or* `Hash`.

4. Test.

5. Find all references to the old method and change them to refer to the new one. Test after each change.

Remove Parameter

6. Remove the old method.

   ⟹ *If the old method is part of the published interface and you cannot get to all of its callers, leave it in place and mark it as deprecated.*

7. Test.

Remove Parameter

A parameter is no longer used by the method body.

Remove it.

Motivation

Programmers often add parameters but are reluctant to remove them. After all, a spurious parameter doesn't cause any problems, and you might need it again later.

This is the demon *Obfuscatis* speaking; purge him from your soul! A parameter indicates information that is needed; different values make a difference. Your caller has to worry about what values to pass. By not removing the parameter you are making further work for everyone who uses the method. That's not a good trade-off, especially because removing parameters is an easy refactoring.

Mechanics

The mechanics of Remove Parameter are similar to those of Rename Method and Add Parameter.

1. Check to see whether this method signature is implemented by a superclass or subclass. Check to see whether the subclass or superclass uses the parameter. If it does, don't do this refactoring.

2. Declare a new method without the parameter. Ruby doesn't allow method overloading, so you'll have to give the new method a different name from

the old one. This will only be temporary. Copy the old body of code to the new method.

⟹ *If you need to remove more than one parameter, it is easier to remove them together.*

3. Change the body of the old method so that it calls the new one.

   ⟹ *If you only have a few references, you can reasonably skip this step.*

4. Test.

5. Find all references to the old method and change them to refer to the new one. Test after each change.

6. Remove the old method.

   ⟹ *If the old method is part of the published interface and you cannot get to all of its callers, leave it in place and mark it as deprecated.*

7. Test.

8. Use Rename Method to change the name of the new method to the old method's name.

9. Because I'm pretty comfortable with adding and removing parameters, I often do a batch in one go.

Separate Query from Modifier

You have a method that returns a value and also changes the state of an object.

Create two methods, one for the query and one for the modification.

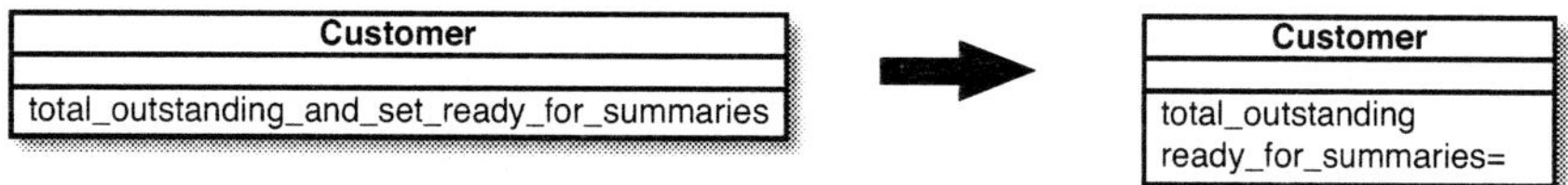

Motivation

When you have a function that gives you a value and has no observable side effects, you have a valuable thing. You can call this function as often as you like. You can move the call to other places in the method. In short, you have a lot less to worry about.

It is a good idea to clearly signal the difference between methods with side effects and those without. A good rule to follow is to say that any method that returns a value should not have observable side effects. Some programmers treat this as an absolute rule, including Bertrand Meyer, author of Object Oriented Software Constructionm [Meyer]. I'm not 100 percent sure on this (as on anything), but I try to follow it most of the time, and it has served me well.

It's worth clarifying that in Ruby, every method returns some value (the return value of the last statement or `nil`). Here we're talking about return values that are actually used by the caller.

If you come across a method that returns a value that is used by the caller and also has side effects, you should try to separate the query from the modifier.

Note I use the phrase *observable* side effects. A common optimization is to cache the value of a query in a field so that repeated calls go perform better. Although this changes the state of the object with the cache, the change is not observable. Any sequence of queries will always return the same results for each query [Meyer].

Mechanics

1. Create a query that returns the same value as the original method.

   ⟹ *Look in the original method to see what is returned. If the returned value is a temporary, look at the location of the temp assignment.*

2. Modify the original method so that it returns the result of a call to the query.

   ⟹ *Every return in the original method should say, "`return new_query`" (where `new_query` is the name of the `new_query` method), instead of returning anything else.*

   ⟹ *If the method used a temp with a single assignment to capture the return value, you should be able to remove it.*

3. Test.

4. For each call, replace the single call to the original method with a call to the query. Add a call to the original method before the line that calls the query. Test after each change to a calling method.

5. Remove the return expressions from the original method.

Example

Here is a function that tells me the name of a miscreant for a security system and sends an alert. The rule is that only one alert is sent even if there is more than one miscreant:

```
def found_miscreant(people)
  people.each do |person|
    if person == "Don"
      send_alert
      return "Don"
    end
    if person == "John"
      send_alert
      return "John"
    end
  end
  ""
end
```

It is called by:

```
def check_security(people)
  found = found_miscreant(people)
  some_later_code(found)
end
```

To separate the query from the modifier, I first need to create a suitable query that returns the same value as the modifier does but without the side effects.

```
def found_person(people)
  people.each do |person|
    return "Don" if person == "Don"
    return "John" if person == "John"
  end
  ""
end
```

Then I replace every return in the original function, one at a time, with calls to the new query. I test after each replacement. When I'm done the original method looks like the following:

```
def found_miscreant(people)
  people.each do |person|
    if person == "Don"
      send_alert
      return found_person(people)
    end
    if person == "John"
      send_alert
      return found_person(people)
    end
  end
  found_person(people)
end
```

Now I alter all the calling methods to do two calls: first to the modifier and then to the query:

```
def check_security(people)
  found_miscreant(people)
  found = found_person(people)
  some_later_code(found)
end
```

Once I have done this for all calls, I can alter the modifier to make it return `nil`:

```
def found_miscreant(people)
  people.each do |person|
    if person == "Don"
      send_alert
      return
    end
    if person == "John"
      send_alert
      return
    end
  end
  nil
end
```

Now it seems better to change the name of the original:

```
def send_alert_if_miscreant_in(people)
```

```
  people.each do |person|
    if person == "Don"
      send_alert
      return
    end
    if person == "John"
      send_alert
      return
    end
  end
  nil
end
```

Of course in this case I have a lot of code duplication because the modifier uses the body of the query to do its work. I can now use Substitute Algorithm on the modifier to take advantage of this:

```
def send_alert_if_miscreant_in(people)
  send_alert unless found_person(people).empty?
end
```

Concurrency Issues

If you are working in a multithreaded system, you know that doing test and set operations as a single action is an important idiom. Does this conflict with Separate Query from Modifier? I discussed this issue with Doug Lea, author of *Concurrent Programming in Java*, and concluded that it doesn't. You do, however, need to do some additional things. It is still valuable to have separate query and modifier operations. However, you need to retain a third method that does both. The query-and-modify operation will call the separate query and modify methods and be synchronized. If the query and modify operations are not synchronized, you also might restrict their visibility to private level. That way you have a safe, synchronized operation decomposed into two easier-to-understand methods. These lower-level methods are then available for other uses.

Parameterize Method

Several methods do similar things but with different values contained in the method body.

Create one method that uses a parameter for the different values.

Employee
five_percent_raise
ten_percent_raise

→

Employee
raise(percentage)

Motivation

You may see a couple of methods that do similar things but vary depending on a few values. In this case you can simplify matters by replacing the separate methods with a single method that handles the variations by parameters. Such a change removes duplicate code and increases flexibility, because you can deal with other variations by adding parameters.

Mechanics

1. Create a parameterized method that can be substituted for each repetitive method.

2. Replace one old method with a call to the new method.

3. Test.

4. Repeat for all the methods, testing after each one.

You may find that you cannot do this for the whole method, but you can for a fragment of a method. In this case, first extract the fragment into a method; then parameterize that method.

Example

The simplest case is methods along the following lines:

```
class Employee
  def ten_percent_raise
    @salary *= 1.1
  end

  def five_percent_raise
    @salary *= 1.05
```

```
  end
end
```

which can be replaced with

```
def raise(factor)
  @salary *= (1 + factor)
end
```

Of course that is so simple that anyone would spot it.

A less obvious case is as follows:

```
def base_charge
  result = [last_usage, 100].min * 0.03

  if last_usage > 100
    result += ([last_usage, 200].min - 100) * 0.05
  end

  if last_usage > 200
    result += (last_usage - 200) * 0.07
  end

  Dollar.new(result)
end

def last_usage
  ...
end
```

this can be replaced with:

```
def base_charge
  result = (usage_in_range 0..100) * 0.03
  result += (usage_in_range 100..200) * 0.05
  result += (usage_in_range 200..last_usage) * 0.07
  Dollar.new(result)
end

def usage_in_range(range)
  if last_usage > range.begin
    [last_usage, range.end].min - range.begin
  else
    0
  end
end
```

The trick is to spot code that is repetitive on the basis of a few values that can be passed in as parameters.

Replace Parameter with Explicit Methods

You have a method that runs different code depending on the values of an enumerated parameter.

Create a separate method for each value of the parameter.

```
def set_value(name, value)
  if name == "height"
    @height = value
  elsif name == "width"
    @width = value
  else
    raise "Should never reach here"
  end
end
```

```
def height=(value)
  @height = value
end

def width=(value)
  @width = value
end
```

Motivation

Replace Parameter with Explicit Methods is the reverse of Parameterize Method. The usual case for the former is that you have discrete values of a parameter, test for those values in a conditional, and do different things. The caller has to decide what it wants to do by setting the parameter, so you might as well provide different methods and avoid the conditional. Furthermore your interface is also clearer. `Switch.turn_on` is a lot clearer than `Switch.set_state(true)`, even when all you are doing is setting an internal boolean field.

With the parameter, any programmer using the method needs not only to look at the methods on the class but also to determine a valid parameter value. The latter is often poorly documented.

You shouldn't use Replace Parameter with Explicit Methods when the parameter values are likely to change a lot. If this happens and you are just setting a field to the passed-in parameter, use a simple setter. If you need conditional behavior, you need Replace Conditional with Polymorphism.

Mechanics

1. Create an explicit method for each value of the parameter.

2. For each leg of the conditional, call the appropriate new method.

3. Test after changing each leg.

4. Replace each caller of the conditional method with a call to the appropriate new method.

5. Test.

6. When all callers are changed, remove the conditional method.

Example

I want to create a subclass of `Employee` on the basis of a passed-in parameter, often the result of Replace Constructor with Factory Method:

```
ENGINEER = 0
SALESPERSON = 1
MANAGER = 2

def self.create(type)
  case type
  when ENGINEER
    Engineer.new
  when SALESPERSON
    Salesperson.new
  when MANAGER
```

```
    Manager.new
  else
    raise ArgumentError, "Incorrect type code value"
  end
end
```

Because this is a factory method, I can't use Replace Conditional with Polymorphism, because I haven't created the object yet. I don't expect too many new subclasses, so an explicit interface makes sense. First I create the new methods:

```
def self.create_engineer
  Engineer.new
end

def self.create_salesperson
  Salesperson.new
end

def self.create_manager
  Manager.new
end
```

One by one I replace the cases in the case statement with calls to the explicit methods:

```
def self.create(type)
  case type
  when ENGINEER
    Employee.create_engineer
  when SALESPERSON
    Salesperson.new
  when MANAGER
    Manager.new
  else
    raise ArgumentError, "Incorrect type code value"
  end
end
```

I test after changing each leg, until I've replaced them all:

```
def self.create(type)
  case type
  when ENGINEER
    Employee.create_engineer
  when SALESPERSON
    Employee.create_salesperson
```

```
  when MANAGER
    Employee.create_manager
  else
    raise ArgumentError, "Incorrect type code value"
  end
end
```

Now I move on to the callers of the old create method. I change code such as:

```
kent = Employee.create(Employee::ENGINEER)
```

to

```
kent = Employee.create_engineer
```

Once I've done that for all the callers of `create`, I can remove the `create` method. I may also be able to get rid of the constants.

Preserve Whole Object

You are getting several values from an object and passing these values as parameters in a method call.

Send the whole object instead.

```
low = days_temperature_range.low
high = days_temperature_range.high
plan.within_range?(low, high)
```

```
plan.within_range?(days_temperature_range)
```

Motivation

This type of situation arises when an object passes several data values from a single object as parameters in a method call. The problem with this is that if the called object needs new data values later, you have to find and change all the calls to this method. You can avoid this by passing in the whole object from which the data came. The called object can then ask for whatever it wants from the whole object.

Preserve Whole Object

In addition to making the parameter list more robust to changes, Preserve Whole Object often makes the code more readable. Long parameter lists can be hard to work with because both caller and callee have to remember which values were there. They also encourage duplicate code because the called object can't take advantage of any other methods on the whole object to calculate intermediate values.

There is a down-side. When you pass in values, the called object has a dependency on the values, but there isn't any dependency to the object from which the values were extracted. Passing in the required object causes a dependency between the required object and the called object. If this is going to mess up your dependency structure, don't use Preserve Whole Object.

Another reason I have heard for not using Preserve Whole Object is that when a calling object needs only one value from the required object, it is better to pass in the value than to pass in the whole object. I don't subscribe to that view. One value and one object amount to the same thing when you pass them in, at least for clarity's sake (there may be a performance cost with pass by value parameters). The driving force is the dependency issue.

That a called method uses a lot of values from another object is a signal that the called method should really be defined on the object from which the values come. When you are considering Preserve Whole Object, consider Move Method as an alternative.

You may not already have the whole object defined. In this case you need Introduce Parameter Object.

A common case is that a calling object passes several of its *own* data values as parameters. In this case you can make the call and pass in `self` instead of these values, if you have the appropriate accessor methods and you don't mind the dependency.

Mechanics

1. Create a new parameter for the whole object from which the data comes.

2. Test.

3. Determine which parameters should be obtained from the whole object.

4. Take one parameter and replace references to it within the method body by invoking an appropriate method on the whole object parameter.

5. Delete the parameter.

6. Test.

7. Repeat for each parameter that can be got from the whole object.

8. Remove the code in the calling method that obtains the deleted parameters.

   ⟹ *Unless, of course, the code is using these parameters somewhere else.*

9. Test.

Motivation

Consider a Room object that records high and low temperatures during the day. It needs to compare this range with a range in a predefined heating plan:

```
class Room...


  def within_plan?(plan)
    low = days_temperature_range.low
    high = days_temperature_range.high
    plan.within_range?(low, high)
  end

class HeatingPlan...

  def within_range?(low, high)
    (low >= @range.low) && (high <= @range.high)
  end
```

Rather than unpack the range information when I pass it, I can pass the whole range object. In this simple case I can do this in one step. When more parameters are involved, I can do it in smaller steps. First I add the whole object to the parameter list:

```
class HeatingPlan...

  def within_range?(room_range, low, high)
    (low >= @range.low) && (high <= @range.high)
  end
```

Preserve Whole Object

```
class Room...

  def within_plan?(plan)
    low = days_temperature_range.low
    high = days_temperature_range.high
    plan.within_range?(days_temperature_range, low, high)
  end
```

Then I use a method on the whole object instead of one of the parameters:

```
class HeatingPlan...

  def within_range?(room_range, high)
    (room_range.low >= @range.low) && (high <= @range.high)
  end

class Room...

  def within_plan?(plan)
    low = days_temperature_range.low
    high = days_temperature_range.high
    plan.within_range?(days_temperature_range, high)
  end
```

I continue until I've changed all I need:

```
class HeatingPlan...

  def within_range?(room_range)
    (room_range.low >= @range.low) && (room_range.high <= @range.high)
  end

class Room...

  def within_plan?(plan)
    low = days_temperature_range.low
    high = days_temperature_range.high
    plan.within_range?(days_temperature_range)
  end
```

Now I don't need the temps anymore:

```
class Room...
  def within_plan?(plan)
    low = days_temperature_range.low
    high = days_temperature_range.high
    plan.within_range?(days_temperature_range)
  end
```

Using whole objects this way soon leads you to realize that you can usefully move behavior into the whole object to make it easier to work with.

```
class HeatingPlan...

  def within_temperature_range?(room_temperature_range)
    @range.includes?(room_temperature_range)
  end

class TempRange...

  def includes?(temperature_range)
    temperature_range.low >= low && temperature_range.high <= high
  end
```

Replace Parameter with Method

An object invokes a method, then passes the result as a parameter for a method. The receiver can also invoke this method.

Remove the parameter and let the receiver invoke the method.

```
base_price = @quantity * @item_price
level_of_discount = discount_level
final_price = discounted_price(base_price, level_of_discount)
```

```
base_price = @quantity * @item_price
final_price = discounted_price(base_price)
```

Motivation

If a method can get a value that is passed in as parameter by another means, it should. Long parameter lists are difficult to understand, and we should reduce them as much as possible.

One way of reducing parameter lists is to look to see whether the receiving method can make the same calculation. If an object is calling a method on itself, and the calculation for the parameter does not reference any of the parameters of the calling method, you should be able to remove the parameter by turning the calculation into its own method. This is also true if you are calling a method on a different object that has a reference to the calling object.

You can't remove the parameter if the calculation relies on a parameter of the calling method, because that parameter may change with each call (unless, of course, that parameter can be replaced with a method). You also can't remove the parameter if the receiver does not have a reference to the sender, and you don't want to give it one.

In some cases the parameter may be there for a future parameterization of the method. In this case I would still get rid of it. Deal with the parameterization when you need it; you may find out that you don't have the right parameter anyway. I would make an exception to this rule only when the resulting change in the interface would have painful consequences around the whole program, such as changing of a lot of embedded code. If this worries you, look into how painful such a change would really be. You should also look to see whether you can reduce the dependencies that cause the change to be so painful. Stable interfaces are good, but freezing a poor interface is a problem.

Mechanics

1. If necessary, extract the calculation of the parameter into a method.

2. Replace references to the parameter in method bodies with references to the method.

3. Test after each replacement.

4. Use Remove Parameter on the parameter.

Example

Another unlikely variation on discounting orders is as follows:

```
def price
  base_price = @quantity * @item_price
  level_of_discount = 1
  level_of_discount = 2 if @quantity > 100
  discounted_price(base_price, level_of_discount)
end

def discounted_price(base_price, level_of_discount)
  return base_price * 0.1 if level_of_discount == 2
  base_price * 0.05
end
```

I can begin by extracting the calculation of the discount level:

```
def price
  base_price = @quantity * @item_price
  level_of_discount = discount_level
  discounted_price(base_price, level_of_discount)
end

def discount_level
  return 2 if @quantity > 100
  return 1
end
```

I then replace references to the parameter in `discounted_price`:

```
def discounted_price(base_price, level_of_discount)
  return base_price * 0.1 if discount_level == 2
  base_price * 0.05
end
```

Then I can use Remove Parameter:

```
def price
  base_price = @quantity * @item_price
  level_of_discount = discount_level
  discounted_price(base_price)
end

def discounted_price(base_price)
  return base_price * 0.1 if discount_level == 2
  base_price * 0.05
end
```

I can now get rid of the temp:

```
def price
  base_price = @quantity * @item_price
  discounted_price(base_price)
end
```

Then it's time to get rid of the other parameter and its temp. I am left with:

```
def price
  discounted_price
end

def discounted_price
  return base_price * 0.1 if discount_level == 2
  base_price * 0.05
end

def base_price
  @quantity * @item_price
end
```

so I might as well use Inline Method on `discounted_price`:

```
def price
  return base_price * 0.1 if discount_level == 2
  base_price * 0.05
end
```

Introduce Parameter Object

You have a group of parameters that naturally go together.

Replace them with an object.

Motivation

Often you see a particular group of parameters that tend to be passed together. Several methods may use this group, either on one class or in several classes.

Such a group of classes is a data clump and can be replaced with an object that carries all of this data. It is worthwhile to turn these parameters into objects just to group the data together. This refactoring is useful because it reduces the size of the parameter lists, and long parameter lists are hard to understand. The defined accessors on the new object also make the code more consistent, which again makes it easier to understand and modify.

You get a deeper benefit, however, because once you have clumped together the parameters, you soon see behavior that you can also move into the new class. Often the bodies of the methods have common manipulations of the parameter values. By moving this behavior into the new object, you can remove a lot of duplicated code.

Mechanics

1. Create a new class to represent the group of parameters you are replacing. Make the class immutable.

2. Use Add Parameter for the new data clump. Use a default value for the new parameter.

3. For each parameter in the data clump, remove the parameter from the signature. Modify the callers and method body to use the parameter object for that value.

4. Test after you remove each parameter.

5. When you have removed the parameters, look for behavior that you can move into the parameter object with Move Method.

   ⟹ *This may be a whole method or part of a method. If it is part of a method, use Extract Method first and then move the new method over.*

6. Be sure to remove the default value for the new parameter. The method is not intended to be used without the parameter. Leaving it in would only cause confusion.

Example

I begin with an account that holds a collection of charges for items. Each charge is determined by a calculation based on base price, tax rate, and whether the item is imported:

Introduce Parameter Object

```
class Account...

  def add_charge(base_price, tax_rate, imported)
    total = base_price + base_price * tax_rate
    total += base_price * 0.1 if imported
    @charges << total
  end

  def total_charge
    @charges.inject(0) { |total, charge| total + charge }
  end

client code...
  account.add_charge(5, 0.1, true)
  account.add_charge(12, 0.125, false)
  ...
  total = account.total_charge
```

The `base_price`, `tax_rate`, and `imported` status naturally go together, so I group them in a Charge object:

```
class Charge
  attr_accessor :base_price, :tax_rate, :imported

  def initialize(base_price, tax_rate, imported)
    @base_price = base_price
    @tax_rate = tax_rate
    @imported = imported
  end
end
```

I've made the `Charge` class immutable; that is, all the values for the charge are set in the constructor, hence there are no methods for modifying the values. This is a wise move to avoid aliasing bugs.

Next I add the charge into the parameter list for the `add_charge` method:

```
class Account...

  def add_charge(base_price, tax_rate, imported, charge=nil)
    total = base_price + base_price * tax_rate
    total += base_price * 0.1 if imported
    @charges << total
  end

  def total_charge
```

```
    @charges.inject(0) { |total, charge| total + charge }
  end
```

At this point I haven't altered any behavior.

The next step is to remove one of the parameters and use the new object instead. To do this I delete the `base_price` parameter and modify the method and its callers to use the new object instead:

```
class Account...

  def add_charge(tax_rate, imported, charge)
    total = charge.base_price + charge.base_price * tax_rate
    total += charge.base_price * 0.1 if imported
    @charges << total
  end

  def total_charge
    @charges.inject(0) { |total, charge| total + charge }
  end

client code...
  account.add_charge(0.1, true, Charge.new(9.0, nil, nil))
  account.add_charge(0.125, true, Charge.new(12.0, nil, nil))
  ...
  total = account.total_charge
```

I then remove the other two parameters:

```
class Account...

  def add_charge(charge)
    total = charge.base_price + charge.base_price * charge.tax_rate
    total += charge.base_price * 0.1 if charge.imported
    @charges << total
  end

  def total_charge
    @charges.inject(0) { |total, charge| total + charge }
  end

client code...
  account.add_charge(Charge.new(9.0, 0.1, true))
  account.add_charge(Charge.new(12.0, 0.125, true))
  ...
  total = account.total_charge
```

I have introduced the parameter object; however, I can get more value from this refactoring by moving behavior from other methods to the new object. In this case I can take the code to perform the charge calculation and use Extract Method and Move Method to add the method to the Charge object. I can also remove the readers on the `Charge` object, improving encapsulation.

```
class Account...

  def add_charge(charge)
    @charges << charge
  end

  def total_charge
    @charges.inject(0) do |total_for_account, charge|
      total_for_account + charge.total
    end
  end

class Charge
  def initialize(base_price, tax_rate, imported)
    @base_price = base_price
    @tax_rate = tax_rate
    @imported = imported
  end

  def total
    result = @base_price + @base_price * @tax_rate
    result += @base_price * 0.1 if @imported
    result
  end
end
```

I usually do simple extracts and moves such as this in one step. If I run into a bug, I can back out and take the two smaller steps.

Remove Setting Method

A field should be set at creation time and never altered.

Remove any setting method for that field.

Motivation

Providing a setting method indicates that a field may be changed. If you don't want that field to change once the object is created, don't provide a setting method. That way your intention is clear and you often remove the possibility that the field will change.

This situation often occurs when programmers blindly use indirect variable access [Beck]. Such programmers then use setters even in a constructor. I guess there is an argument for consistency but not compared with the confusion that the setting method will cause later on.

Mechanics

1. Check that the setting method is called only in the constructor, or in a method called by the constructor.

2. Modify the constructor to access the variables directly.

3. Test.

4. Remove the setting method.

5. Test.

Example

A simple example is as follows:

```
class Account

  def initialize(id)
    self.id = id
  end
```

```
# you may have an attr_writer instead of this method - it
# should be removed also
  def id=(value)
    @id = value
  end
```

which can be replaced with

```
class Account

  def initialize(id)
    @id = id
  end
```

The problems come in some variations. First is the case in which you are doing computation on the argument:

```
class Account

  def initialize(id)
    self.id = id
  end

  def id=(value)
    @id = "ZZ#{value}"
  end
```

If the change is simple (as here), I can make the change in the constructor. If the change is complex or I need to call it from separate methods, I need to provide a method. In that case I need to name the method to make its intention clear:

```
class Account

  def initialize(id)
    initialize_id(id)
  end

  def initialize_id(value)
    @id = "ZZ#{value}"
  end
```

Another case to consider is setting the value of a collection:

```
class Person
  attr_accessor :courses

  def initialize
    @courses = []
  end

end
```

Here I want to replace the setter with add and remove operations. I talk about this in Encapsulate Collection.

Hide Method

A method is not used by any other class.

Make the method private.

Motivation

Refactoring often causes you to change decisions about the visibility of methods. It is easy to spot cases in which you need to make a method more visible: Another class needs it and you thus relax the visibility. It is somewhat more difficult to tell when a method is too visible. Ideally a tool should check all methods to see whether they can be hidden. If it doesn't, you should make this check at regular intervals.

A particularly common case is hiding, getting, and setting methods as you work up a richer interface that provides more behavior. This case is most common when you are starting with a class that is little more than an encapsulated data holder. As more behavior is built into the class, you may find that many of the getting and setting methods are no longer needed publicly, in which case they can be hidden. If you make a getting or setting method private and you are using direct variable access, you can remove the method.

Mechanics

1. Check regularly for opportunities to make a method more private.

   ⟹ *Use a lint-style tool, do manual checks every so often, and check when you remove a call to a method in another class.*

   ⟹ *Particularly look for cases such as this with setting methods.*

2. Make each method as private as you can.

3. Test after doing a group of hidings.

Replace Constructor with Factory Method

You want to do more than simple construction when you create an object.

Replace the constructor with a factory method.

```
class ProductController...

  def create
    ...
    @product = if imported
      ImportedProduct.new(base_price)
    else
      if base_price > 1000
        LuxuryProduct.new(base_price)
      else
        Product.new(base_price)
      end
    end
    ...
  end
```

```
class ProductController...

  def create
    ...
    @product = Product.create(base_price, imported)
    ...
  end

class Product

  def self.create(base_price, imported=false)
    if imported
      ImportedProduct.new(base_price)
    else
      if base_price > 1000
        LuxuryProduct.new(base_price)
      else
        Product.new(base_price)
      end
    end
  end
```

Motivation

The most obvious motivation for Replace Constructor with Factory Method is when you have conditional logic to determine the kind of object to create. If you need to do this conditional logic in more than one place, it's time for a Factory Method.

You can use factory methods for other situations in which constructors are too limited. Factory methods are essential for Change Value to Reference. They also can be used to signal different creation behavior that goes beyond the number and types of parameters.

Mechanics

1. Perform Extract Method to isolate the construction logic.

   ⟹ *Make the newly extracted method a class method. Pass in any required data as parameters.*

2. Test.

Replace Constructor with Factory Method

3. If the factory method is not on the desired object, use Move Method.

4. Test.

5. Remove the original constructor if no one else is using it.

6. Test.

Example

In this example we are creating products. The type of product we want to create depends on the product's base price, and whether it is imported from another country.

```
class ProductController...

  def create
    ...
    @product = if imported
      ImportedProduct.new(base_price)
    else
      if base_price > 1000
        LuxuryProduct.new(base_price)
      else
        Product.new(base_price)
      end
    end
    ...
  end
```

We might have an inheritance hierarchy to represent the products.

```
class Product...

  def initialize(base_price)
    @base_price = base_price
  end

  def total_price
    @base_price
  end

end
```

```
class LuxuryProduct < Product...
  def total_price
    super + 0.1 * super
  end
end

class ImportedProduct < Product...

  def total_price
    super + 0.25 * super
  end

end
```

There are two motivations here for using Replace Constructor with Factory Method. The first comes about if we need to perform this construction logic in more than one place. We don't want to introduce duplication, so extracting this construction logic to a factory method makes sense. The second motivation is encapsulation. If we can push this logic that uses the product's attributes onto the product object itself, we'll be able to accommodate changes to this logic more easily in the future.

The first step is to perform Extract Method on the construction logic. We'll make the extracted method a class method (so that it's easy to turn into a factory method).

```
def create
  ...
  @product = self.class.create_product(base_price, imported)
  ...
end

def self.create_product(base_price, imported)
  if imported
    ImportedProduct.new(base_price)
  else
    if base_price > 1000
      LuxuryProduct.new(base_price)
    else
      Product.new(base_price)
    end
  end
end
```

We can then use Move Method to move the method to a more appropriate place—the `Product` class.

```
class ProductController...

  def create
    ...
    @product = Product.create(base_price, imported)
    ...
  end

class Product

  def self.create(base_price, imported=false)
    if imported
      ImportedProduct.new(base_price)
    else
      if base_price > 1000
        LuxuryProduct.new(base_price)
      else
        Product.new(base_price)
      end
    end
  end
```

Since no one else is using `Product`'s `initialize` method, we can remove it.

Replace Error Code with Exception

A method returns a special code to indicate an error.

Raise an exception instead.

```
def withdraw(amount)
  return -1 if amount > @balance
  @balance -= amount
  0
end
```

```
def withdraw(amount)
  raise BalanceError.new if amount > @balance
  @balance -= amount
end
```

Motivation

In computers, as in life, things go wrong occasionally. When things go wrong, you need to do something about it. In the simplest case, you can stop the program with an error code. This is the software equivalent of committing suicide because you miss a flight. (If I did that I wouldn't be alive even if I were a cat.) Despite my glib attempt at humor, there is merit to the software suicide option. If the cost of a program crash is small and the user is tolerant, stopping the program is fine. However, more important programs need more important measures.

The problem is that the part of a program that spots an error isn't always the part that can figure out what to do about it. When such a routine finds an error, it needs to let its caller know, and the caller may pass the error up the chain. In many languages a special output is used to indicate error. Unix and C-based systems traditionally use a return code to signal success or failure of a routine.

Ruby has a better way: exceptions. Exceptions are better because they clearly separate normal processing from error processing. This makes programs easier to understand, and as I hope you now believe, understandability is next to godliness.

Mechanics

1. Find all the callers and adjust them to use the exception.

   ⟹ *Decide whether the caller should check for the condition before making the call or rescue the exception.*

2. Test after each such change.

3. Use Rename Method if there is a more appropriate name for the method given the changes.

If you have many callers, this can be too big a change. You can make it more gradual with the following steps:

1. Create a new method that uses the exception.

Replace Error Code with Exception

2. Modify the body of the old method to call the new method.

3. Test.

4. Adjust each caller of the old method to call the new method. Test after each change.

5. Delete the old method.

Example

Isn't it strange that computer textbooks often assume you can't withdraw more than your balance from an account, although in real life you often can?

```
class Account...

  def withdraw(amount)
    return -1 if amount > @balance
    @balance -= amount
    return 0
  end
```

In Ruby, there are no "checked" exceptions, as there are in Java. So all that is left to decide is how to handle the error. Should the caller check for the error condition before calling the method, or should it rescue the exception? I look to the likelihood of the error condition occurring to help me decide. If the error is likely to occur in normal processing, then I would make the caller check the condition before calling. If the error is not likely to occur, then I would rescue the exception.

Example: Caller Checks Condition Before Calling

First I look at the callers. In this case nobody should be using the return code because it is a programmer error to do so. If I see code such as:

```
if account.withdraw(amount) == -1
  handle_overdrawn
else
  do_the_usual_thing
end
```

I need to replace it with code such as:

```
if !account.can_withdraw?(amount)
  handle_overdrawn
else
  account.withdraw(amount)
end
```

I can test after each change.

Now I need to remove the error code and raise an exception for the error case. Because the behavior is (by definition) exceptional, I should use a guard clause for the condition check:

```
def withdraw(amount)
  raise ArgumentError.new if amount > @balance
  @balance -= amount
end
```

Because it is a programmer error, I should signal even more clearly by using an assertion:

```
class Account
  include Assertions
  ...

  def withdraw(amount)
    assert("amount too large") { amount <= @balance }
    @balance -= amount
  end

module Assertions
  class AssertionFailedError < StandardError; end

  def assert(message, &condition)
    unless condition.call
      raise AssertionFailedError.new("Assertion Failed: #{message}")
    end
  end
```

Example: Caller Catches Exception

I handle the "caller catches exception" case slightly differently. First I create (or use) an appropriate new exception:

```
class BalanceError < StandardError ; end
```

Then I adjust the callers to look like:

```
begin
  account.withdraw(amount)
  do_the_usual_thing
rescue BalanceError
  handle_overdrawn
end
```

Now I change the `withdraw` method to use the exception:

```
def withdraw(amount)
  raise BalanceError.new if amount > @balance
  @balance -= amount
end
```

If there are a lot of callers, this can be too large a change without being able to test as you go.

For these cases I can use a temporary intermediate method. I begin with the same case as before:

```
if account.withdraw(amount) == -1
  handle_overdrawn
else
  do_the_usual_thing
end

class Account...

  def withdraw(amount)
    return -1 if amount > @balance
    @balance -= amount
    return 0
  end
```

The first step is to create a new `withdraw` method that uses the exception:

```
def new_withdraw(amount)
  raise BalanceError.new if amount > @balance
  @balance -= amount
end
```

Next I adjust the current withdraw method to use the new one:

```
def withdraw(amount)
  begin
```

```
    new_withdraw(amount)
    return 0
  rescue BalanceException
    return -1
  end
end
```

With that done, I can test. Now I can replace each of the calls to the old method with a call to the new one:

```
begin
  account.new_withdraw(amount)
  do_the_usual_thing
rescue BalanceError
  handle_overdrawn
end
```

With both old and new methods in place, I can test after each change. When I'm finished, I can delete the old method and use Rename Method to give the new method the old name.

Replace Exception with Test

You are raising an exception on a condition the caller could have checked first.

Change the caller to make the test first.

```
def execute(command)
  command.prepare rescue nil
  command.execute
end
```

```
def execute(command)
  command.prepare if command.respond_to? :prepare
  command.execute
end
```

Motivation

Exceptions are an important advance in programming languages. They allow us to avoid complex codes by use of Replace Error Code with Exception. Like so many pleasures, exceptions can be used to excess, and they cease to be pleasurable. Exceptions should be used for exceptional behavior: behavior that is an unexpected error. They should not act as a substitute for conditional tests. If you can reasonably expect the caller to check the condition before calling the operation, you should provide a test, and the caller should use it.

Mechanics

1. Put a test up front and copy the code from the rescue clause into the appropriate leg of the `if` statement.

2. Add an assertion to the rescue clause to notify you whether the rescue clause is executed.

3. Test.

4. Remove the rescue clause and the begin block if there are no other rescue clauses.

5. Test.

Example

For this example I use an object that manages resources that are expensive to create but can be reused. Database connections are a good example of this. Such a manager has two pools of resources, one that is available for use and one that is allocated. When a client wants a resource, the pool hands it out and transfers it from the available pool to the allocated pool. When a client releases a resource, the manager passes it back. If a client requests a resource and none is available, the manager creates a new one.

The method for giving out resources might look like this:

```
class ResourceStack...

  def pop
    ... #raises EmptyStackError if the stack is empty
  end
```

```
class ResourcePool
  def initialize
    @available = ResourceStack.new
    @allocated = ResourceStack.new
  end

  def resource
    begin
      result = @available.pop
      @allocated.push(result)
      return result
    rescue EmptyStackError
      result = Resource.new
      @allocated.push(result)
      return result
    end
  end

end
```

In this case running out of resources is not an unexpected occurrence, so I should not use an exception.

To remove the exception I first add an appropriate up-front test and do the empty behavior there:

```
def resource
  if @available.empty?
    result = Resource.new
    @allocated.push(result)
    return result
  else
    begin
      result = @available.pop
      @allocated.push(result)
      return result
    rescue EmptyStackError
      result = Resource.new
      @allocated.push(result)
      return result
    end
  end
end
```

With this the exception should never occur. I can add an assertion to check this:

```
def resource
  if @available.empty?
    result = Resource.new
    @allocated.push(result)
    return result
  else
    begin
      result = @available.pop
      @allocated.push(result)
      return result
    rescue EmptyStackError
      Assert.should_never_reach_here("available was empty on pop")
      result = Resource.new
      @allocated.push(result)
      return result
    end
  end
end

class Assert...
  def self.should_never_reach_here(message)
    raise message
  end
```

Now I can test. If all goes well, I can remove the begin-rescue block completely:

```
def resource
  if @available.empty?
    result = Resource.new
    @allocated.push(result)
    return result
  else
    result = @available.pop
    @allocated.push(result)
    return result
  end
end
```

After this I usually find I can clean up the conditional code. Here I can use Consolidate Duplicate Conditional Fragments:

```
def resource
  if @available.empty?
    result = Resource.new
  else
    result = @available.pop
  end
  @allocated.push(result)
  result
end
```

Introduce Gateway

You want to interact with a complex API of an external system or resource in a simplified way.

Introduce a Gateway that encapsulates access to an external system or resource.

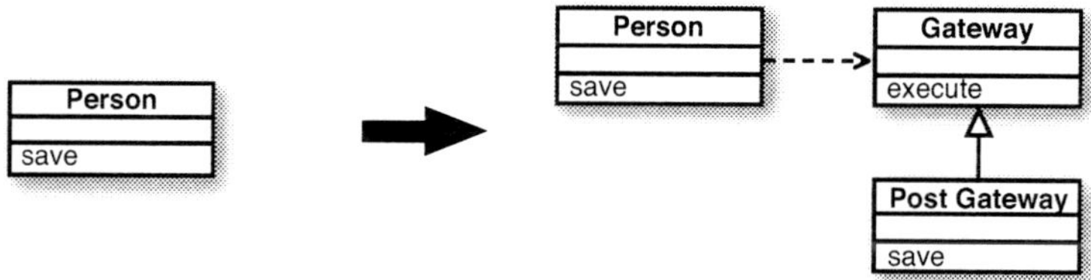

Motivation

Interesting software rarely lives in isolation. Even the purest Object-Oriented system often has to deal with things that aren't objects. The majority of Rails applications use `ActiveRecord` as a Gateway to a relational database. Additionally, Ruby applications often make use of YAML files and connection to one or more Web services.

When accessing external systems or resources, you'll usually get APIs for them. However, these APIs are naturally going to be somewhat complicated because they are designed to be flexible and reusable for various consumers. Anyone who needs to understand a resource needs to understand its API. Not only does this make the software harder to understand, it also makes it much

Introduce Gateway

harder to change should you shift some data from a relational database to an XML message at some point in the future.

Mechanics

1. Introduce a Gateway that uses the underlying API.
2. Change one use of the API to use the Gateway instead.
3. Test.
4. Change all other uses of the API to use the Gateway instead.
5. Test.

Example

Imagine we are working with an application that uses Web Services to persist all its data. The save methods of the domain objects could be implemented using the `net/http` library included in the Ruby Standard Library.

```
class Person
  attr_accessor :first_name, :last_name, :ssn

  def save
    url = URI.parse('http://www.example.com/person')
    request = Net::HTTP::Post.new(url.path)
    request.set_form_data(
      "first_name" => first_name,
      "last_name" => last_name,
      "ssn" => ssn
    )
    Net::HTTP.new(url.host, url.port).start {|http| http.request(request) }
  end
end
```

Unfortunately, we are working with a few different services provided by different teams. Because the teams are different they've chosen to create their Web services in different ways. Some teams allow you to post form data; others require that you send over get requests. Additionally, there's the matter of authentication. Some use IPs to trust internal calls, but others require you to use basic HTTP authentication. In the end, each save method is similar, but not similar enough that Form Template Method can be easily applied.

The following are a few more example domain objects that demonstrate the differences between the save methods.

```
class Company
  attr_accessor :name, :tax_id

  def save
    url = URI.parse('http://www.example.com/companies')
    request = Net::HTTP::Get.new(url.path + "?name=#{name}&tax_id=#{tax_id}")
    Net::HTTP.new(url.host, url.port).start {|http| http.request(request) }
  end
end

class Laptop
  attr_accessor :assigned_to, :serial_number

  def save
    url = URI.parse('http://www.example.com/issued_laptop')
    request = Net::HTTP::Post.new(url.path)
    request.basic_auth 'username', 'password'
    request.set_form_data(
      "assigned_to" => assigned_to,
      "serial_number" => serial_number
    )
    Net::HTTP.new(url.host, url.port).start {|http| http.request(request) }
  end
end
```

The solution is to create a Gateway that simplifies the API for consumption, but simply delegates behind the scenes to `net/http`.

We'll begin by creating the Gateway and only giving it the methods required by the `Person` class.

```
class Gateway
  attr_accessor :subject, :attributes, :to

  def self.save
    gateway = self.new
    yield gateway
    gateway.execute
  end

  def execute
    request = Net::HTTP::Post.new(url.path)
    attribute_hash = attributes.inject({}) do |result, attribute|
      result[attribute.to_s] = subject.send attribute
```

```
      result
    end
    request.set_form_data(attribute_hash)
    Net::HTTP.new(url.host, url.port).start {|http| http.request(request) }
  end

  def url
    URI.parse(to)
  end
end
```

Now the Person class can be updated to use the new Gateway class.

```
class Person
  attr_accessor :first_name, :last_name, :ssn

  def save
    Gateway.save do |persist|
      persist.subject = self
      persist.attributes = [:first_name, :last_name, :ssn]
      persist.to = 'http://www.example.com/person'
    end
  end
end
```

Next we update the Gateway to support the Company class. The Company class introduces the need for supporting both get and post. To support both we're going to introduce the PostGateway and the GetGateway.

```
class Gateway
  # ...

  def self.save
    gateway = self.new
    yield gateway
    gateway.execute
  end

  def execute
    Net::HTTP.new(url.host, url.port).start do |http|
      http.request(build_request)
    end
  end

class PostGateway < Gateway
```

```
  def build_request
    request = Net::HTTP::Post.new(url.path)
    attribute_hash = attributes.inject({}) do |result, attribute|
      result[attribute.to_s] = subject.send attribute
      result
    end
    request.set_form_data(attribute_hash)
  end
end

class GetGateway < Gateway
  def build_request
    parameters = attributes.collect do |attribute|
      "#{attribute}=#{subject.send(attribute)}"
    end
    Net::HTTP::Get.new("#{url.path}?#{parameters.join("&")}")
  end
end
```

The `Company` class can now use the `GetGateway`, and the `Person` class can use the `PostGateway`.

```
class Company
  attr_accessor :name, :tax_id

  def save
    GetGateway.save do |persist|
      persist.subject = self
      persist.attributes = [:name, :tax_id]
      persist.to = 'http://www.example.com/companies'
    end
  end
end

class Person
  attr_accessor :first_name, :last_name, :ssn

  def save
    PostGateway.save do |persist|
      persist.subject = self
      persist.attributes = [:first_name, :last_name, :ssn]
      persist.to = 'http://www.example.com/person'
    end
  end
end
```

Next, authentication support must be added to the Gateway for the Laptop class.

```
class Gateway
  attr_accessor :subject, :attributes, :to, :authenticate

  def execute
    request = build_request(url)
    request.basic_auth 'username', 'password' if authenticate
    Net::HTTP.new(url.host, url.port).start {|http| http.request(request) }
  end

  # ...
end
```

With support in place for authentication the last thing to do is change the Laptop to take advantage of the Gateway.

```
class Laptop
  attr_accessor :assigned_to, :serial_number

  def save
    PostGateway.save do |persist|
      persist.subject = self
      persist.attributes = [:assigned_to, :serial_number]
      persist.authenticate = true
      persist.to = 'http://www.example.com/issued_laptop'
    end
  end
end
```

We can then use Introduce Expression Builder to interact with the Gateway in a more fluent manner. This example is continued there.

Introduce Expression Builder

You want to interact with a public interface in a more fluent manner and not muddy the interface of an existing object.

Introduce an Expression Builder and create an interface specific to your application.

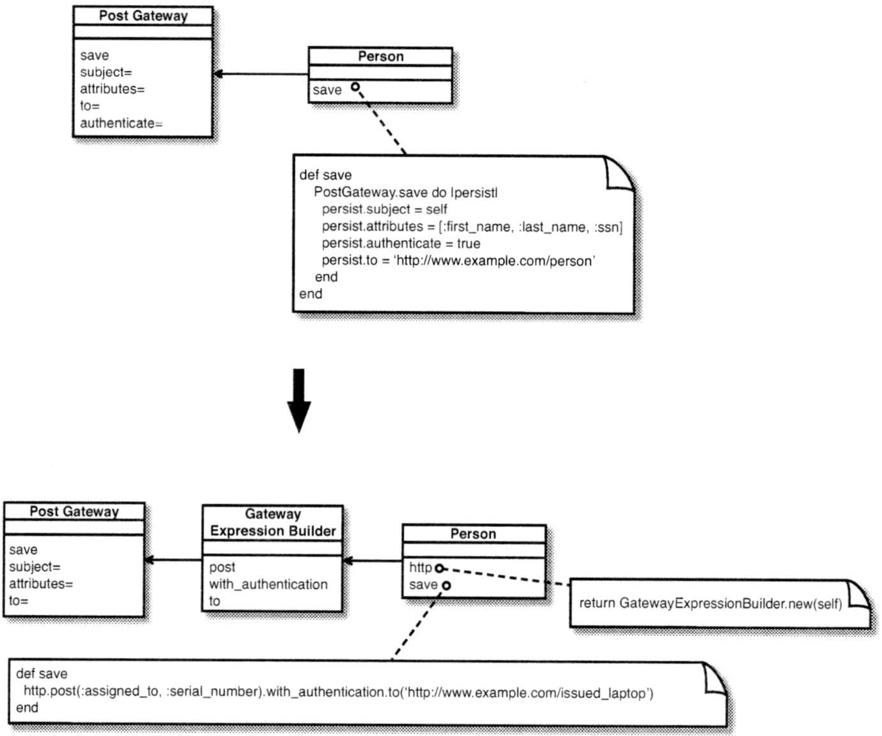

Motivation

APIs are usually designed to provide a set of self-standing methods on objects; ideally these methods can be understood individually. This is in contrast to a fluent interface that is designed around the readability of a whole expression. Fluent interfaces often lead to methods that make little sense individually.

An Expression Builder provides a fluent interface as a separate layer on top of the regular API. It has one job—to supply the fluent interface—leaving the original object to provide the interface that can be understood on a method-by-method basis.

Mechanics

1. Change the calling code to use the fluent interface.

Introduce Expression Builder

⟹ *The fluent interface is much easier to design by writing the client code first.*

2. Create an Expression Builder that uses the original object.
3. Change one use of the original object to use the Expression Builder instead.
4. Test.
5. Change all other uses of the original object to use the Expression Builder instead.
6. Test.

Example

Imagine we are working with an application that uses Web services to persist all its data. We're going to build on the example used in Introduce Gateway.

Currently, the `Person`, `Company`, and `Laptop` classes are defined as follows.

```
class Person
  attr_accessor :first_name, :last_name, :ssn

  def save
    PostGateway.save do |persist|
      persist.subject = self
      persist.attributes = [:first_name, :last_name, :ssn]
      persist.to = 'http://www.example.com/person'
    end
  end
end

class Company
  attr_accessor :name, :tax_id

  def save
    GetGateway.save do |persist|
      persist.subject = self
      persist.attributes = [:name, :tax_id]
      persist.to = 'http://www.example.com/companies'
```

```
    end
  end
end

class Laptop
  attr_accessor :assigned_to, :serial_number

  def save
    PostGateway.save do |persist|
      persist.subject = self
      persist.attributes = [:assigned_to, :serial_number]
      persist.authenticate = true
      persist.to = 'http://www.example.com/issued_laptop'
    end
  end
end
```

The `Person`, `Company`, and `Laptop` classes use the Gateway to hide the complexity of the underlying API, but the Gateway interface can be made more fluent.

The solution is to create an Expression Builder that exposes a fluent interface for consumption, but simply delegates behind the scenes to the Gateway.

We'll begin by writing the Ruby that we'd like to use in our `Person` class.

```
class Person
  attr_accessor :first_name, :last_name, :ssn
  def save
    http.post(:first_name, :last_name, :ssn).to(
      'http://www.example.com/person'
    )
  end
end
```

There's a couple of ways that we could implement this interface. We could make the `http` method return the relevant `Gateway` class, and add a `post` method and `to` method to the `Gateway`. The problem with this is that a method called "`to`" makes no sense outside the context of the fluent expression. Defining `to` on the `Gateway` class would muddy its interface.

A better option is to create a class whose sole responsibility is to provide our desired fluent interface. It can delegate to the relevant `Gateway` object to do the real work. That way, the `Gateway` objects' interfaces can all be easily understood in isolation, yet we can still have our fluent calling code.

In this example we'll create a `GatewayExpressionBuilder` class to provide the fluency. Our `http` method will return an instance of this class.

```
class Person
  def save
    http.post(:first_name, :last_name, :ssn).to(
      'http://www.example.com/person'
    )
  end

  private

  def http
    GatewayExpressionBuilder.new(self)
  end

end

class GatewayExpressionBuilder
  def initialize(subject)
    @subject = subject
  end

  def post(attributes)
    @attributes = attributes
  end

  def to(address)
    PostGateway.save do |persist|
      persist.subject = @subject
      persist.attributes = @attributes
      persist.to = address
    end
  end
end
```

Next we'll change the `Company` class to use a fluent interface. Again we will create the fluent interface before worrying about the implementation.

```
class Company < DomainObject
  attr_accessor :name, :tax_id

  def save
    http.get(:name, :tax_id).to('http://www.example.com/companies')
  end
```

```
end
```

As the preceding example shows, while creating our fluent interface we noticed that the `http` method was common and went ahead with extracting that to a base class.

```
class DomainObject
  def http
    GatewayExpressionBuilder.new(self)
  end
end
```

Now that we know what interface the `Company` class would like to use we can update the `GatewayExpressionBuilder` class. The `Company` class introduces the need for supporting both the `GetGateway` and the `PostGateway`. This is fairly easily handled by storing the desired `Gateway` subclass class as an instance variable. In the `to` method we'll use the `@gateway` instead of hard-coding which Gateway to use.

```
class GatewayExpressionBuilder
  # ...

  def post(attributes)
    @attributes = attributes
    @gateway = PostGateway
  end

  def get(attributes)
    @attributes = attributes
    @gateway = GetGateway
  end

  def to(address)
    @gateway.save do |persist|
      persist.subject = @subject
      persist.attributes = @attributes
      persist.to = address
    end
  end
end
```

Again, we'll create our fluent interface for `Laptop` first and worry about implementing the required methods when we know what we want.

```
class Laptop
```

Introduce Expression Builder

```
  attr_accessor :assigned_to, :serial_number

  def save
    http.post(:assigned_to, :serial_number).with_authentication.to(
      'http://www.example.com/issued_laptop'
    )
  end
end
```

The final change to GatewayExpressionBuilder is to add support for authentication.

```
class GatewayExpressionBuilder
  # ...

  def with_authentication
    @with_authentication = true
  end

  def to(address)
    @gateway.save do |persist|
      persist.subject = @subject
      persist.attributes = @attributes
      persist.authenticate = @with_authentication
      persist.to = address
    end
  end
end
```

Chapter 11

Dealing with Generalization

Generalization produces its own batch of refactorings, mostly dealing with moving methods around a hierarchy of inheritance, or a module hierarchy. Pull Up Method and Push Down Method promote function up and down a hierarchy, respectively. Rather than pushing down a constructor, it is often useful to use Replace Constructor with Factory Method.

If you have methods that have a similar outline body but vary in details, you can use Form Template Method to separate the differences from the similarities.

In addition to moving functionality around a hierarchy, you can change the hierarchy by creating new classes or modules. Extract Module, Extract Subclass, and Introduce Inheritance all do this by forming new elements out of various points. If you find yourself with unnecessary classes or modules in your hierarchy, you can use Collapse Hierarchy or Inline Module to remove them.

Sometimes you find that inheritance is not the best way of handling a situation and that you need delegation instead. Replace Inheritance with Delegation helps make this change. Sometimes life is the other way around and you have to use Replace Delegation with Hierarchy.

It is a good idea to use Replace Abstract Superclass with Module if you never intend to directly instantiate your superclass, to better communicate this intention.

Pull Up Method

You have methods with identical results on subclasses.

Move them to the superclass.

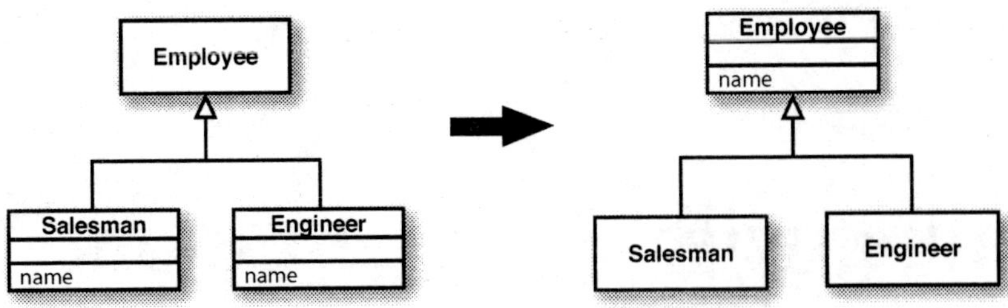

Motivation

Eliminating duplicate behavior is important. Although two duplicate methods work fine as they are, they are nothing more than a breeding ground for bugs in the future. Whenever there is duplication, you face the risk that an alteration to one will not be made to the other. Usually it is difficult to find the duplicates.

The easiest case of using Pull Up Method occurs when the methods have the same body, implying there's been a copy and paste. Of course it's not always as obvious as that. You could just do the refactoring and see if the tests croak, but that puts a lot of reliance on your tests. I usually find it valuable to look for the differences; often they show up behavior that I forgot to test for.

Often Pull Up Method comes after other steps. You see two methods in different classes that can be parameterized in such a way that they end up as essentially the same method. In that case the smallest step is to parameterize each method separately and then generalize them. Do it in one go if you feel confident enough.

A special case of the need for Pull Up Method occurs when you have a subclass method that overrides a superclass method yet does the same thing.

The most awkward element of Pull Up Method is that the body of the methods may refer to features that are on the subclass but not on the superclass. If the feature is a method, you may be able to generalize the other method. You may need to change a method's signature or create a delegating method to get this to work.

If you have two methods that are similar but not the same, you may be able to use Form Template Method.

This refactoring also applies to a module hierarchy, where a method is duplicated on two or more classes that include a module. Move the methods onto the module itself.

Mechanics

1. Inspect the methods to ensure they are identical.

   ⟹ *If the methods look like they do the same thing but are not identical, use Substitute Algorithm on one of them to make them identical.*

2. If the methods have different signatures, change the signatures to the one you want to use in the superclass.

3. Create a new method in the superclass, copy the body of one of the methods to it, and adjust.

4. Delete one subclass method.

5. Test.

6. Keep deleting subclass methods and testing until only the superclass method remains.

Example

Consider a customer with two subclasses: regular customer and preferred customer (see Figure 11.1).

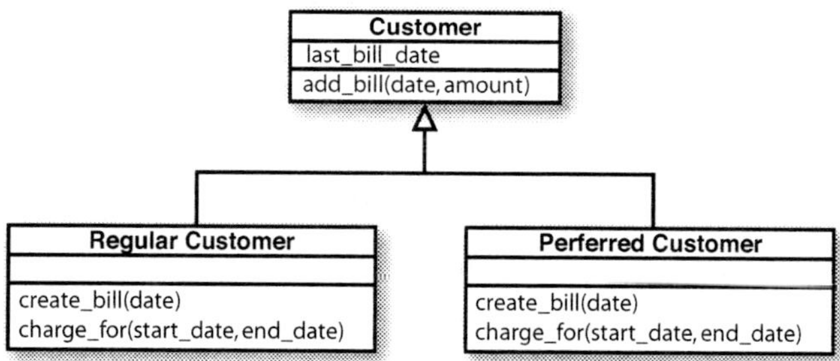

Figure 11.1 Regular customer and preferred customer.

The `create_bill` method is identical for each class:

```
def create_bill(date)
  charge_amount = charge_for(last_bill_date, date)
```

```
  add_bill(date, charge_amount)
end
```

I copy `create_bill` from one of the subclasses. I then remove the `create_bill` method from one of the subclasses and test. I then remove it from the other and test (see Figure 11.2).

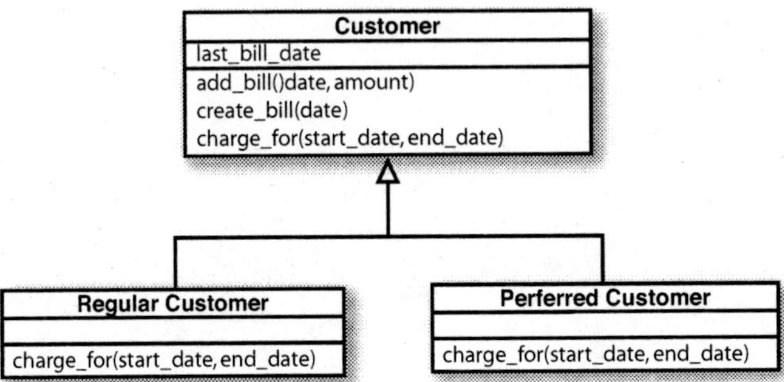

Figure 11.2 Inheritance hierarchy after pulling the `create_bill` method up to the superclass.

Push Down Method

Behavior on a superclass is relevant only for some of its subclasses.

Move it to those subclasses.

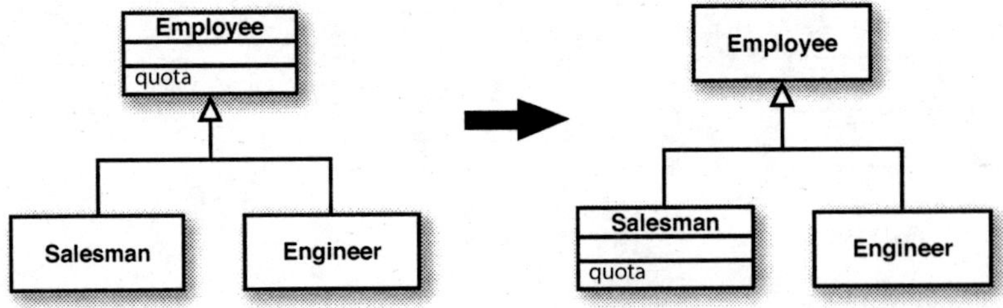

Motivation

Pull Down Method is the opposite of Pull Up Method. I use it when I need to move behavior from a superclass to a specific subclass, usually because it makes sense only there. You often do this when you use Extract Subclass. Pull Down Method is also used to move methods from a module onto a class that includes that module.

Mechanics

1. Declare a method in all subclasses and copy the body into each subclass.

   ⟹ *Use an accessor on the superclass to access any fields on the superclass. Make the accessor protected if public access isn't required.*

2. Remove method from superclass.

3. Test.

4. Remove the method from each subclass that does not need it.

5. Test.

Extract Module

You have duplicated behavior in two or more classes.

Create a new module and move the relevant behavior from the old class into the module, and include the module in the class.

```
class Bid...

  before_save :capture_account_number

  def capture_account_number
    self.account_number = buyer.preferred_account_number
  end
end
```

```
class Bid...
  include AccountNumberCapture
end

module AccountNumberCapture

  def self.included(klass)
    klass.class_eval do
      before_save :capture_account_number
    end
  end

  def capture_account_number
    self.account_number = buyer.preferred_account_number
  end
end
```

Motivation

There are a number of reasons to use Extract Module, the primary one being the removal of duplication. It's relatively straightforward to create a new module, move methods to the module, and include the module in the appropriate classes. But Extract Module should be used with care. A module should have a single responsibility, just like a class. The methods within a module should be cohesive: They should make sense as a group. Too often I've seen modules become "junk-drawers" for behavior. They are created with the noble goal of removing duplication, but over time they become bloated. The methods don't make sense together, and it becomes difficult to find a particular piece of behavior. And when existing behavior is hard to find, identifying and removing duplication is an onerous task. A module that is difficult to name without using words like "Helper" or "Assistant" is probably doing too much.

So the question becomes, when do you choose Extract Module over Extract Class? When we're talking about the removal of duplication, use Extract Class whenever possible. Let's say you have class A and class B. Behavior X is duplicated in A and B. If you can remove behavior X entirely from class A and B by extracting the behavior to class C and having instances of A and A delegate to an instance of C, then that's great. A and B both have one less responsibility, the duplication has been removed, and C is now able to be reused and tested in isolation.

If, however, behavior X only makes sense on class A and B, then Extract Module is a better choice. Perhaps a framework you are using looks for the behavior on class A and B, and the introduction of delegation would be messy.

Mechanics

1. Create a blank module; include the module into the original classes.
2. Start with the instance methods. One by one, use Pull Up Method to move the common elements to the module.

   ⇒ *If you have methods in the including classes that have different signatures but the same purpose, use Rename Method to get them to the same name and then use Pull Up Method.*

   ⇒ *If you have methods with different bodies that do the same thing, you may try using Substitute Algorithm to copy one body into the other. If this works, you can then use Pull Up Method.*
3. Test after each pull.
4. For class methods that you want to call directly on the module, use Move Method just as you did for the instance methods. Change the callers to call the method using the module reference.
5. If you have class methods that you want to call on either of the including classes, create an included hook on the module. Move the class method definitions to the included hook.
6. Test after each change.
7. Examine the methods left on the including classes. See if there are common parts, if there are you can use Extract Method followed by Pull Up Method on the common parts. If the overall flow is similar, you may be able to use Form Template Method.

Extract Module

Example

In this example, we are using a framework that makes use of a before_save hook to perform work before the object is saved to a database. In our case, we want to update an account number on both the Bid and Sale objects before they are saved to the database.

```
class Bid...

  before_save :capture_account_number

  def capture_account_number
    self.account_number = buyer.preferred_account_number
  end
end

class Sale...

  before_save :capture_account_number

  def capture_account_number
    self.account_number = buyer.preferred_account_number
  end

end
```

At this point I ask myself whether I should use Extract Class or Extract Module. Since we want our bid and sale objects to respond to before_save (so that the framework can call it), we're stuck with writing some sort of code to make Bid and Sale respond to before_save. We could conceivably implement capture_account_number on Bid and Sale, and use it to delegate to another object, but this object would have to be aware of the caller so that it could set the account_number. We would be delegating to an object only to have it call back to our bid and sale, which is undesirable. Extract Module is the way to go.

Let's start by creating an AccountNumberCapture module.

```
module AccountNumberCapture

end
```

Next we'll include this module into Bid and Sale.

```
class Bid...
  include AccountNumberCapture
```

```
end

class Sale...
  include AccountNumberCapture

end
```


We're now ready to perform Move Method on the first (and only) instance method. We remove it from `Bid`, and add it to `AccountNumberCapture`.

```
module AccountNumberCapture

  def capture_account_number
    self.account_number = buyer.preferred_account_number
  end
end
```

All going well, our tests should pass.

We don't have any class methods to move—if we did, we'd have to decide whether we wanted to call them directly on the module (for example, `AccountNumberCapture.my_class_method`), or on one of the including classes (for example, `Bid.my_class_method`). If we choose the former, we can move the class method in the same way as we did the instance methods. But if the class method calls something specific on the including class, the method has to go on the including class itself. For that, we would need an `included` hook. The same applies to our `before_save` class annotation, which needs to be executed on the including class, not on the `AccountNumberCapture` module. We'll need to open up the class that's including our module using `class_eval` and make the call to `before_save`.

```
module AccountNumberCapture...

  def self.included(klass)
    klass.class_eval do
      before_save :capture_account_number
    end
  end
```

This can be an awkward step at first if you're not used to opening up classes in this fashion, but if all goes well, the tests should pass.

We can then remove the duplicated methods from the Sale class.

The full definition of `AccountNumberCapture` looks like this:

```
module AccountNumberCapture

  def self.included(klass)
    klass.class_eval do
      before_save :capture_account_number
    end
  end

  def capture_account_number
    self.account_number = buyer.preferred_account_number
  end
end
```


Inline Module

The resultant indirection of the included module is no longer worth the duplication it is preventing.

Merge the module into the including class.

Motivation

Modules introduce a level of indirection—to find the behavior you first have to go to the class definition, find the name of the included module, and then go to the module definition. This indirection is worthwhile if you can remove duplication. But if a module is no longer pulling its weight—if the level of indirection is not worth the savings in duplication—merge the module into the class that is including it.

Mechanics

1. Use Push Down Method to move all the behavior out of the module onto the class that is including the module.

2. Test with each move.

3. Remove the empty module.

4. Test.

Extract Subclass

A class has features that are used only in some instances.

Create a subclass for that subset of features.

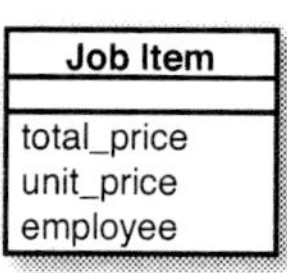

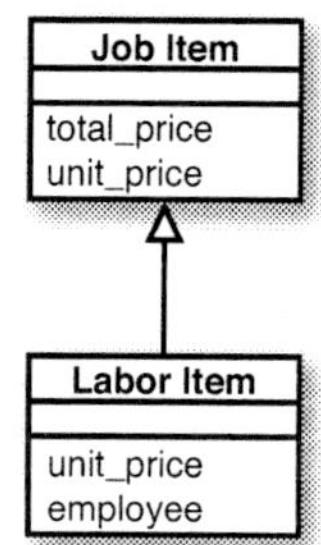

Motivation

The main trigger for use of Extract Subclass is the realization that a class has behavior used for some instances of the class and not for others. Sometimes this is signaled by a type code, in which case you can use Replace Type Code with Polymorphism, Replace Type Code with Module Extension, or Replace Type Code with State/Strategy. Another alternative to Extract Subclass is Extract Class. This is a choice between delegation and inheritance. Extract Subclass is usually simpler to do, but it has limitations. You can't change the class-based behavior of an object once the object is created. You can change the class-based behavior with Extract Class simply by plugging in different components. Another limitation of subclasses is that you're also only able to represent one variation, as a given class in Ruby can only inherit from one superclass directly. If you want the class to vary in several different ways, you have to use delegation or module extension for all but one of them.

Mechanics

1. Define a new subclass of the source class.

2. Look for places where the subclass should be created instead of the superclass.

⟹ *If you need conditional logic to determine which type to create, consider using Replace Constructor with Factory Method.*

3. One by one use Push Down Method to move features onto the subclass.

4. Look for any field that designates information now indicated by the hierarchy (usually a boolean or type code). Eliminate it by using Self Encapsulate Field and replacing the getter with polymorphic constant methods. All users of this field should be refactored with Replace Conditional with Polymorphism.

   ⟹ *For any methods outside the class that use an accessor, consider using Move Method to move the method into this class; then use Replace Conditional with Polymorphism.*

5. Test after each push down.

Example

I'll start with a `JobItem` class that determines prices for items of work at a local garage:

```
class JobItem
  def initialize(unit_price, quantity, is_labor, employee)
    @unit_price = unit_price
    @quantity = quantity
    @is_labor = is_labor
    @employee = employee
  end

  def total_price
    unit_price * @quantity
  end

  def unit_price
    labor? ? @employee.rate : @unit_price
  end

  def labor?; @is_labor end

  attr_reader :quantity, :employee
```

```
class Employee...
  attr_reader :rate

  def initialize(rate)
    @rate = rate
  end
```

I extract a LaborItem subclass from this class because some of the behavior and data are needed only in that case. I begin by creating the new class:

```
class LaborItem < JobItem
end
```

The first thing I need is a constructor for the labor item because job item does not have a no-arg constructor. For this I copy the signature of the parent constructor:

```
def initialize(unit_price, quantity, is_labor, employee)
  super
end
```

Although this may be enough to get the tests to pass, the constructor is messy; some arguments are needed by the labor item, and some are not. I deal with that later.

The next step is to look for calls to the constructor of the job item, and to look for cases where the constructor of the labor item should be called instead. So statements like:

```
j1 = JobItem.new(0, 5, true, kent)
```

become

```
j1 = LaborItem.new(0, 5, true, kent)
```

Now is a good time to clean up the constructor parameter lists. I work with the superclass first. I use a default value of false for is_labor so that I can change the callers one-by-one:

```
class JobItem...

  def initialize(unit_price, quantity, is_labor=false, employee=nil)
    @unit_price = unit_price
    @quantity = quantity
    @is_labor = is_labor
    @employee = employee
  end
```

Callers can now take advantage of the default values:

```
j2 = JobItem.new(10, 15)
```

Once I've run the tests, I use Remove Parameter on the subclass constructor:

```
class LaborItem

  def initialize(quantity, employee)
    super(0, quantity, true, employee)
  end
```

Now I can start pushing down the features of the job item. I begin with the methods. I start with using Push Down Method on the `employee` attribute reader:

```
class LaborItem...
  attr_reader :employee

class JobItem...
  attr_reader :employee
```

I can clean up the constructors so that employee is set only in the subclass into which it is being pushed down:

```
class JobItem...
  def initialize(unit_price, quantity, is_labor=false)
    @unit_price, @quantity, @is_labor = unit_price, quantity, is_labor
  end


class LaborItem...
  def initialize(quantity, employee)
    super(0, quantity, true)
    @employee = employee
  end
```

The field `@is_labor` is used to indicate information that is now inherent in the hierarchy. So I can remove the field. The best way to do this is to first use Self Encapsulate Field and then change the accessor to use a polymorphic constant method. A polymorphic constant method is one whereby each implementation returns a (different) fixed value:

```
class JobItem...
  protected
```

```
  def labor?
    false
  end

class LaborItem...
  protected

  def labor?
    true
  end
```

Then I can get rid of the `@labor` field.

Now I can look at users of the `labor?` methods. These should be refactored with Replace Conditional with Polymorphism. I take the method:

```
class JobItem...
  def unit_price
    labor? ? @employee.rate : @unit_price
  end
```

and replace it with

```
class JobItem...
  attr_reader :unit_price

class LaborItem
  def unit_price
    @employee.rate
  end
```

Because `unit_price` is used only by items that are nonlabor (parts job items), I can use Extract Subclass on job item again to create a parts item class. When I've done that, the job item class will not be instantiated explicitly. It will only be used as the superclass of `LaborItem` and `PartsItem`. In this case, I could use Replace Abstract Superclass with Module.

Introduce Inheritance

You have two classes with similar features.

Make one of the classes a superclass and move the common features to the superclass.

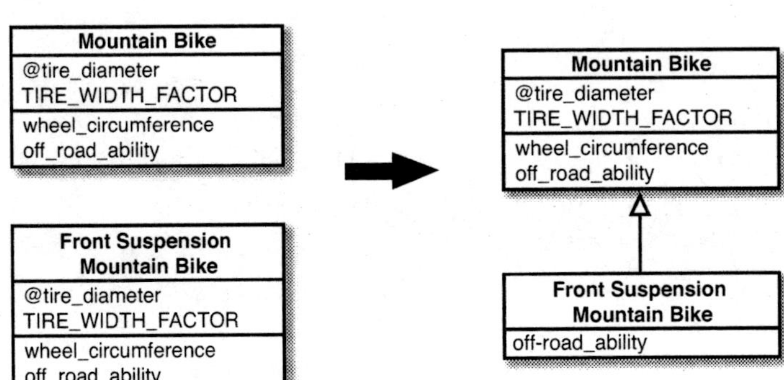

Motivation

Duplicate code is one of the principal bad things in systems. If you say things in multiple places, then when it comes time to change what you say, you have more things to change than you should.

One form of duplicate code is two classes that do similar things in the same way or similar things in different ways. Objects provide a built-in mechanism to simplify this situation with inheritance. However, you often don't notice the commonalities until you have created some classes, in which case you need to create the inheritance structure later.

An alternative to Introduce Inheritance is Extract Class. The choice is essentially between inheritance and delegation. Inheritance is the simpler choice if the two classes share interface as well as behavior. If you make the wrong choice, you can always use Replace Inheritance with Delegation later.

If you can't use Extract Class, consider Extract Module. If you never intend to directly instantiate the superclass, the use of a module instead will better communicate this intention. If you make the wrong choice, it's no big deal—you can always use Replace Abstract Superclass with Module later.

Mechanics

1. Choose one of the classes to be a superclass. Make the other classes inherit it.

2. One by one, use Pull Up Method to move common elements to the superclass.

   ⟹ *If you have subclass methods that have different signatures but the same purpose, use Rename Method to get them to the same name and then use Pull Up Method.*

   ⟹ *If you have methods with different bodies that do the same thing, you may try using Substitute Algorithm to copy one body into the other. If this works, you can then use Pull Up Method.*

3. Test after each pull.

4. Examine the methods left on the subclass. See if there are common parts, if there are you can use Extract Method followed by Pull Up Method on the common parts. If the overall flow is similar, you may be able to use Form Template Method.

Example

Again we'll use the mountain bike example. An instance of the `MountainBike` class has no suspension, whereas `FrontSuspensionMountainBike` has front suspension:

```
class MountainBike
  TIRE_WIDTH_FACTOR = 6
  attr_accessor :tire_diameter

  def wheel_circumference
     Math::PI * (@wheel_diameter + @tire_diameter)
  end

  def off_road_ability
    @tire_diameter * TIRE_WIDTH_FACTOR
  end
end
```

```
class FrontSuspensionMountainBike

  TIRE_WIDTH_FACTOR = 6
  FRONT_SUSPENSION_FACTOR = 8

  attr_accessor :tire_diameter, :front_fork_travel

  def wheel_circumference
     Math::PI * (@wheel_diameter + @tire_diameter)
  end

  def off_road_ability
    @tire_diameter * TIRE_WIDTH_FACTOR + @front_fork_travel *
    FRONT_SUSPENSION_FACTOR
  end
end
```

There are a couple of areas of commonality here. First, both kinds of bicycles have the `wheel_circumference` and `off_road_ability` calculation, as well as the `tire_diameter` attribute and `TIRE_WIDTH_FACTOR`. `wheel_circumference` is identical for both, whereas `off_road_ability` is slightly different. `FrontSuspensionMountainBike` looks like a specialization of `MountainBike` so I'll make `MountainBike` the superclass:

```
class FrontSuspensionMountainBike < MountainBike

  TIRE_WIDTH_FACTOR = 6
  FRONT_SUSPENSION_FACTOR = 8

  attr_accessor :tire_diameter, :front_fork_travel

  def wheel_circumference
     Math::PI * (@wheel_diameter + @tire_diameter)
  end

  def off_road_ability
    @tire_diameter * TIRE_WIDTH_FACTOR + @front_fork_travel *
    FRONT_SUSPENSION_FACTOR
  end
end
```

Now I begin to pull up features to the superclass. I can start by deleting the `wheel_circumference` method, `tire_diameter`, and `TIRE_WIDTH_FACTOR`, which are exactly the same on both classes. Then I can make `off_road_ability` in `FrontSuspensionMountainBike` use `MountainBike`:

```
class FrontSuspensionMountainBike < MountainBike

  FRONT_SUSPENSION_FACTOR = 8

  attr_accessor :front_fork_travel

  def off_road_ability
    super + @front_fork_travel * FRONT_SUSPENSION_FACTOR
  end

end
```

Collapse Hierarchy

A superclass and subclass (or module and the class that includes the module) are not very different.

Merge them together.

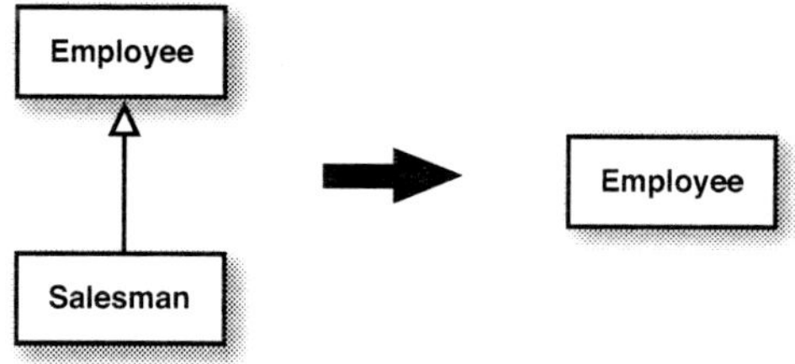

Motivation

If you have been working for a while with a class or module hierarchy, it can easily become too tangled for its own good. Refactoring the hierarchy often involves pushing methods and fields up and down the hierarchy. After you've done this you can well find you have a subclass or module that isn't adding any value, so you need to merge the hierarchy together.

Mechanics

We describe here the mechanics for merging an inheritance hierarchy, but the refactoring is the same for modules.

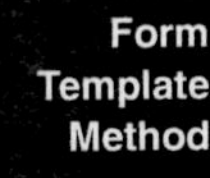

1. Choose which class is going to be removed: the superclass or the subclasses.

2. Use Pull Up Method or Push Down Method to move all the behavior of the removed class to the class with which it is being merged.

3. Test with each move.

4. Adjust references to the class that will be removed to use the merged class.

5. Remove the empty class.

6. Test.

Form Template Method

You have two methods in subclasses that perform similar steps in the same order, yet the steps are different.

Get the steps into methods with the same signature, so that the original methods become the same. Then you can pull them up.

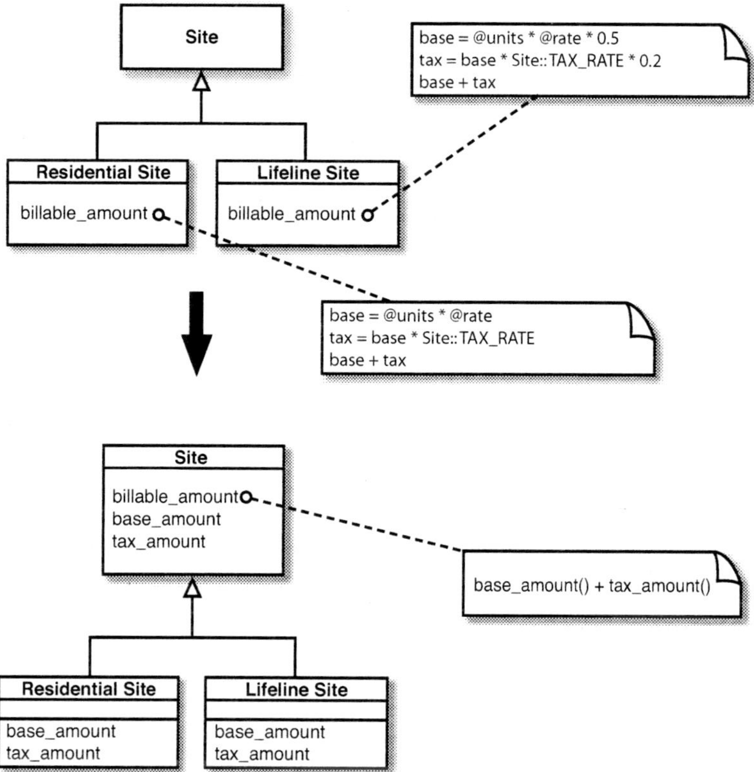

Motivation

Inheritance is a powerful tool for eliminating duplicate behavior. Whenever we see two similar methods in a subclass, we want to bring them together in a superclass. But what if they are not exactly the same? What do we do then? We still need to eliminate all the duplication we can but keep the essential differences.

A common case is two methods that seem to carry out broadly similar steps in the same sequence, but the steps are not the same. In this case we can move the sequence to the superclass and allow polymorphism to play its role in ensuring the different steps do their things differently. This kind of method is called a template method [Gang of Four].

In Ruby, it is also possible to Form Template Method using the extension of modules. The class that extends the modules plays the role of the superclass, housing the sequence, while the modules implement the specific behavior.

Mechanics

1. Decompose the methods so that all the extracted methods are either identical or completely different.

2. Use Pull Up Method to pull the identical methods into the superclass (when using inheritance) or the class that extends the modules (when using module extension).

3. For the different methods use Rename Method so the signatures for all the methods at each step are the same.

   ⟹ *This makes the original methods the same in that they all issue the same set of method calls, but the subclasses/modules handle the calls differently.*

4. Test after each signature change.

5. Use Pull Up Method on one of the original methods.

6. Test.

7. Remove the other methods. Test after each removal.

Example 1: Template Method Using Inheritance

I finish where I left off in Chapter 1, "Refactoring, a First Example." I had a customer class with two methods for printing statements. The `statement` method prints statements in ASCII:

```
def statement
  result = "Rental Record for #{name}\n"
  @rentals.each do |rental|
    # show figures for this rental
    result << "\t#{rental.movie.title}\t#{rental.charge}\n"
  end
  # add footer lines
  result << "Amount owed is #{total_charge}\n"
  result << "You earned #{total_frequent_renter_points} frequent renter\
points"
  result
end
```

while the `html_statement` does them in HTML:

```
def html_statement
  result = "<H1>Rentals for <EM>#{name}</EM></H1><P>\n"
  @rentals.each do |rental|
    # show figures for this rental
    result << "#{rental.movie.title}: \t#{rental.charge}<BR/>\n"
  end
  # add footer lines
  result << "<P>You owe <EM>#{total_charge}</EM></P>\n"
  result << "On this rental you earned <EM>#{total_frequent_renter_points}</\
EM> frequent renter points</P>"
end
```

Before I can use Form Template Method I need to arrange things so that the two methods are subclasses of some common superclass. I do this by using a method object [Beck] to create a separate strategy hierarchy for printing the statements (refer to Figure 11.3).

```
class Statement; end
class TextStatement < Statement; end
class HtmlStatement < Statement; end
```

Now I use Move Method to move the two statement methods over to the subclasses:

```
class Customer
  def statement
    TextStatement.value(self)
  end

  def html_statement
    HtmlStatement.value(self)
  end
```

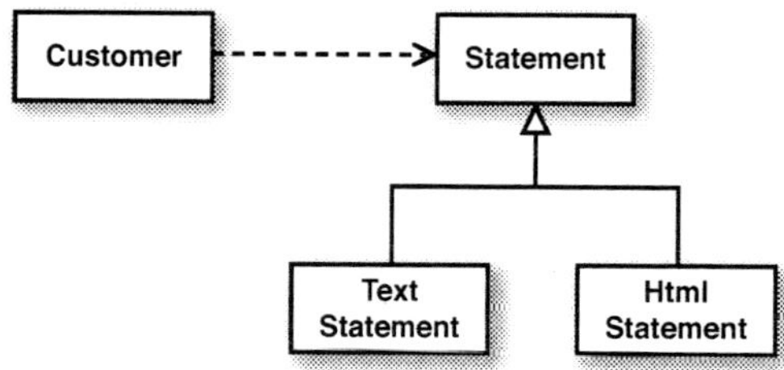

Figure 11.3 Using a strategy for statements.

Form Template Method

```
class TextStatement < Statement
  def value(customer)
    result = "Rental Record for #{customer.name}\n"
    customer.rentals.each do |rental|
      # show figures for this rental
      result << "\t#{rental.movie.title}\t#{rental.charge}\n"
    end
    # add footer lines
    result << "Amount owed is #{customer.total_charge}\n"
    result << "You earned #{customer.total_frequent_renter_points} frequent\
renter points"
  end
end

class HtmlStatement < Statement
  def value(customer)
    result = "<H1>Rentals for <EM>#{customer.name}</EM></H1><P>\n"
    customer.rentals.each do |rental|
      # show figures for this rental
      result << "#{rental.movie.title}: \t#{rental.charge}<BR/>\n"
    end
    # add footer lines
    result << "<P>You owe <EM>#{customer.total_charge}</EM></P>\n"
    result << "On this rental you earned <EM>\
#{customer.total_frequent_renter_points}</EM> frequent renter points</P>"
  end
end
```

As I moved them I renamed the `statement` methods to better fit the strategy. I gave them the same name because the difference between the two now lies in the class rather than the method. (For those trying this from the example, I also had to add a rentals method to customer and relax the visibility of `total_charge` and `total_frequent_renter_points`.

With two similar methods on subclasses, I can start to use Form Template Method. The key to this refactoring is to separate the varying code from the similar code by using Extract Method to extract the pieces that are different between the two methods. Each time I extract I create methods with different bodies but the same signature.

The first example is the printing of the header. Both methods use the customer to obtain information, but the resulting string is formatted differently. I can extract the formatting of this string into separate methods with the same signature:

```
class TextStatement < Statement
  def value(customer)
```

```
    result = header_string(customer)
    customer.rentals.each do |rental|
      # show figures for this rental
      result << "\t#{rental.movie.title}\t#{rental.charge}\n"
    end
    # add footer lines
    result << "Amount owed is #{customer.total_charge}\n"
    result << "You earned #{customer.total_frequent_renter_points} frequent\
renter points"
  end

  def header_string(customer)
    "Rental Record for #{customer.name}\n"
  end
end

class HtmlStatement < Statement

  def value(customer)
    result = header_string(customer)
    customer.rentals.each do |rental|
      # show figures for this rental
      result << "#{rental.movie.title}: \t#{rental.charge}<BR/>\n"
    end
    # add footer lines
    result << "<P>You owe <EM>#{customer.total_charge}</EM></P>\n"
    result << "On this rental you earned <EM>\
#{customer.total_frequent_renter_points}</EM> frequent renter points</P>"
  end

  def header_string(customer)
    "<H1>Rentals for <EM>#{customer.name}</EM></H1><P>\n"
  end
end
```

I test and then continue with the other elements. I did the steps one at a time. Here is the result:

```
class TextStatement < Statement
  def value(customer)
    result = header_string(customer)
    customer.rentals.each do |rental|
      result << each_rental_string(rental)
    end
```

```
    result << footer_string(customer)
  end

  def header_string(customer)
    "Rental Record for #{customer.name}\n"
  end

  def each_rental_string(rental)
    "\t#{rental.movie.title}\t#{rental.charge}\n"
  end

  def footer_string(customer)
    <<-EOS
      Amount owed is #{customer.total_charge}
      You earned #{customer.total_frequent_renter_points} frequent renter
points
    EOS
  end
end

class HtmlStatement < Statement
  def value(customer)
    result = header_string(customer)
    customer.rentals.each do |rental|
      result << each_rental_string(rental)
    end
    result << footer_string(customer)
  end

  def header_string(customer)
    "<h1>Rentals for <em>#{customer.name}</em></h1><p>\n"
  end

  def each_rental_string(rental)
    "#{rental.movie.title}: \t#{rental.charge}<BR/>\n"
  end

  def footer_string(customer)
    <<-EOS
      <P>You owe <EM>#{customer.total_charge}</EM></P>
      On this rental you earned <EM>#{customer.
      total_frequent_renter_points}</EM> frequent renter points</P>
    EOS
  end
```

```
end
```

Once these changes have been made, the two `value` methods look remarkably similar. So I use Pull Up Method on one of them, picking the text version at random:

```
class Statement...
  def value(customer)
    result = header_string(customer)
    customer.rentals.each do |rental|
      result << each_rental_string(rental)
    end
    result << footer_string(customer)
  end
```

I remove the `value` method from text statement and test. When that works I remove the value method from the HTML statement and test again. The result is shown in Figure 11.4.

After this refactoring, it is easy to add new kinds of statements. All you have to do is create a subclass of statement that implements the three methods.

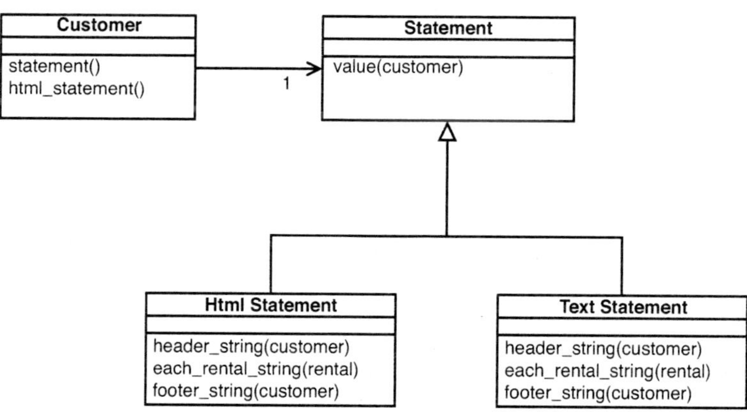

Figure 11.4 Classes after forming the template method.

Technically, if the `Statement` class was never to be instantiated directly, I would make it a module. (See Replace Abstract Superclass with Module later in this chapter for an explanation.) I'd then include the `Statement` module in each of the `HtmlStatement` and `TextStatement` classes. But the traditional Template Method pattern is done with inheritance, so I thought an example would be useful.

Example 2: Template Method Using Extension of Modules

For this example, we'll go back to the code as it stood at the end of Chapter 1:

Form Template Method

```
def statement
  result = "Rental Record for #{name}\n"
  @rentals.each do |rental|
    # show figures for this rental
    result << "\t#{rental.movie.title}\t#{rental.charge}\n"
  end
  # add footer lines
  result << "Amount owed is #{total_charge}\n"
  result << "You earned #{total_frequent_renter_points} frequent renter\
points"
  result
end

def html_statement
  result = "<H1>Rentals for <EM>#{name}</EM></H1><P>\n"
  @rentals.each do |rental|
    # show figures for this rental
    result << "#{rental.movie.title}: \t#{rental.charge}<BR/>\n"
  end
  # add footer lines
  result << "<P>You owe <EM>#{total_charge}</EM></P>\n"
  result << "On this rental you earned <EM>\
#{total_frequent_renter_points}</EM> frequent renter points</P>"
end
```

Similarly to the inheritance example, I first create a `Statement` class. Instead of creating two subclasses of Statement, I create two modules to house the unique behavior:

```
class Statement
end

module TextStatement
end

module HtmlStatement
end
```

I use Move Method to move the two `statement` methods over to the modules:

```
class Customer
  def statement
```

```
    Statement.new.extend(TextStatement).value(self)
  end

  def html_statement
    Statement.new.extend(HtmlStatement).value(self)
  end
end

module TextStatement
  def value(customer)
    result = "Rental Record for #{customer.name}\n"
    customer.rentals.each do |rental|
      # show figures for this rental
      result << "\t#{rental.movie.title}\t#{rental.charge}\n"
    end
    # add footer lines
    result << "Amount owed is #{customer.total_charge}\n"
    result << "You earned #{customer.total_frequent_renter_points} frequent\
renter points"
  end
end

module HtmlStatement
  def value(customer)
    result = "<H1>Rentals for <EM>#{customer.name}</EM></H1><P>\n"
    customer.rentals.each do |rental|
      # show figures for this rental
      result << "#{rental.movie.title}: \t#{rental.charge}<BR/>\n"
    end
    # add footer lines
    result << "<P>You owe <EM>#{customer.total_charge}</EM></P>\n"
    result << "On this rental you earned <EM>\
#{customer.total_frequent_renter_points}</EM> frequent renter points</P>"
  end
end
```

As with the inheritance example, I use Extract Method on any unique behavior:

```
module TextStatement...
  def value(customer)
    result = header_string(customer)
    customer.rentals.each do |rental|
      result << each_rental_string(rental)
```

```
    end
    result << footer_string(customer)
  end

  def header_string(customer)
    "Rental Record for #{customer.name}\n"
  end

  def each_rental_string(rental)
    "\t#{rental.movie.title}\t#{rental.charge}\n"
  end

  def footer_string(customer)
    <<-EOS
      Amount owed is #{customer.total_charge}
      You earned #{customer.total_frequent_renter_points} frequent renter 
points
    EOS
  end
end

module HtmlStatement...
  def value(customer)
    result = header_string(customer)
    cusotmer.rentals.each do |rental|
      result << each_rental_string(rental)
    end
    result << footer_string(customer)
  end

  def header_string(customer)
    "<H1>Rentals for <EM>#{customer.name}</EM></H1><P>\n"
  end

  def each_rental_string(rental)
    "#{rental.movie.title}: \t#{rental.charge}<BR/>\n"
  end

  def footer_string(customer)
    <<-EOS
      <P>You owe <EM>#{customer.total_charge}</EM></P>
      On this rental you earned <EM>#{customer.
      total_frequent_renter_points}</EM> frequent renter points</P>
    EOS
  end
```

```
end
```

The final step is to pull up the value method.

```
class Statement...
  def value(customer)
    result = header_string(customer)
    customer.rentals.each do |rental|
      result << each_rental_string(rental)
    end
    result << footer_string(customer)
  end

module TextStatement...
  def header_string(customer)
    "Rental Record for #{customer.name}\n"
  end

  def each_rental_string(rental)
    "\t#{rental.movie.title}\t#{rental.charge}\n"
  end

  def footer_string(customer)
    <<-EOS
      Amount owed is #{customer.total_charge}
      You earned #{customer.total_frequent_renter_points} frequent renter
points
    EOS
  end
end

module HtmlStatement...
  def header_string(customer)
    "<h1>Rentals for <em>#{customer.name}</em></h1><p>\n"
  end

  def each_rental_string(rental)
    "#{rental.movie.title}: \t#{rental.charge}<BR/>\n"
  end

  def footer_string(customer)
    <<-EOS
```

```
      <P>You owe <EM>#{customer.total_charge}</EM></P>
      On this rental you earned <EM>#{customer.
      total_frequent_renter_points}</EM> frequent renter points</P>
    EOS
  end
end
```

Form Template Method

And finally we're left with the structure shown in Figure 11.5.

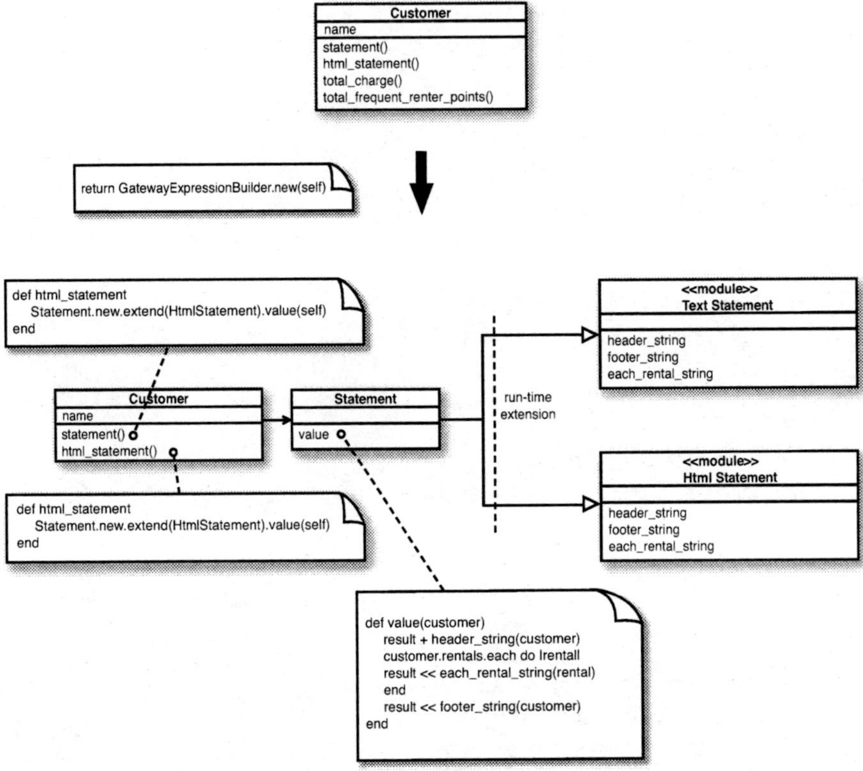

Figure 11.5 Using dynamic extension of modules to implement Form Template Method.

Notice that the implementation using extension of modules is similar to the inheritance example. So why use extend instead of inheritance? The answer is that you would use extend if the modules you were creating could be used to extend various classes.

For example, let's imagine that the next requirement of our application is to display the preceding information for only the previous month. The current statement class gives a list of each rental associated with a customer for all months. To satisfy our new requirement we could create a `MonthlyStatement` class similar to the following code.


```
MonthlyStatement
  def value(customer)
    result = header_string(customer)
    rentals = customer.rentals.select do |rental|
      rental.date > DateTime.now -30
    end
    rentals.each do |rental|
      result << each_rental_string(rental)
    end
    result << footer_string(customer)
  end
end
```

The advantage of module extension is now clear: Because a given class in Ruby can inherit directly from only one other class, the inheritance approach would have forced us to implement both a `TextMonthlyStatement` class and an `HtmlMonthlyStatement` class, instead of our `MonthlyStatement` class. Each new subclass would have had to decide whether to output the rental based on the rental date, which is not ideal. The module extension approach allows us to avoid the complexity of another level of inheritance and consolidates the date-checking code into one method.

```
class Customer
  def statement
    Statement.new.extend(TextStatement).value(self)
  end

  def html_statement
    Statement.new.extend(HtmlStatement).value(self)
  end

  def monthly_statement
    MonthlyStatement.new.extend(TextStatement).value(self)
  end

  def monthly_html_statement
    MonthlyStatement.new.extend(HtmlStatement).value(self)
  end
end
```

Replace Inheritance with Delegation

Replace Inheritance with Delegation

A subclass uses only part of a superclass interface or does not want to inherit data.

Create a field for the superclass, adjust methods to delegate to the superclass, and remove the subclassing.

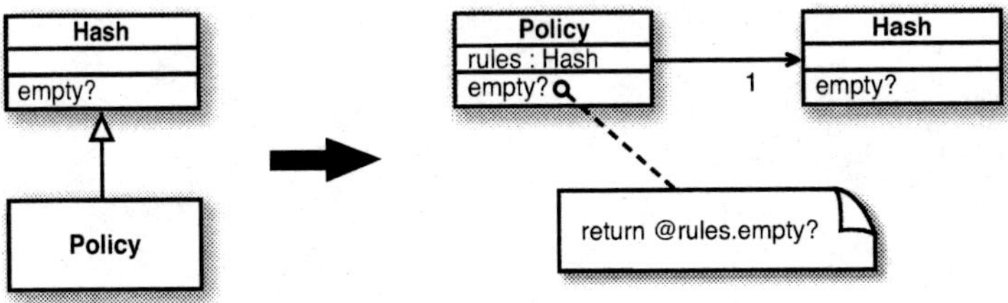

Motivation

Inheritance is a wonderful thing, but sometimes it isn't what you want. Often you start inheriting from a class but then find that many of the superclass operations aren't really true of the subclass. In this case you have an interface that's not a true reflection of what the class does. Or you may find that you are inheriting a whole load of data that is not appropriate for the subclass. Or you may find that there are protected superclass methods that don't make much sense with the subclass.

You can live with the situation and use convention to say that although it is a subclass, it's using only part of the superclass function. But that results in code that says one thing when your intention is something else—a confusion you should remove.

By using delegation instead, you make it clear that you are making only partial use of the delegated class. You control which aspects of the interface to take and which to ignore. The cost is extra delegating methods that are boring to write but are too simple to go wrong.

Mechanics

1. Create a field in the subclass that refers to an instance of the superclass. Initialize it to self.

2. Change each method defined in the subclass to use the delegate field. Test after changing each method.

   ⟹ *You won't be able to replace any methods that invoke a method on super that is defined on the subclass, or they may get into an infinite recurse. These methods can be replaced only after you have broken the inheritance.*

3. Remove the subclass declaration and replace the delegate assignment with an assignment to a new object.

4. For each superclass method used by a client, add a simple delegating method.

5. Test.

Example

One of the classic examples of inappropriate inheritance is inheriting from a collection. Here I have a `Policy` class that inherits from `Hash`. Each `Hash` element is an `Array` of `Rules`, and `Policy` gives the `Hash` an `Array`like interface by implementing the << operator:

```
class Policy < Hash
  attr_reader :name

  def initialize(name)
    @name = name
  end

  def <<(rule)
    key = rule.attribute
    self[key] ||= []
    self[key] << rule
  end

  def apply(account)
    self.each do |attribute, rules|
      rules.each { |rule| rule.apply(account) }
    end
  end

end
```

The Rule class has an attribute and default value:

```
class Rule...
  attr_reader :attribute, :default_value

  def initialize(attribute, default_value)
    @attribute, @default_value = attribute, default_value
  end

  def apply(account)
    ...
  end
```

Looking at the users of Policy, I realize that clients do only five things: <<, apply, [], size, and empty?. The latter three are inherited from Hash.

I begin the delegation by creating a field for the delegated Hash. I link this field to self so that I can mix delegation and inheritance while I carry out the refactoring:

```
class Policy < Hash...

  def initialize(name)
    @name = name
    @rules = self
  end
```

Now I start replacing methods to get them to use the delegation. I begin with <<:

```
def <<(rule)
  key = rule.attribute.to_sym
  @rules[key] ||= []
  @rules[key] << rule
end
```

I can test here, and everything will still work. Now the apply method:

```
def apply(account)
  @rules.each do |attribute, rules|
    rules.each { |rule| rule.apply(account) }
  end
end
```

Once I've completed these subclass methods, I need to break the link to the superclass:

```
class Policy < Hash

  def initialize(name)
    @name = name
    @rules = {}
  end
```


I then extend `Forwardable` to add simple delegating methods for superclass methods used by clients:

```
require 'forwardable'

class Policy...
  extend Forwardable

  def_delegators :@rules, :size, :empty?, :[]

  def initialize(name)
    @name = name
    @rules = {}
  end
```

Now I can test. If I forgot to add a delegating method, the tests will tell me.

Replace Delegation with Hierarchy

You're using delegation and are often writing many simple delegations for the entire interface.

Make the delegate a module and include it into the delegating class.

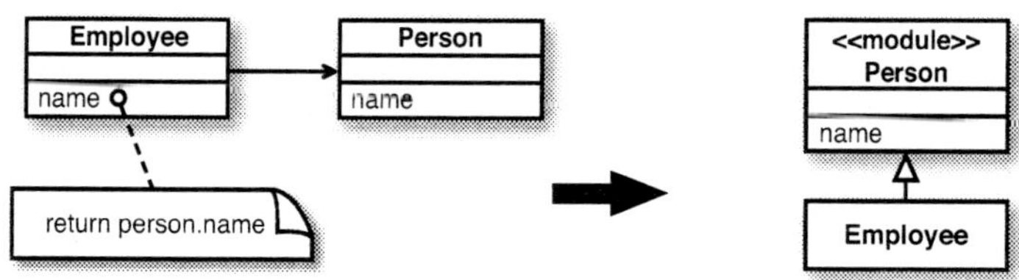

Motivation

This is the flip side of Replace Delegation with Inheritance, though generally we'll end up with a module hierarchy rather than inheritance.

If you find yourself using all the methods of the delegate and are sick of writing all those simple delegating methods, you can switch back to a hierarchy pretty easily.

One situation to beware of is that in which the delegate is shared by more than one object and is mutable. In this case you can't replace the delegate with a hierarchy because you'll no longer share the data. Data sharing is a responsibility that cannot be transferred back to a module hierarchy. When the object is immutable, data sharing is not a problem, because you can just copy and nobody can tell.

Mechanics

1. Make the delegate a module. Include the module in the delegating object.

2. Remove the simple delegation methods.

3. Set the delegate instance variable to `self`.

4. Test.

5. Replace all other delegations with calls to the object itself.

6. Remove the delegate field.

Example

A simple `Employee` delegates to a simple `Person`:

```
class Employee
  extend Forwardable
  def_delegators :@person, :name, :name=

  def initialize
    @person = Person.new
  end

  def to_s
```

```
    "Emp: #{@person.last_name}"
  end
end

class Person
  attr_accessor :name

  def last_name
    @name.split(' ').last
  end
end
```

The first step is to make `Person` a module and include it into `Employee`:

```
module Person
  attr_accessor :name

  def last_name
    @name.split(' ').last
  end
end

class Employee...
  include Person

end
```

The next step is to make the delegate field refer to `self`. I must remove all simple delegation methods such as name and `name=`. If I leave any in, I will get a stack overflow error caused by infinite recursion. In this case I need to remove name and `name=` from `Employee`. Now that `Employee` includes the `Person` module, these methods have already been mixed into the Employee, so it is just a matter of removing the `def_delegators` declaration.

```
class Employee
  include Person
  extend Forwardable
  def_delegators :@person, :name, :name=

  def initialize
    @person = self
  end

  def to_s
    "Emp: #{@person.last_name}"
```

```
  end
end
```

Next I can change the methods that use the delegate. I switch them to use calls to implicit `self`:


```
def to_s
  "Emp: #{last_name}"
end
```

Once I've gotten rid of all methods that use delegate methods, I can get rid of the `@person` field.

Replace Abstract Superclass with Module

You have an inheritance hierarchy, but never intend to explicitly instantiate an instance of the superclass.

Replace the superclass with a module to better communicate your intention.

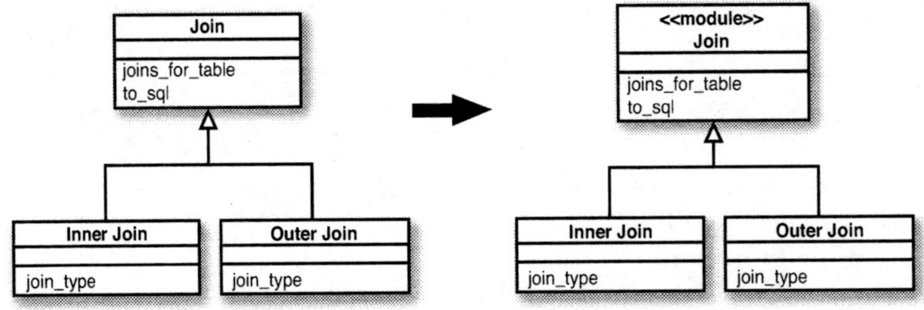

Motivation

In Java, it is possible to designate a class as abstract to prevent objects of that class from being instantiated explicitly. There is no such feature in Ruby. Writing intentional code is important, and it would be nice if we could communicate that instances of our abstract superclass are not meant to be instantiated directly. We could write some code to raise an error when the constructor is invoked, but if instead we replace the abstract superclass with a module, we can communicate our intention in a more idiomatic fashion.

Mechanics

1. If the superclass has any class methods that you want to call using the subclass class, define an `inherited` hook and use the hook to move the class methods onto the subclasses themselves.

2. Test.

3. Make the class a module, and replace the inheritance declaration with an `include` in each of the base classes.

4. Make the `inherited` hook an `included` hook.

5. Test.

Example

Let's start with some subclass objects that we are using to construct SQL joins:

```
class LeftOuterJoin < Join

  def join_type
    "LEFT OUTER"
  end
end

class InnerJoin < Join

  def join_type
    "INNER"
  end
end
```

They can be used like so:

```
InnerJoin.new(
  :equipment_listings,
  :on => "equipment_listings.listing_id =listings.id"
).to_sql
```

And we have a class method for returning all joins for a given table:

```
InnerJoin.joins_for_table(:books)
```

The superclass looks like this:

```
class Join...
```

```
  def initialize(table, options)
    @table = table
    @on = options[:on]
  end

  def self.joins_for_table(table_name)
    # ...some code for querying the database for the given table's joins of
    # the base class's join type
  end

  def to_sql
    "#{join_type} JOIN #{@table} ON #{@on}"
  end

end
```

When we change `Join` to a module, the `joins_for_table` method will not be available using the `InnerJoin.joins_for_table` syntax. To enable this, we have to add the `joins_for_table` method to both of thesubclasses. To do so without duplicating the method, we can use the `inherited` hook. We define the `inherited` hook on the `Join` class, and within the definition we open up the class that is doing the inheriting, and add the `joins_for_table` method:

```
class Join...

  def self.inherited(klass)
    klass.class_eval do
      def self.joins_for_table(table_name)
        table_name.to_s
      end
    end
  end

end
```

If we're successful, our tests should pass.

Then we can make `Join` a module:

~~class~~ module Join...

```
end
```

And include the `Join` module into our subclasses, removing the inheritance as we go:

```
class LeftOuterJoin < Join
  include Join

  def join_type
    "LEFT OUTER"
  end
end

class InnerJoin < Join
  include Join

  def join_type
    "INNER"
  end
end
```


Finally, our `inherited` hook will no longer be executed, because we're not inheriting—we're including. Luckily for us, Ruby has an `included` hook, with similar syntax:

```
def self.included(mod)
  mod.class_eval do
    def self.joins_for_table(table_name)
      table_name.to_s
    end
  end
end
```

Chapter 12

Big Refactorings

The preceding chapters present the individual "moves" of refactoring. What is missing is a sense of the whole "game." You are refactoring to some purpose, not just to avoid making progress (at least usually you are refactoring to some purpose). What does the whole game look like?

The Nature of the Game

One thing you'll surely notice in what follows is that the steps aren't nearly as carefully spelled out as in the previous refactorings. That's because the situations change so much in the big refactorings. We can't tell you exactly what to do, because we don't know exactly what you'll be seeing when you do it. When you are adding a parameter to a method, the mechanics are clear because the scope is clear. When you are untangling an inheritance mess, every mess is different.

Another thing to realize about these refactorings is that they take time. All the refactorings in Chapters 6 through 11 can be accomplished in a few minutes or an hour at most. We have worked at some of the big refactorings for months or years on running systems. When you have a system and it's in production and you need to add functionality, you'll have a hard time persuading managers that they should stop progress for a couple of months while you tidy up. Instead, you have to make like Hansel and Gretel and nibble around the edges, a little today, a little more tomorrow.

As you do this, you should be guided by your need to do something else. Do the refactorings as you need to add function and fix bugs. You don't have to complete the refactoring when you begin. Do as much as you need to achieve your real task. You can always come back tomorrow.

This philosophy is reflected in the examples. To show you each of the refactorings in this book it would easily take a hundred pages each. We know this, because Martin tried it. So we've compressed the examples into a few sketchy diagrams.

Because they can take such a long time, the big refactorings also don't have the instant gratification of the refactorings in the other chapters. You will have to have faith that you are making the world a little safer for your program each day.

The big refactorings require a degree of agreement among the entire programming team that isn't needed with the smaller refactorings. The big refactorings set the direction for many, many changes. The whole team has to recognize that one of the big refactorings is "in play" and make their moves accordingly. You don't want to get in the situation of the two guys whose car stops near the top of a hill. They get out to push, one on each end of the car. After a fruitless half-hour the guy in front says, "I never thought pushing a car downhill would be so hard." To which the other guy replies, "What do you mean 'downhill'?"

Why Big Refactorings Are Important

If the big refactorings lack so many of the qualities that make the little refactorings valuable (predictability, visible progress, instant satisfaction), why are they important enough that we wanted to put them in this book? Because without them you run the risk of investing time and effort into learning to refactor and then actually refactoring and not getting the benefit. That would reflect badly on us. We can't stand that.

Seriously, you refactor not because it is fun but because there are things you expect to be able to do with your programs if you refactor that you just can't do if you don't refactor.

Accumulation of half-understood design decisions eventually chokes a program as a water weed chokes a canal. By refactoring you can ensure that your full understanding of how the program should be designed is always reflected in the program. As a water weed quickly spreads its tendrils, partially understood design decisions quickly spread their effects throughout your program. No one or two or even ten individual actions will be enough to eradicate the problem.

Four Big Refactorings

In this chapter we describe four examples of big refactorings. These are examples of the kind of things that you might face, rather than an attempt to cover the whole ground.

Tease Apart Inheritance deals with a tangled inheritance hierarchy that seems to combine several variations in a confusing way. Convert Procedural Design to Objects helps solve the classic problem of what to do with procedural code. A lot of programmers use Object-Oriented languages without really knowing about objects, so this is a refactoring you often have to do. If you see code written with the classic two-tier approach to user interfaces and databases, you'll find you need Separate Domain from Presentation when you want to isolate business logic from user interface code. Experienced Object-Oriented developers have learned that this separation is vital to a long-lived and prosperous system. Extract Hierarchy simplifies an overly complex class by turning it into a group of subclasses.

Tease Apart Inheritance

You have an inheritance hierarchy that is doing two jobs at once.

Create two hierarchies and use delegation to invoke one from the other.

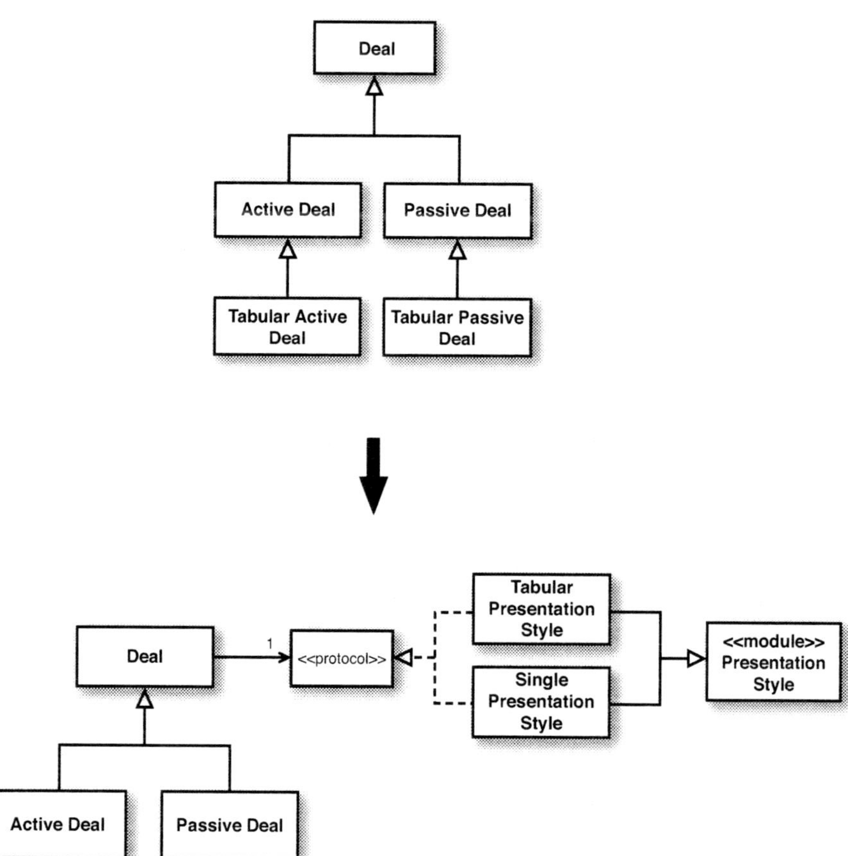

Motivation

Inheritance is great. It helps you write dramatically "compressed" code in subclasses. A single method can take on importance out of proportion with its size because of where it sits in the hierarchy.

Not surprisingly for such a powerful mechanism, it is easy to misuse inheritance. And the misuse can easily creep up on you. One day you are adding one little subclass to do a little job. The next day you are adding other subclasses to do the same job in other parts of the hierarchy. A week (or month or year) later you are swimming in spaghetti. Without a paddle.

Tangled inheritance is a problem because it leads to code duplication, the bane of the programmer's existence. It makes changes more difficult, because the strategies for solving a certain kind of problem are spread around. Finally, the resulting code is hard to understand. You can't just say, "This hierarchy here, it computes results." You have to say, "Well, it computes results, and there are subclasses for the tabular versions, and each of those has subclasses for each of the countries."

You can easily spot a single inheritance hierarchy that is doing two jobs. If every class at a certain level in the hierarchy has subclasses that begin with the same adjective, you probably are doing two jobs with one hierarchy.

Mechanics

1. Identify the different jobs being done by the hierarchy. Create a two-dimensional grid (or three- or four-dimensional, if your hierarchy is a real mess and you have some really cool graph paper) and label the axes with the different jobs. We assume two or more dimensions require repeated applications of this refactoring (one at a time, of course).

2. Decide which job is more important and which is to be retained in the current hierarchy and which is to be moved to another hierarchy.

3. Use Extract Class (see Chapter 6, "Composing Methods") at the common superclass to create an object for each of the subclasses in the original hierarchy.

4. Add an instance variable on the superclass to hold the new object. Initialize the instance variable to the appropriate new class.

5. Extract a module to house the common code that will be shared between the new classes. Include this module in the new classes.

6. Use Move Method (see Chapter 7, "Moving Features Between Objects") on each of the subclasses to move the behavior in the subclass to the relevant extracted object.

7. When the subclass has no more code, eliminate it.

8. Continue until all the subsidiary subclasses are gone. Look at the new hierarchy for possible further refactorings such as Pull Up Method (see Chapter 11, "Dealing with Generalization").

Examples

Let's take the example of a tangled hierarchy (see Figure 12.1).

This hierarchy got the way it did because `Deal` was originally being used only to display a single deal. Then someone got the bright idea of displaying a table of deals. A little experiment with the quick subclass Active Deal shows you can indeed display a table with little work. Oh, you want tables of passive deals, too? No problem, another little subclass and away we go.

Two months later the table code has become complicated but there is no simple place to put it, time is pressing, the usual story. Now adding a new kind of deal is hard, because the deal logic is tangled with the presentation logic.

Following the recipe, the first step is to identify the jobs being done by the hierarchy. One job is capturing variation according to type of deal. Another job is capturing variation according to presentation style. So here's our grid:

Deal	**Active Deal**	**Passive Deal**
Tabular Deal		

The next step tells us to decide which job is more important. The dealness of the object is far more important than the presentation style, so we leave `Deal` alone and extract the presentation style to its own hierarchy. Practically speaking, we should probably leave alone the job that has the most code associated with it, so there is less code to move.

The next step tells us to use Extract Class to create a presentation style for each of the subclasses (see Figure 12.2).

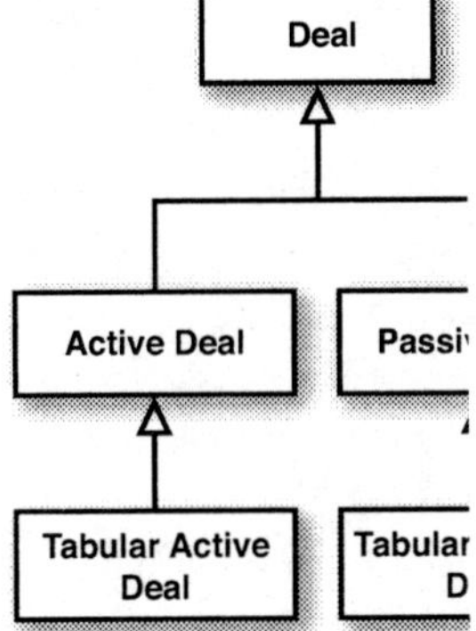

Tease Apart Inheritance

Figure 12.1 A tangled hierarchy.

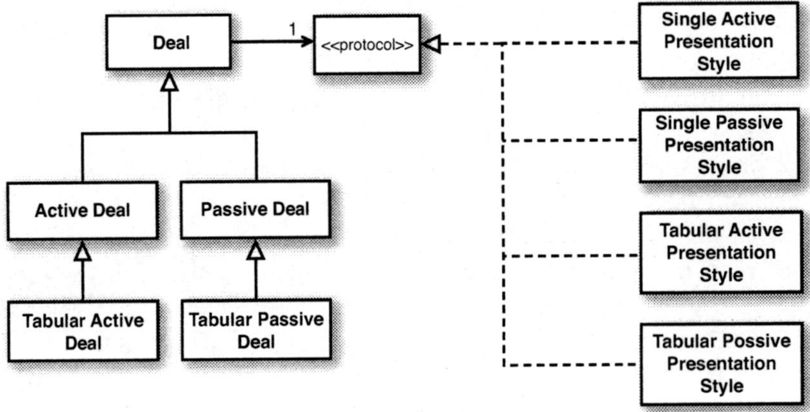

Figure 12.2 Adding a presentation style.

We'll then use Extract Module to house the common behavior shared between our new objects (see Figure 12.3) and initialize the instance variable to the appropriate new class:

```
class ActiveDeal

  def initialize
    ...
    @presentation = SingleActivePresentationStyle.new...
```


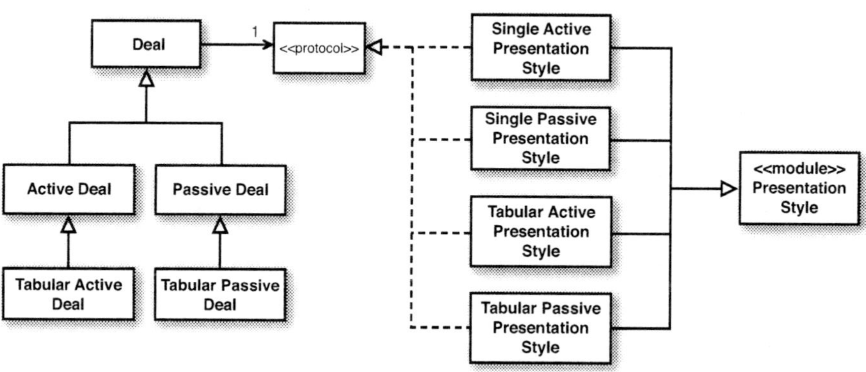

Figure 12.3 Adding subclasses of presentation style.

You may well be saying, "Don't we have more classes now than we did before? How is this supposed to make my life better?" It is true that sometimes you have to take a step backward before you can take two steps forward. In cases such as this tangled hierarchy, the hierarchy of the extracted object can almost always be dramatically simplified once the object has been extracted. However, it is safer to take the refactoring one step at a time than to jump ten steps ahead to the already simplified design.

Now we use Move Method and Move Field to move the presentation-related methods and variables of the deal subclasses to the presentation style classes. We don't have a good way of simulating this with the example as drawn, so we ask you to imagine it happening. When we're done, though, there should be no code left in the classes `Tabular Active Deal` and `Tabular Passive Deal`, so we remove them (see Figure 12.4).

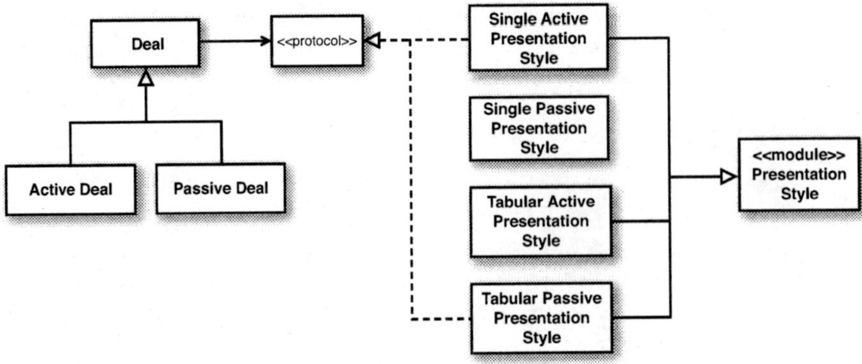

Figure 12.4 The tabular subclasses of Deal have been removed.

Now that we've separated the two jobs, we can work to simplify each separately. When we've done this refactoring, we've always been able to dramatically simplify the extracted classes and often further simplify the original object. The next move will get rid of the active-passive distinction in the presentation style in Figure 12.5.

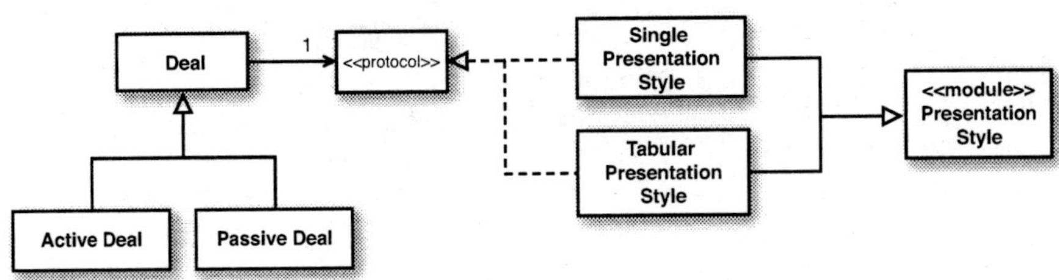

Figure 12.5 The hierarchies are now separated.

Even the distinction between single and tabular can be captured by the values of a few variables. You don't need the module hierarchy at all (see Figure 12.6).

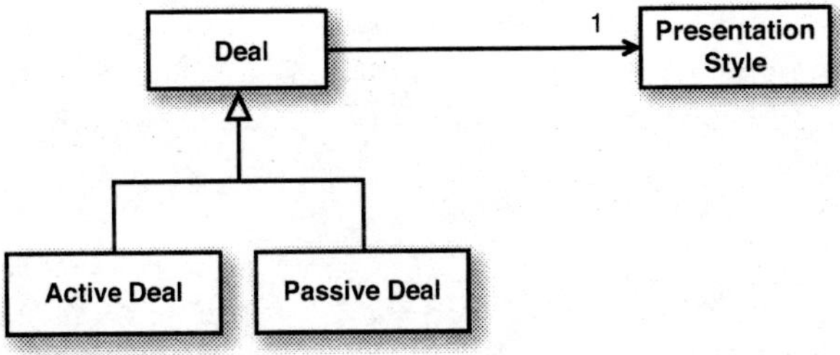

Figure 12.6 Presentation differences can be handled with a couple of variables.

Convert Procedural Design to Objects

You have code written in a procedural style.

Turn the data records into objects, break up the behavior, and move the behavior to the objects.

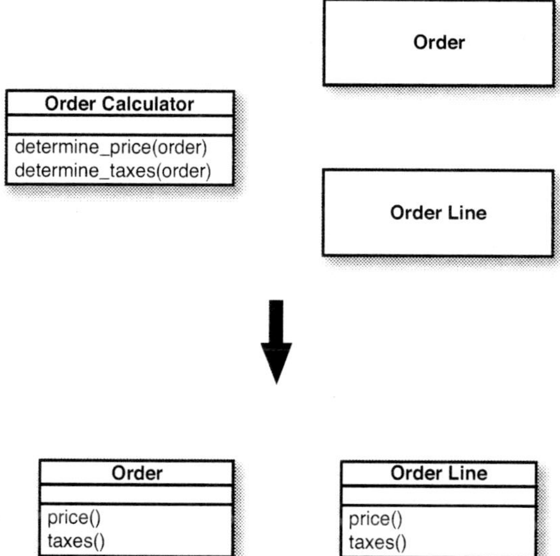

Motivation

A client of ours once started a project with two absolute principles the developers had to follow: (1) You must use Java; (2) you must not use objects.

We may laugh, but although Java, like Ruby, is an Object-Oriented language, there is more to using objects than calling an initializer. Using objects well takes time to learn. Often you're faced with the problem of procedurelike code that has to be more Object-Oriented. The typical situation is long procedural methods on a class with little data and dumb data objects with nothing more than accessors. If you are converting from a purely procedural program, you may not even have this, but it's a good place to start.

We are not saying that you should never have objects with behavior and little or no data. We often use small strategy objects when we need to vary behavior. However, such procedural objects usually are small and are used when we have a particular need for flexibility.

Mechanics

1. Take each record type and turn it into a dumb data object with accessors.

   ⇒ *If you have a relational database, take each table and turn it into a dumb data object.*

2. Take all the procedural code and put it into a single class.

   ⇒ *You can make the methods class methods.*

3. Take each long procedure and apply Extract Method and the related refactorings to break it down. As you break down the procedures, use Move Method to move each one to the appropriate dumb data class.

4. Continue until you've removed all the behavior away from the original class. If the original class was a purely procedural class, it's very gratifying to delete it.

Example

Chapter 1, "Refactoring, a First Example," illustrates the need for Convert Procedural Design to Objects, particularly the first stage, in which the `statement` method is broken up and distributed. When you're finished, you can work on now-intelligent data objects with other refactorings.

Separate Domain from Presentation

You have views and controller classes that contain domain logic.

Move the domain logic into the model.

Motivation

Whenever you hear people talking about objects, you hear about model-view-controller (MVC). This idea underpinned the relationship between the graphical user interface (GUI) and domain objects in Smalltalk-80.

The gold at the heart of MVC is the separation of the user interface code (the view) and the domain logic (the model). The views contain only the logic needed to deal with the user interface. Domain objects contain no visual code but all the business logic. This separates two complicated parts of the program into pieces that are easier to modify. It also allows multiple presentations of the same business logic. Those experienced in working with objects use this separation instinctively, and it has proven its worth.

Unfortunately, many programming environments with client-server GUIs use a logical two-tier design: The data sits in the database and the logic sits in the view. The environment often forces you toward this style of design, making it hard for you to put the logic anywhere else.

The designers of the Ruby on Rails framework, in contrast, believed fundamentally in an MVC-style architecture; they even defined a file structure that has places to house models, views, and controllers, and an object-relational mapper. As such, Rails naturally leads programmers to separate code into the model-view-controller hierarchy. But that doesn't mean that this separation is always performed correctly. I often find that domain logic begins to creep into the controller, and even the view. When the same logic is needed in other parts of the system, it is often duplicated in another controller or view, leading to inconsistencies and bugs. Controllers should only be responsible for accepting user requests, organizing for the model to do its work, and triggering the appropriate view to be displayed.

Mechanics

1. Identify functionality in the controllers that does not have anything to do with accepting user requests, organizing for the model to do its work, or triggering the appropriate views to be displayed.

2. Examine this code to determine a domain object on which it could be put.

   ⟹ *Add a new domain object if necessary.*

   ⟹ *Use of Extract Method may be required prior to moving the offending code. The shortcuts that lead to domain logic landing in views and controllers also often mix up presentation and domain logic within the methods.*

3. Use Move Method to move it to the domain object.

4. Test.

5. Identify code in the views that is not concerned with display logic.

6. Examine this code to determine a domain object on which it could be put.

   ⇒ *Add a new domain object if necessary.*

   ⇒ *Again, use of Extract Method may be required prior to moving the offending code.*

7. Use Move Method to move it to the domain object.

8. Test.

9. When you are finished, you will have views that handle the GUI, controllers that handle request marshaling, and domain objects that contain all the business logic. The domain objects may be well factored, but further refactorings will deal with that.

Example

In this example, we have a program that allows users to enter and view orders. The GUI for entering orders looks like Figure 12.7. The views and controllers interact with models that are backed by a relational database laid out like Figure 12.8.

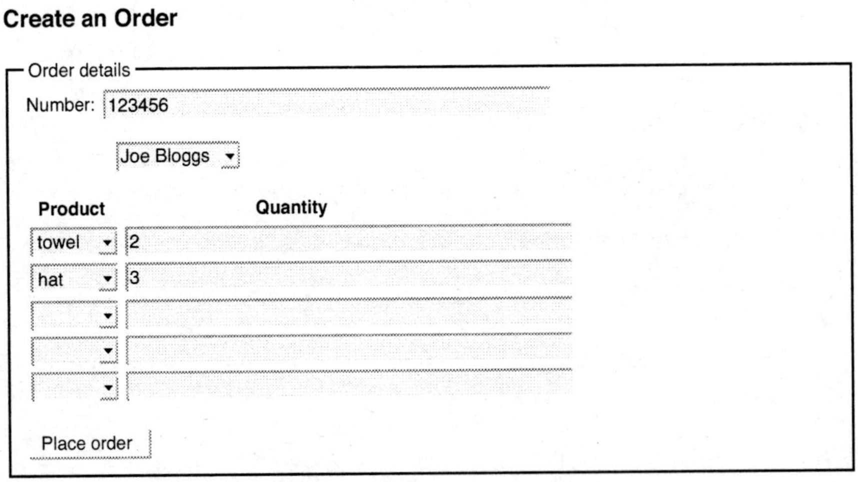

Create an Order

Order details

Number: 123456

Joe Bloggs

Product	Quantity
towel	2
hat	3

Place order

Figure 12.7 The user interface for creating an order.

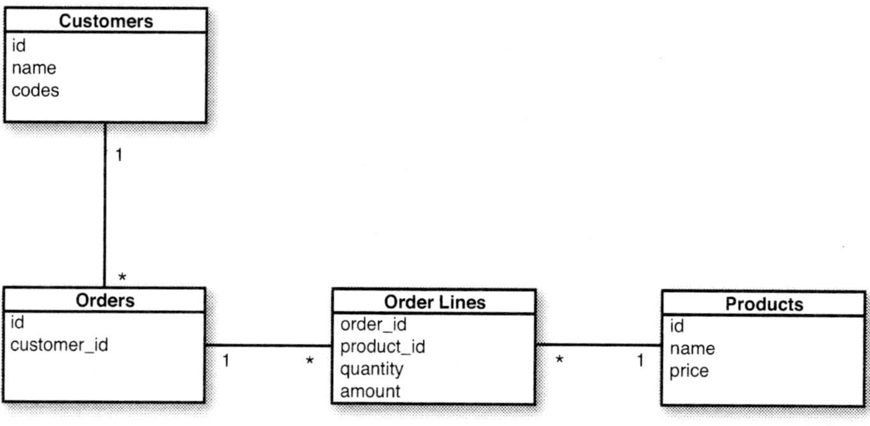

Figure 12.8 The database for the order program.

There is a minimum order of $100, so the create action in the controller calculates the total for the order and determines whether the order meets the minimum limit:

```
class OrdersController < ApplicationController...

  MINIMUM_ORDER_AMOUNT = 100

  def create
    @order_lines = []
    params[:order_line].each_value do |order_line_params|
      unless all_values_blank?(order_line_params)
        amount = Product.find(order_line_params[:product_id]).price
        @order_lines << OrderLine.new(
          order_line_params.merge(:amount =>amount)
        )
      end
    end

    @order = Order.new(params[:order])

    if total_amount_for_order_lines(@order_lines) >= MINIMUM_ORDER_AMOUNT
      begin
        Order.transaction do
          @order.order_lines = @order_lines
          @order.save!
        end
      rescue ActiveRecord::ActiveRecordError
```

```
      render_new
      return
    end
  else
    flash[:error] = "An order must be at least $#{MINIMUM_ORDER_AMOUNT}"
    render_new
    return
  end
  redirect_to :action => 'index'
end
```

Separate Domain from Presentation

```
private

  def render_new
    @order_lines = [OrderLine.new] * 5 if @order_lines.empty?
    render :action => 'new'
  end

  def total_amount_for_order_lines(order_lines)
    order_lines.inject(0) do |total, order_line|
      total + (order_line.amount * order_line.quantity)
    end
  end
```

The index view displays a list of orders. It also calculates the total for each order in the table:

```
<h3>Orders</h3>
<p><%= link_to 'Add a new Order', new_order_url %></p>
<table>
  <tr>
    <th>Number</th>
    <th>Customer</th>
    <th>Amount</th>
    <th> </th>
  </tr>
  <% @orders.each do |order| %>
    <%
      total = order.order_lines.inject(0) do |total, order_line|
        total + (order_line.amount * order_line.quantity)
      end
    %>
    <tr>
      <td><%=order.number%></td>
```

```
      <td><%=order.customer%></td>
      <td><%=total%></td>
      <td><%= link_to 'Show', order_url(order) %></td>
    </tr>
  <% end %>
</table>
```

The duplication of the calculation logic for the total charge of an order is one problem. It could be solved by using Move Method to place the `total_amount_for_order_lines` method in a place accessible to both the view and the controller (perhaps in a helper that is included by the controller). But the choice of where to place that method is also important. An order is never valid if it is less than $100, so the logic to perform this validation should go in the model:


```
class Order < ActiveRecord::Base...

  MINIMUM_ORDER_AMOUNT = 100

  def validate
    if total < MINIMUM_ORDER_AMOUNT
      errors.add_to_base("An order must be at least $#{MINIMUM_ORDER_AMOUNT}")
    end
  end

  def total
    order_lines.inject(0) do |total, order_line|
      total + (order_line.amount * order_line.quantity)
    end
  end
```

We can then make use of this method in the controller. By making the validation an `ActiveRecord` validation, the logic in the controller becomes simpler:

```
def create
  @order_lines = []
  params[:order_line].each_value do |order_line_params|
    unless all_values_blank?(order_line_params)
      amount = Product.find(order_line_params[:product_id]).price
      @order_lines << OrderLine.new(
        order_line_params.merge(:amount =>amount)
      )
    end
  end

  @order = Order.new(params[:order])
  begin
    Order.transaction do
```

```
      @order.order_lines = @order_lines
      @order.save!
    end
  rescue ActiveRecord::ActiveRecordError
    @order_lines = [OrderLine.new] * 5 if @order_lines.empty?
    render :action => 'new'
    return
  end
  redirect_to :action => 'index'
end
```


And the duplicated code is removed from the view:

```
<h3>Orders</h3>
<p><%= link_to 'Add a new Order', new_order_url %></p>
<table>
  <tr>
    <th>Number</th>
    <th>Customer</th>
    <th>Amount</th>
    <th> </th>
  </tr>
  <% @orders.each do |order| %>
    <tr>
      <td><%=order.number%></td>
      <td><%=order.customer%></td>
        <td><%=order.total%></td>
      <td><%= link_to 'Show', order_url(order) %></td>
    </tr>
  <% end %>
</table>
```

As you do this refactoring you have to pay attention to where your risk is. If the intermingling of presentation and domain logic is the biggest risk, get them completely separated before you do much else. If other things are more important, such as pricing strategies for the products, get the logic for the important part out of the view and controller and refactor around that logic to create a suitable structure for the area of high risk.

Extract Hierarchy

You have a class that is doing too much work, at least in part through many conditional statements.

Create a hierarchy of classes in which each subclass represents a special case.

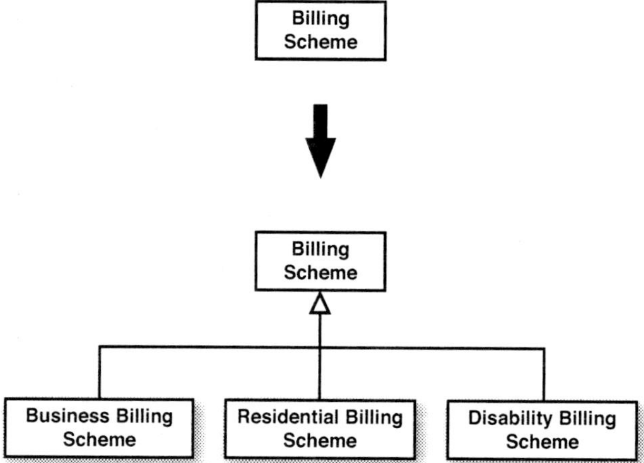

Motivation

In evolutionary design, it is common to think of a class as implementing one idea and come to realize later that it is really implementing two or three or ten. You create the class simply at first. A few days or weeks later you see that if only you add a flag and a couple of tests, you can use it in a new case. A month later you have another such opportunity. A year later you have a real mess: flags and conditional expressions all over the place.

When you encounter a Swiss-Army-knife class that has grown to open cans, cut down small trees, shine a laser point at reluctant presentation bullet items, and, oh yes, I suppose cut things, you need a strategy for teasing apart the various strands. The strategy here works only if your conditional logic remains static during the life of the object. If not, you may have to use Extract Class before you can begin separating the cases from each other.

Don't be discouraged if Extract Hierarchy is a refactoring that you can't finish in a day. It can take weeks or months to untangle a design that has become snarled. Do the steps that are easy and obvious and then take a break. Do some visibly productive work for a few days. When you've learned something, come back and do a few more easy and obvious steps.

Mechanics

We've put in two sets of mechanics. In the first case you aren't sure what the variations should be. In this case you want to take one step at a time, as follows:

1. Identify a variation.

   ⟹ *If the variations can change during the life of the object, use Extract Class to pull that aspect into a separate class.*

2. Create a subclass for that special case and use Replace Constructor with Factory Method on the original. Alter the factory method to return an instance of the subclass where appropriate.

3. One at a time, copy methods that contain conditional logic to the subclass, and then simplify the methods given what you can say for certain about instances of the subclass that you can't say about instances of the superclass.

   ⟹ *Use Extract Method in the superclass if necessary to isolate the conditional parts of methods from the unconditional parts.*

4. Continue isolating special cases until all superclass methods have subclass implementations.

5. Delete the methods in the superclass that are overridden in all subclasses.

6. If the superclass is no longer instantiated directly, use Replace Abstract Superclass with Module.

When the variations are clear from the outset, you can use a different strategy, as follows: If the superclass is no longer instantiated directly, use Replace Abstract Superclass with Module.

Example

The example is a nonobvious case. You can follow the refactorings for Replace Type Code with Polymorphism, Replace Type Code with Module Extension, and Replace Type Code with State/Strategy to see how the obvious case works.

We start with a program that calculates an electricity bill. The initial objects look like Figure 12.9.

The billing scheme contains a lot of conditional logic for billing in different circumstances. Different charges are used for summer and winter, and different billing plans are used for residential, small business, customers receiving Social Security (lifeline), and those with a disability. The resulting complex logic makes the `Billing Scheme` class complex.

Our first step is to pick a variant aspect that keeps cropping up in the conditional logic. This might be various conditions that depend on whether the customer is on a disability plan. This can be a flag in `Customer`, `Billing Scheme`, or somewhere else.

We create a subclass for the variation. To use the subclass we need to make sure it is created and used. So we look at the constructor for `Billing Scheme`. First we use Replace Constructor with Factory Method. Then we look at the factory method and see how the logic depends on disability. We then create a clause that returns a disability billing scheme when appropriate.

We look at the various methods on `Billing Scheme` and look for those that contain conditional logic that varies on the basis of disability. `create_bill` is one of those methods, so we copy it to the subclass (see Figure 12.10).

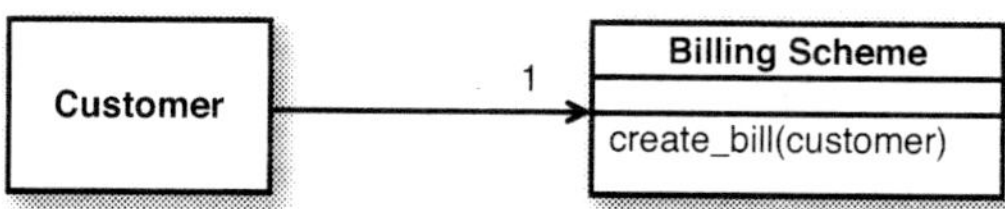

Figure 12.9 Customer and billing scheme.

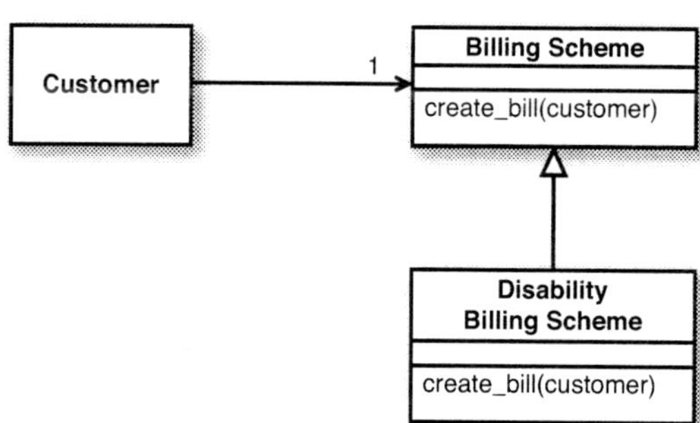

Figure 12.10 Adding a subclass for disability.

Now we examine the subclass copy of `create_bill` and simplify it on the basis that we know it is now within the context of a disability scheme. So code that says:

```
do_something if disability_scheme
```

can be replaced with

```
do_something
```

If disabilities are exclusive of the business scheme we can eliminate any code that is conditional on the business scheme.

As we do this, we like to ensure that varying code is separated from code that stays the same. We use Extract Method and Decompose Conditional to do that. We continue doing this for various methods of Billing Scheme until we feel we've dealt with most of the disability conditionals. Then we pick another variation, say lifeline, and do the same for that.

As we do the second variation, however, we look at how the variations for lifeline compare with those for disability. We want to identify cases in which we can have methods that have the same intention but carry it out differently in the two separate cases. We might have variation in the calculation of taxes for the two cases. We want to ensure that we have two methods on the subclasses that have the same signature. This may mean altering disability so we can line up the subclasses. Usually we find that as we do more variations, the pattern of similar and varying methods tends to stabilize, making additional variations easier.

Chapter 13

Putting It All Together

Now you have all the pieces of the puzzle. You've learned the refactorings. You've studied the catalog. You've practiced all of the checklists. You've gotten good at testing, so you aren't afraid. Now you may think you know how to refactor. Not yet.

The list of techniques is only the beginning. It is the gate you must pass through. Without the techniques, you can't manipulate the design of running programs. With them, you still can't, but at least you can start.

Why are all these wonderful techniques really only the beginning? Because you don't yet know when to use them and when not to, when to start and when to stop, when to go and when to wait. It is the rhythm that makes for refactoring, not the individual notes.

How will you know when you are really getting it? You'll know when you start to calm down. When you feel absolute confidence that no matter how screwed up someone left it, you can make the code better, enough better to keep making progress.

Mostly, though, you'll know you're getting it when you can stop with confidence. Stopping is the strongest move in the refactorer's repertoire. You see a big goal—a host of subclasses can be eliminated. You begin to move toward that goal, each step small and sure, each step backed up by keeping all the tests running. You're getting close. You only have two methods to unify in each of the subclasses, and then they can go away.

That's when it happens. You run out of gas. Maybe it's getting late and you are becoming fatigued. Maybe you were wrong in the first place and you can't really get rid of all of those subclasses. Maybe you don't have the tests to back you up. Whatever the cause, your confidence is gone. You can't make the next step with certainty. You don't think you will screw anything up, but you're not sure.

That's when you stop. If the code is already better, integrate and release what you've done. If it isn't better, walk away. Flush it. Glad to have learned a lesson, pity it didn't work out. What's on for tomorrow?

Tomorrow or the next day or the next month or maybe even next year (my personal record is nine years waiting for the second half of a refactoring), the insight comes. Either you understand why you were wrong, or you understand why you were right. In any case, the next step is clear. You take the step with the confidence you had when you started. Maybe you're even a little abashed at how stupid you could have been not to have seen it all along. Don't be. It happens to everyone.

It's a little like walking along a narrow trail above a 1,000-foot drop. As long as the light holds, you can step forward cautiously but with confidence. As soon as the sun sets, though, you'd better stop. You bed down for the night, sure the sun will rise again in the morning.

This may sound mystical and vague. In a sense it is, because it is a new kind of relationship with your program. When you really understand refactoring, the design of the system is as fluid and plastic and moldable to you as the individual characters in a source code file. You can feel the whole design at once. You can see how it might flex and change—a little this way and this is possible; a little that way and that is possible.

In another sense, though, it is not at all mystical or vague. Refactoring is a learnable skill, the components of which you have read about in this book and begun to learn about. You get those little skills together and polished. Then you begin to see development in a new light.

I said this was a learnable skill. How do you learn it?

Get used to picking a goal. Somewhere your code smells bad. Resolve to get rid of the problem. Then march toward that goal. You aren't refactoring to pursue truth and beauty (at least that's not all there is to it). You are trying to make your world easier to understand, to regain control of a program that is flapping loose.

Stop when you are unsure. As you move toward your goal, a time may come when you can't exactly prove to yourself and others that what you are doing will preserve the semantics of your program. Stop. If the code is already better, go ahead and release your progress. If it isn't, throw away your changes.

Backtrack. The discipline of refactoring is hard to learn and easy to lose sight of, even if only for a moment. I still lose sight more often than I care to admit. I'll do two or three or four refactorings in a row without rerunning the test cases. Of course I can get away with it. I'm confident. I've practiced. Boom! A test fails, and I can't see which of my changes caused the problem.

At this moment you will be mightily tempted to just debug your way out of trouble. After all, you got those tests to run in the first place. How hard could it be to get them running again? Stop. You are out of control, and you have no idea what it will take to get back in control by going forward. Go back to your last known good configuration. Replay your changes one by one. Run the tests after each one.

This may sound obvious here in the comfort of your recliner. When you are hacking and you can smell a big simplification centimeters away, it is the hardest thing to do to stop and back up. But think about it now, while your head is clear. If you have refactored for an hour, it will take only about ten minutes to replay what you did. So you can be guaranteed to be back on track in ten minutes. If, however, you try to move forward, you might be debugging for five seconds or for two hours.

It is easy for me to tell you what to do now. It is brutally hard to actually do it. I think my personal record for failing to follow my own advice is four hours and three separate tries. I got out of control, backtracked, moved forward slowly at first, got out of control again, and again, for four painful hours. It is no fun. That's why you need help.

Duets. For goodness' sake, refactor with someone. There are many advantages to working in pairs for all kinds of development. The advantages work in spades for refactoring. In refactoring there is a premium on working carefully and methodically. Your partner is there to keep you moving step by step, and you are there for him or her. In refactoring there is a premium on seeing possibly far-ranging consequences. Your partner is there to see things you don't see and know things you don't know. In refactoring, there is a premium on knowing when to quit. When your partner doesn't understand what you are doing, it is a sure sign that you don't either. Above all, in refactoring there is an absolute premium on quiet confidence. Your partner is there to gently encourage you when you might otherwise stop.

Another aspect of working with a partner is talking. You want to talk about what you think is about to happen, so the two of you are pointed in the same direction. You want to talk about what you think is happening, so you can spot trouble as soon as possible. You want to talk about what just happened, so you'll know better next time. All that talking cements in your mind exactly where the individual refactorings fit into the rhythm of refactoring.

You are likely to see new possibilities in your code, even if you have worked with it for years, once you know about the smells and the refactorings that can sterilize them. You may even want to jump in and clean up every problem in sight. Don't. No manager wants to hear the team say it has to stop for three months to clean up the mess it has created. And, well, they shouldn't. A big refactoring is a recipe for disaster.

As ugly as the mess looks now, discipline yourself to nibble away at the problem. When you are going to add some new functionality to an area, take a few minutes to clean it up first. If you have to add some tests before you can clean up with confidence, add them. You'll be glad you did. Refactoring first is less dangerous than adding new code. Touching the code will remind you how it works. You'll get done faster, and you'll have the satisfaction of knowing that the next time you pass this way, the code will look better than it did this time.

When you decide to undertake a large refactoring, try to pick off pieces that can be integrated back into the main development branch as quickly as possible. There's nothing worse than completing some great work on an alternative branch and finding that the main development branch has shifted so far from you that you can no longer integrate it. When contemplating a large refactoring it's tempting to say, "I can't improve that code without adopting a big-bang approach that will take 3 days." Rarely do I find this to actually be the case. My first idea for the refactoring might prescribe a large design change as the first step, but usually I can attack the problem at a different angle. I find a piece to slice off to get me started. Then I slice off another piece. And then another, integrating each piece back to the main development branch as I go. I might need to write some extra code to help the new design integrate with the old design; code that will eventually be thrown away. But the extra time spent writing this throw-away adaptive code is worth the benefit of continual integration with the development branch.

The final thought I'll leave you with is this: Never forget the two hats: The refactoring hat, and the new functionality hat. Only wear one hat at a time. When you refactor, you will inevitably discover code that doesn't work correctly. You'll find bugs, test cases to add or change, and other unrelated refactorings. Some of these might even be more important than the refactoring you're currently working on. Resist temptation to mix an unfinished refactoring with one of these newfound tasks. If the newfound task truly is an immediate priority, abandon your refactoring. Revert the code and start a fresh. But if you decide to wear the refactoring hat, your goal is to leave the code computing exactly the same answers that it was when you found it; nothing more, nothing less. Once you develop the discipline and rhythm to juggle the two hats, you'll find refactoring to be a rewarding and productive experience. Happy coding!

References

[Auer] Ken. Auer "Reusability through Self-Encapsulation." In Pattern Languages of Program Design 1, Coplien J.O. Schmidt.D.C. Reading, Mass.: Addison-Wesley, 1995. Patterns paper on the concept of self-encapsulation.

[Bäumer and Riehle] Bäumer, Riehle and Riehle. Dirk "Product Trader." In Pattern Languages of Program Design 3, R. MartinF. BuschmannD. Riehle. Reading, Mass.: Addison-Wesley, 1998. A pattern for flexibly creating objects without knowing in what class they should be.

[Beck] Kent. Beck Smalltalk Best Practice Patterns. Upper Saddle River, N.J.: Prentice Hall, 1997a. An essential book for any Smalltalker, and a damn useful book for any object-oriented developer.

[Beck, XP] Kent. Beck eXtreme Programming eXplained: Embrace Change. Reading, Mass.: Addison-Wesley, 2000.

[Fowler, UML] Fowler M. Scott. K. UML Distilled, Second Edition: A Brief Guide to the Standard Object Modeling Language. Reading, Mass.: Addison-Wesley, 2000. A concise guide to the Unified Modeling Language used for various diagrams in this book.

[Gang of Four] E. Gamma, R. Helm, R. Johnsonand J. Vlissides. Design Patterns: Elements of Reusable Object Oriented Software. Reading, Mass.: Addison-Wesley, 1995. Probably the single most valuable book on object-oriented design. It's now impossible to look as if you know anything about objects if you can't talk intelligently about strategy, singleton, and chain of responsibility.

[Goetz] Goetz, Brian, Java Concurrency in Practice, Addison-Wesley Professional, 2006. The compiler should stop anyone implementing Runnable who hasn't read this book.

[Lea] Doug. Lea, Concurrent Programming in Java: Design Principles and Patterns, Reading, Mass.: Addison-Wesley, 1997.

[McConnell] Steve. McConnell, Code Complete: A Practical Handbook of Software Construction. Redmond, Wash.: Microsoft Press, 1993. An excellent guide to programming style and software construction.

[Meyer] Bertrand. Meyer, Object Oriented Software Construction. 2 ed. Upper Saddle River, N.J.: Prentice Hall, 1997. A very good, if very large, book on object-oriented design. Includes a thorough discussion of design by contract.

[Sadalage] Pramodkumar. J. Sadalage, Refactoring Databases: Evolutionary Database Design (Addison-Wesley Signature Series) (Hardcover)

[Woolf] Bobby. Woolf, "Null Object." In Pattern Languages of Program Design 3, Martin, R. Riehle. D. Buschmann F. Reading, Mass.: Addison-Wesley, 1998. A discussion on the null object pattern.

Index

Symbols

A

B

C

G

H

I

J-K

L

M

N

O

P

T

W-X-Y-Z

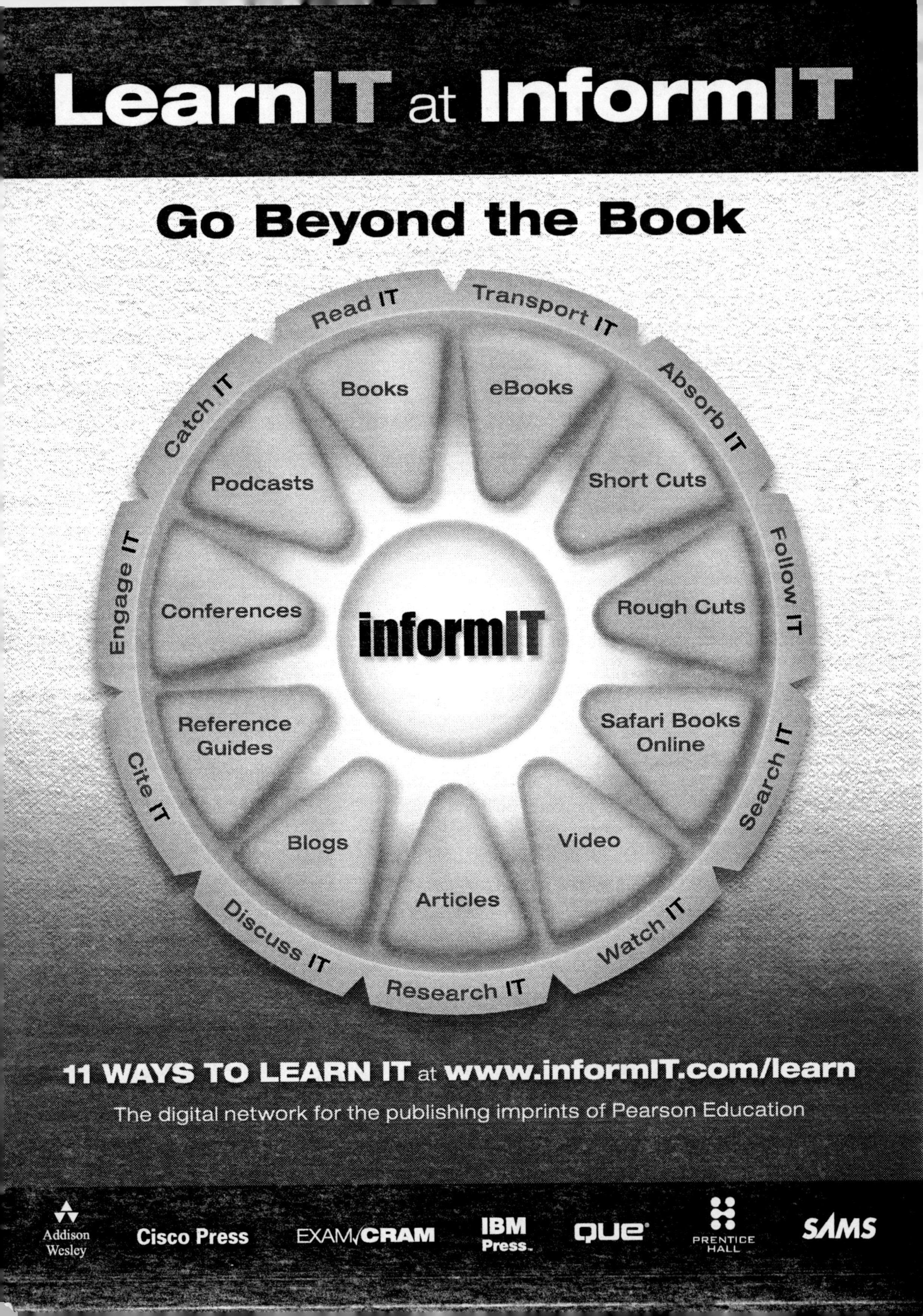
LearnIT at InformIT
Go Beyond the Book
Read IT
Transport IT
Absorb IT
Follow IT
Search IT
Watch IT
Research IT
Discuss IT
Cite IT
Engage IT
Catch IT
Books
eBooks
Short Cuts
Rough Cuts
Safari Books Online
Video
Articles
Blogs
Reference Guides
Conferences
Podcasts
informIT
11 WAYS TO LEARN IT at www.informIT.com/learn
The digital network for the publishing imprints of Pearson Education
Addison Wesley
Cisco Press
EXAM/CRAM
IBM Press
QUE
PRENTICE HALL
SAMS